The Cavalier
King Charles Spaniel

The World of Dogs

Margaret Workman

Front Cover:
Whyteplace Apollo (Mat)
Title Page:
A black-and-tan posing. Photo: Jays Photography
Below:
US/Can Ch Harana Horace. Photo: David Dalton
Back Cover:
Ch Volney Cheerleader with Volney By Jove Jeeves.
Photo: David Warne

t.f.h.
KINGDOM

Contents

Foreword 4

Acknowledgements 4

Chapter   1: Why choose a Cavalier? 5

Chapter   2: Choosing your first Cavalier 9

Chapter   3: Looking after your Cavalier 16

Chapter   4: The evolution of the Cavalier King Charles Spaniel . . .28

Cavalier portrait gallery 40

Chapter   5: The breed standard 47

Chapter   6: So you want to breed your own pups 61

Chapter   7: Problems associated with whelping 81

Chapter   8: Showing your Cavalier 90

Chapter   9: Genetics and successful breeding 103

Chapter   10: The Cavalier's health 114

Chapter   11: Crufts 1973 and afterwards 133

Chapter   12: The Cavalier world-wide 150

Chapter   13: The last chapter 187

Appendix   A: Top twenty breeds 1997 190

Appendix   B: Definitions of classes that
                   may be held at a show 191

Appendix   C: Colour breeding charts 193

Appendix   D: Abbreviations 199

Book list 200

Useful addresses 201

Index 204

Foreword

My family has always had dogs, and at the moment we have two dearly-loved Borders. My oldest friend – the late Paul Maze, distinguished artist and 'the bravest of the brave' in World War 1 – always had Cavaliers who, I believe, were more than human to him. They were always with him and were the subjects of many of his beautiful paintings. How he would have enjoyed and appreciated the book to which I am privileged to write this brief *Foreword*.

Margaret Workman is clearly a complete master of her subject, and the reader will sense her love for the Cavalier in this book. It is a comprehensive and authoritative guide to every aspect of the breed, from the first chapter entitled 'Why choose a Cavalier?' through history, breeding and showing to the finale, where she concludes with Senator George Vest's *Tribute to a Dog*, written in 1870. He wrote: *When all other friends desert, he remains.*

This is a book to enjoy and refer to for advice, beautifully written by a talented expert.

Michael Gow

General Sir Michael Gow GCB served in the Scots Guards and is a former Commander In Chief BAOR. He is a member of the Royal Company of Archers, the Queen's Bodyguard in Scotland.

Acknowledgements

I have greatly enjoyed writing this book and I hope my readers also will get a great deal of pleasure and information from it. I want to begin by thanking all the fellow Cavalier owners who so willingly lent me photographs of their dogs, often very precious ones for which there were no duplicates. They sent them not only from the United Kingdom but also from the United States of America, Canada, Australia and many other countries. Without all these lovely photographs, this book would be nothing.

I also wish to thank all those people who gave help, advice and support, in particular Ken Town, well-known to all Cavalier folk, Moira Jones, herself a vet as well as a Cavalier owner, and my own vet, Ian Butt.

I much appreciate the trouble taken by all the overseas contributors who wrote about Cavaliers in their own countries, namely Joan Twigg, Jeanie Montford, Dianne Tyssen, Dr Annukka Palaheimo, Wendy Hilberts Goodman and Erna Britt Nordin and her daughter, Sara. Several Irish Cavalier owners were very helpful, in particular Geoffrey Porter and Sean Martin.

I would especially like to thank my husband for his patience while I was so preoccupied with the book and Christine Miller, yet another Cavalier owner, who helped with the typing.

Finally, although they will not be able to read what I have written, I owe so much to my own Cavaliers over so many years for the love and affection they have given me and my family. Without them, I would not have been able to write anything at all about Cavaliers!

Margaret Workman

Chapter One
Why choose a Cavalier?

People want dogs for many different reasons, and their choice of breed will depend on what they have in mind. Some people want sporting dogs who will accompany them when they go out for long walks in the country or are out shooting, so they may make their selection from the Gundog group. This includes many of the most popular breeds, such as Retrievers, Spaniels, Pointers, and Setters, all of whom were originally bred to work outdoors. Then there are the people who want smaller, very sporty little dogs, game for anything (and more!), and the choice here would be one of the Terriers. Again, some very popular breeds come into this group, such as the Westie (West Highland Terrier), the Cairn, or the Border Terrier. The Hound group also contains a wide variety of dogs, ranging from the small Miniature Dachshund to large, elegant hounds such as the Afghan Hound or the Borzoi.

Penny among the flowers.

Fire spaniels: Phoebe and Jessica.

Hazel (Retriever) with Pippa and Penny – but Hazel knows better than to take her paw off the bone!

A great many people want their dog to be a guard dog first and foremost, and in this case they will go for a dog from the Working group, such as a German Shepherd Dog (also known as an Alsatian), a Dobermann or a Rottweiler. This group also includes all the dogs originally bred to herd, such as collies and other sheepdogs. You will notice that so far there has been no mention of the somewhat 'different' breeds such as the Bulldog, the Poodle, the Dalmatian, and the Lhasa Apso. These are all found in the Utility group, which is really just a mixture of breeds that do not seem to fit in anywhere else. Finally, there are the Toy dogs, so called because they are all small and toy-like. This includes Chihuahuas, Pekingese, Yorkshire Terriers and a number of other small breeds. It also includes Cavalier King Charles Spaniels, though they are larger than the other 'toy' breeds, and their cousins, the King Charles Spaniels.

You can see that there is a large range of dogs from which you can make your choice, and it must be obvious by now that, before you choose your dog, you need to decide why you want it, what you want it to do and what type of dog most appeals to you. In any case, all people about to acquire a dog need to ask themselves if they really want one, or if what they like is the *idea* of having one rather than the actuality. Having a dog will change your whole lifestyle; it cannot be left alone for too long, it needs regular adequate feeds, and it needs regular exercise (preferably *not* just running round the garden). It also needs to know that it is loved and cared for. If you want to go away, special arrangements have to be made. In a sense, your life is no longer your own; having a dog is a major commitment. Sadly, too many people get a dog without realising what it involves and soon become fed up with it; the poor dog is then either neglected or passed on to someone else. These are the dogs that end up in rescue centres or dog homes.

A family group.

I chose to have a Cavalier many years ago and have never regretted it. There have been many more since my first, and all the others have been descended from her. The first thing that you will notice when you meet a Cavalier is how friendly he (or she) is. His large shining eyes look straight up at you and his elegant, feathery tail never stops wagging. If invited, he will jump up and talk to you; everyone is his friend.

Nowadays, Cavaliers are one of the most popular breeds in the country (see appendix A). Interestingly, though, it has often been said that Cavaliers should not be in the Toy Group at all but should be in the Gundog group; after all, they are spaniels and an extremely sporting breed. They love to rush around in the woods or bushes, putting up and then chasing rabbits or the other wonderful things they scent. They love water and splash happily into the nearest stream. They enjoy a long country walk more than anything else in life and never seem to tire. Yet the Cavalier, unlike many larger dogs, can be satisfied with quite a short walk in spite of its enthusiasm for long ones. This means that your Cavalier should be content with a shorter walk (or walks) on weekdays and a long walk once or even twice at weekends.

Cavaliers are extremely pretty little dogs (see all the photographs in this book) and a real pleasure to have around. They are very affectionate and, while loyal to their owners, still manage to be friendly with everyone else they meet. They are good with children although, as with all dogs, there should always be supervision when they are with very small children and children should never be allowed to hit or torment dogs. Cavaliers are non-aggressive with other dogs, their ever-wagging tails showing just how good-natured they are and how easy to please. They are devoted companions, perfectly happy sitting with their owners by the fire and will give him (or is it her... or both?) a lifetime of love and devotion. For me, they are the ideal, and I would not change them for any other breed. I am certain that, if you do decide to have one for yourself, you will never regret it and your new friend will give you many years of happiness.

Chapter Two
Choosing your first Cavalier

Which one would you choose? A tricolour bitch with two blenheim puppies and one tricolour.

Now that you have finally decided that you want a Cavalier, it is time to talk about what sort of Cavalier to get and where to find one. Cavaliers are very popular little dogs and sometimes it takes a few weeks to find what you want, but it is worth persevering to find the right one for you.

Dog or bitch?

Perhaps the first matter to decide is whether you want a dog or a bitch; both make lovely pets but there are differences between them.

The biggest difference is that a bitch comes *on heat* (or *in season*, either phrase can be used) every six to eight months. This means she is ready to be mated to a male dog and, if mated, will probably have puppies. There is some loss of blood, sometimes very little and sometimes enough to make rather a mess, and this is obviously a nuisance. She cannot be taken out where she will meet other dogs when she is in season as the males will be attracted by her smell and will follow her – you may even find devoted males hanging about outside your house. It is possible to have a bitch spayed (neutered), but this should not be done too soon and may cause her to grow too much coat. However, bitches are very loving and home-centred, gentle and

9

pretty, and you might feel, as many people do, that the disadvantage of her coming into season for three weeks twice a year is a small price to pay. Also, you may want to breed your own puppies, in which case you have no problem over what to choose!

Cavalier dogs are also very devoted and cheerful. They tend to be slightly larger and more outgoing than bitches and, of course, have the great advantage of not coming into season. On the other hand, some dogs, especially if kept as an only dog, can get rather 'sexy' and be quite a nuisance in this way. It often does not happen, but it is a possibility that you have to think about when considering what you want.

Colour

So you may have decided which sex you want, or you may have an open mind, depending on what puppies you see that you really like or what is available. The next matter to think about is the colour.

Paula (ruby) sitting on Rosemary's lap.

There are four colours in Cavaliers (see chapter 5 for details). The red and white ones, known as *blenheims*, are very attractive and popular and therefore usually easier to obtain. The black and white ones with tan eyebrows, tan under tail and in other significant places are called *tricolours,* and they too are popular, though more difficult to find than blenheims. Then there are the all-red Cavaliers, or *rubies,* and the ones known as *black-and-tans* (this *tan* just means red), which are black except for tan on the face, front, feet, and eye-brows. These last two types of Cavalier are known as *wholecolours,* because they do not (or should not) have any white patches. Some people do not like the wholecolours as much as the *particolours* (blenheims and tricolours), but they are very attractive, as many of the pictures in this book will show you. They are usually more difficult to obtain than the particolours, although they are becoming increasingly popular nowadays.

Adult dog or puppy?

So far I have assumed that you want to buy a puppy aged about eight weeks, but you may prefer an older or slightly older dog. The advantage of an older dog is that you do not have the difficult period when you are training your puppy and he keeps having little accidents all over the house. You also avoid the period when he chews everything he can find and cannot be allowed to go on a walk to use up his surplus energy as he has not been inoculated (see also chapter 3).

Certainly, acquiring an older puppy or dog does save a lot of trouble, but the disadvantage is that he will have been brought up and given his basic training by someone else, and there is a great deal to be said for training him (is it time I said 'her'?) to do things in your own way. Incidentally, it is easier to get a young (eight-week-old or so) puppy than one aged about six months, and older puppies are often more expensive. Sometimes a breeder will have a puppy she has intended to keep, but has then changed her mind and decided to sell after all, but this does not happen very often.

If you want an adult Cavalier perhaps aged two or three years, or even older, this may also be difficult. However, the groups that rescue and rehome Cavaliers whose owner cannot keep them any more might know of an unwanted dog who would be overjoyed to have a loving home with you (see

Katie, a lovely blenheim bitch.

chapter 13). Also, Cavalier breeders sometimes have an older dog or bitch available for sale whom they no longer want to keep for showing or breeding. Many breeders keep their dogs for life, but a telephone call to a well-known breeder might produce results. The list of people who handle Cavalier Rescue at present is in **Useful Addresses** but, if there is a problem contacting them, ask the Secretary of your Cavalier club if he or she can help.

Where to obtain your Cavalier

Next we have the very important question of where your new Cavalier will come from and how you find out where you can get a suitable puppy. There are sometimes advertisements in the newspapers, but these need to be treated with care. Unfortunately, there are a number of people in the United Kingdom who breed puppies just for money, have as many litters as they can from their bitches and usually do not give their puppies the human contact they need to become happy and well-adjusted youngsters. These people are sometimes called 'puppy farmers'. It is always

Magda, a one-year-old black-and-tan.

Playtime: Cavaliers are full of fun.

advisable to see the puppies with their mother; often you can see them at about four weeks old and 'book' your puppy. Puppies that are house-reared (born and brought up in a loving owner's house) and handled frequently by the owner will end up happy, fearless little dogs.

The temperament of your puppy is obviously very important, and puppies in constant contact with their owners should be happy to meet any new person and settle down well with them. Sometimes a person with one pet bitch will have puppies that have been brought up in the home, and the owner then advertises in the local paper; so not all advertisements in newspapers come from puppy farmers. Too many do, however. These little puppies need homes too, one feels, but the more often people buy them, the longer puppy farming will continue. Also, there is a strong probability that the puppies, not being used to much human contact, will be nervous and withdrawn. They might also be unhealthy, requiring a large amount of money to be paid out for veterinary attention. This does not always happen but, sadly, it happens far too often.

Sometimes a friend who has a Cavalier will tell you where he or she acquired it, and you could telephone that person. Even if the person you telephone does not have puppies, they might well put you in touch with someone who has. There are various Cavalier clubs all over Great Britain, and the names and addresses of their secretaries (at time of writing) are listed in **Useful Addresses**. These secretaries can often recommend available puppies. The Kennel Club and the Scottish Kennel Club will send a list of approved and recognised breeders. The Kennel Club list, covering all of the United Kingdom, is a list of people who actually have puppies at time of printing; although very often the puppies will have been sold by the time the enquirer gets the current list. The Scottish one is a list of breeders with a special note beside all those who do actually have puppies. You may telephone quite a number of these people and find none of them has puppies; but often if you ask they may know someone else who has pups or who might be able to help you. I am sorry for the people who telephone me (note my name begins with 'W'!), as they have often been all through the list only to find no-one has any puppies left. I always do all I can to help them, but it can mean a wait for a suitable puppy. If you find someone expecting a litter, you could even put your name on a waiting list. This does not commit you to anything. Nor, I am afraid, does it commit the owner of the puppies, but it will certainly help. There is more demand for Cavalier puppies in some areas than others. In Scotland where I live, puppies seem to be booked almost as soon as they are born, yet in other parts of the country (North West England for instance) it seems to be easier to obtain one.

There are various dog papers and magazines available. The Kennel Club produces a high quality monthly called *The Kennel Gazette*, and two papers called *Dog World* and *Our Dogs* are published weekly. These two are mainly for people who breed and show dogs and they

Pippa.

sometimes contain helpful advertisements. They also tell you when and where dog shows are held. These dog shows take place right through the year, all over Britain, ranging from large Championship shows where all breeds are shown to smaller local shows, called Open shows (also see Chapter 8). If you go to a local show and find the area where Cavaliers are being exhibited, the people there will almost certainly give you advice on where to get a puppy and what is best to get.

If you plan to show your Cavalier and later breed from her, you should go to several shows, including one or two large Championship shows, look at the Cavalier classes and decide which dogs you really like, and then go and talk to the owner or breeder of those dogs. You would hope in due course to be able to buy a puppy that would turn out to be quite like the dogs you admired.

When you buy a puppy from a breeder hoping to show it and later breed from it, you must remember that at eight or nine weeks of age you cannot be sure it will be a show dog and it should not be sold to you as a show dog. If the breeder thinks it shows some promise, that is the best you can hope for. The other point to remember is that a breeder will normally keep the best puppy in the litter; the only time you will get first choice is when you breed your litter yourself. However, if you have gone to a reputable breeder with winning dogs, you know the bloodlines are there, and that means you are making a good start when you come to breed your own pups. One further important point is that you should be sure to see the pedigree and check that there is not too much inbreeding, though there will always be some (also see further explanation of this in Chapter 9).

Which puppy?

So at last you have found someone with a suitable litter of puppies and you are going to see them and, all being well, choose your very own puppy and friend. When you get there, they will all be completely adorable but, as one or two may be of the wrong sex and one or two may not be for sale, that leaves you with a choice from two or three rather than all of them. So you talk to them, look at them, cuddle them (but ask the owner first!) and choose the one you like best. As long as the puppy you choose is active and outgoing, playful and friendly, you cannot go wrong. It is better not to choose the quiet little puppy retiring in a corner, but make sure it is not doing this because it played so hard just before you arrived that it has worn itself out.

The puppies should have solid little bodies and nice shiny coats, with round, bright eyes. You will want to take them all away with you! When I sell puppies, prospective purchasers usually come to choose a puppy when the pups are about five or six weeks old, and they come back for it in a few weeks when it is old enough to leave its mother. Sometimes they drop in for another visit as well, or they may bring their children to see it.

Of course, if you are hoping for a puppy you can show, there are a few more things to look out for (see Chapter 8). These are not as important as the points I have just mentioned; just what non-show people call 'cosmetic'.

However, choosing your puppy is not all that is expected of you. You will find (or should find, if the owner of the puppies is conscientious and concerned) that you will be asked all sorts of questions about your lifestyle, such as:

- Do you have a garden?
- Are you out at work all day?
- Do you have very small children?
- Have you any previous experience with dogs?

Me and my bone!

Do not be annoyed by this; it is being done for the benefit of your puppy, as the breeder is very anxious that the little one goes to a suitable home and that you get just what you want.

How much?

You will also, of course, be expected to pay for your puppy. It is difficult to quote a price; they are, on the whole, more expensive in London and the Home Counties. One that the breeder thinks very highly of will cost more than one which cannot be shown because (for instance) it is a ruby with a white front. An older puppy of about 10 months who has done very well in the show ring could be sold for four figures; but then it is very unlikely it would be sold at all.

Collecting your puppy

So at last you have come to a decision and are about to get your puppy. Make sure the breeder gives you its diet sheet so that you can give it just what it is used to; preferably before you come to collect puppy so you can stock up in advance. Ask her if it has been wormed and get details of when it is due to be done again and what was used. Do not be put off by this, as all puppies have roundworms and they can easily be eradicated by medication recommended by your veterinary surgeon. Too many worms can stop the puppy from thriving properly (see also chapters 6 and 10).

When you go to collect your new friend, have a little box (cardboard will do), with a clean blanket, in which to carry your puppy home. Ideally, two of you should go to collect the puppy, particularly if you are travelling by car, so that the driver is not distracted by Puppy trying to play about or climb out of the box. Make sure you note all the breeder's instructions carefully; she will want you to contact her next day to make sure all is well, anyway.

So now you're off, the devoted owner of the sweetest little puppy you ever saw.

Chapter Three
Looking after your Cavalier

Arriving home

Now that you have arrived safely home with Puppy, be sure to remember that the first thing she will need to do is relieve herself. Before you even go into the house with her, put her down in the garden (which is presumably fenced so that it is dog-proof, or you would surely not have acquired Puppy in the first place). Stay with her, and she will probably spend a penny fairly quickly. Now you can carry her into the house, probably the kitchen as she is untrained and will do quite a number of 'wets' at first. Put down some sheets of newspaper near the back door 'just in

Beware of the dog!

case' and let her run around and explore her new home. I mean by this she should be exploring just the one room, not wandering all over the house; and you, her new owner, will be with her at least for a while, to play with her and see that she does not feel too strange in her new environment. One or two nice chewy toys are always very welcome at this stage, kept in her own little toy box.

Sleeping quarters

Every puppy, and adult dog too, should have its own bed, a special place where it can lie and feel safe, and in which it can sleep at night. Dog beds and baskets can be bought at pet-shops and the bigger dog-shows also have them for sale. Cavalier puppies love to chew things, so that a bed

Beginning of a friendship.

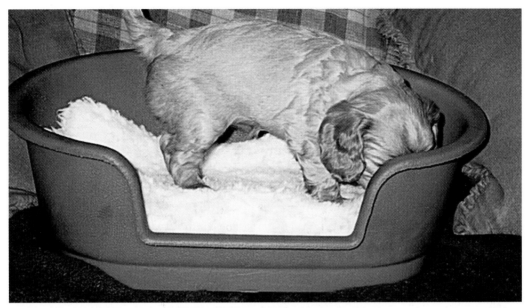

Small bed suitable for young Cavalier.

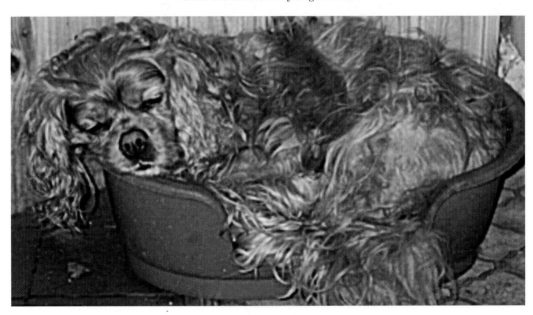

Same small bed with large, old dog, asleep.

made of soft, padded material or basketware may not last very long. Beds made of a hard plastic material are available at all pet outlets; they are either oval or round with an entrance section in front and come in many sizes. A small one, about 40cm (15in) across the base, is excellent for a small Cavalier. I actually have a rather large Cavalier who loves to snuggle up in this small bed (see above); and yes, there are larger beds available for her! Having acquired the bed, put some soft material in it to let Puppy feel really cosy; a folded (small) blanket in the bottom of the bed or a piece of a special material called Vet-bed is ideal. When Puppy is too old to chew it up, you could use a small cushion.

The first night

Puppy's first night in her new home is always a difficult time, both for owner and pup; she is bound to miss her mum and her brothers and sisters, and will never have spent a night alone before. Her bed should be in its regular place in a warm corner of the kitchen and she should be put to bed in there while her new owner goes off to her own bed, leaving the puppy to sleep quietly till next morning...

What a hope! She will almost certainly wake up fairly quickly (assuming she ever went to sleep at all) and start to whimper, possibly quite loudly. This is in fact a critical moment because, if her owner feels sorry for her (with good reason on her first night) and takes her upstairs, she will cry even louder, and for longer, the next night. The sensible thing to do is be quite firm and, after a couple of nights, she will get used to the situation and sleep in the kitchen quite happily. Some people suggest putting a ticking clock in her bed so that she does not feel so alone, though there is always the risk that she might chew it or mess up the bed to get at it. The ticking clock is comforting, but might be better just out of reach. Some owners do allow their dogs to sleep in the same room as them, in their own doggy beds. A few owners even allow their dogs on (or sometimes in!) their own beds. I had better come clean and admit that I have done this myself before now though not with a pup. However, if little Puppy is taken into the bedroom as young as this, she will almost certainly wet on the carpet, so it really would be much wiser to be firm and train her to sleep in the kitchen or wherever you wish her to be. She can come into the bedroom when she is house-trained if that is what you, her owner and best friend, feel you want for her. Meanwhile, be sure to leave newspaper down in the kitchen in case she performs during the night.

House training

House training Puppy (by which I mean teaching her to be clean in the house) is one of the most important things you have to teach her, if not *the* most important. She may not have had any training at all when you get her, although she will at least be used to doing her business on newspaper, since most breeders let their pups run around on this when they are in their puppy run. Therefore, if you leave paper down in the kitchen, she will very probably use that if necessary. This is not what you want, however; she has to be trained not to use paper at all but to wait till she gets outside.

A puppy will want to spend a penny whenever it wakes up after being asleep, after feeding and after exciting play. First thing in the morning, put Puppy in the garden and, if possible, stay with her until she has performed; then let her come in if she wishes, or stay out and play for a while. Do this after every feed, after she has been to sleep, or if she has been active for a while and seems to need to go out again. If you see her in a corner of the room sniffing at the carpet, this means she is looking for a place to perform (that is, unless you have managed to drop some delicious edible material on the floor), so take her outside at once. Whenever she spends her penny outside, be sure to praise her so that she gets the idea that this is what she is expected to do. When she spends her penny in the house, do not be angry, especially at first, but put her outside for a minute or two to build up the connection between 'wetting' and 'out'. Being angry with a young puppy when it wets can have the potentially disastrous effect of making it think that it is naughty to urinate anywhere; I have heard of this actually happening, though not with a Cavalier, and although the owner would take that dog out and walk her for an hour or two, when she got back, she still found somewhere in the house to hide and perform. I thought this was very sad both for the dog and the owner, and I do not know what finally happened, but the owner was seriously considering rehoming her dog. When an older dog, who knows perfectly well what is expected of him, performs in the house, he should certainly be told off firmly; but on the whole, Cavaliers are clean little dogs.

As you can see, training young puppies is hard work, but they soon learn if you persevere. Remember, all the dogs you know went through this stage once; and they are all clean now.

Feeding your Cavalier

Feeding the puppy

When you first bring Puppy home, follow carefully the diet on the sheet which the owner has given you, as she might well get a tummy upset from a sudden change of diet. If you feel you want to change this diet for any (good) reason, this is no problem; it is just a matter of gradually changing it a meal at a time over a period of a week or two. There are many different diets suitable for young puppies. As they are still so small and so recently weaned (this means that they have been taught to eat food other than their mother's milk), they need about five small meals every day. Here follows a suggested diet, the one I use myself and give to the people who buy my puppies:

First thing:	Small saucer of milk
Breakfast:	Weetabix and milk
Lunch:	45g (1¹/2oz) best mince with fine puppy meal soaked in stock.
Dinner:	60g (2oz) minced (or finely-chopped) chicken or fish with some cooked rice.
Last thing:	Saucer of milk and a very small biscuit.

Important points about the above:

- *Milk:* A bitch's milk is different from a cow's milk. Various specially-made powdered milks suitable for young puppies are available; the one I use is Lactol, one of the oldest brands of all. These powdered milks are mixed up as instructed on the packet (quite simple). As Puppy gets older, she can be introduced gradually to cow's milk until, by the time she is about $4^1/2$ months old or even earlier, she will be entirely on cow's milk. If Puppy is on cow's milk when she arrives and she seems to be thriving on it, then just carry on with it. There are a few people who still use it for puppies. Some puppies and adult dogs cannot tolerate cow's milk; they cannot digest it easily, so develop diarrhoea.
- *Variations on above:* Various diets are suitable for young puppies; I expect the one your breeder has given you, even if different from the above, will be completely satisfactory. Some tinned foods and some dried foods are made especially for puppies. As long as Puppy eats happily and seems fit and very active, has a healthy coat and neat, well-formed motions, and grows at a satisfactory rate, you can take it that her diet agrees with her; but always keep watching. Goat's milk also is good for puppies.
- *Cutting down on feeds:* After a few days, you will notice that Puppy may not want all her feeds; perhaps she will turn against her Weetabix and milk. This is quite natural, as five small feeds are far too many for an older dog or even an older puppy. So you begin to cut out some of the feeds at this stage. I suggest cutting out the first saucer of milk and giving the cereal as first meal. About a fortnight later, another feed will go. By the time Puppy is five months old, she should be on just two meals: a main evening meal and a smaller

breakfast. She can still have a saucer of milk last thing if you feel she wants this. Some puppies never go off any of their feeds, but in this case you gradually cut the feeds anyway. The feeds will get larger as Puppy grows up to make up for the fact that there are fewer of them.

Feeding a full-grown Cavalier

There are many different foods available to suit Cavaliers: tinned, dried and fresh. Nowadays dried complete foods are very popular; the best ones contain necessary supplements, such as vitamins and calcium, as well as the food itself. They are also very quick and convenient at feeding time. The good tinned dog foods contain quality meat and also the required supplements. The best-known manufacturers of dog food do a great deal of research on what keeps dogs really fit, making due allowance for size and breed. When buying prepared foods, do remember that on the whole you get what you pay for; so buy a good quality food if you can.

It is also possible to buy fresh dog meat, usually frozen. I am a believer in fresh meat myself, but it is more trouble; it has to be defrosted and cooked and is usually messier. My dogs get one main meal a day, consisting of 140–170g (5–6oz) meat mixed with a (small lady's) handful of finely-broken biscuit. Added to this are half a dessertspoonful of corn oil, a large pinch of seaweed powder and a pinch of garlic granules. The larger dogs have 170g meat, while the smaller ones have just a little less. Both the corn oil and the garlic come from the supermarket, and the seaweed powder comes from the canine herb specialists. My dogs also get a small biscuit first thing, and a saucer of milk and two chocolate drops last thing at night.

Cavaliers are not supposed to get titbits and certainly should not be allowed to beg at meals. Be sure not to overfeed your Cavalier; if he gets fat, he will not look so nice and it is bad for him. Notice that 140g meat and a handful of biscuit is not all that much.

Special diets

Some Cavaliers need special diets. Some owners encourage fussy feeders by giving them nice things like chicken with rice; others maintain you should not give in to them and that they will eat if they are hungry. I'm afraid I come into the former group. If a Cavalier regularly has rather runny motions, a complete dried food (possibly mixed in with the fresh or tinned meat) can be very helpful. There is more about this in chapter 10.

Inoculation

When Puppy first comes home, she will not be able to go outside for a walk until she is about four months old. This is because all Cavalier puppies (all pups actually) have to be protected by inoculation against several very dangerous diseases which would probably cause death if they were to pick one of them up in the street outside. These are distemper (hardpad), hepatitis, parvovirus, leptospirosis and para-influenza and, because so many dogs are inoculated against them, they are seldom met with today.

One of the first things you do with Puppy is take her to visit your vet. This is to check that you have been sold a fit puppy with no incipient problems and to get, or arrange to get, her first inoculation. Normally there are just two inoculations, occasionally three; but be guided by your vet on this. After the final inoculation, you still have to wait for a week or 10 days for the inoculation to take effect; then at last Puppy can go out into the big wide world!

Exercise and lead training

While Puppy is unable to go beyond the home she can spend a lot of time playing in the house and even more running in the garden. Most Cavaliers living alone like human company when playing, so you also may spend time with her in the garden.

During this period she can learn to wear a collar and walk on the lead. Begin by putting on a small collar and leaving it on for half an hour or so, possibly less if she objects very strongly to it. Do this a couple of times a day until she is quite accustomed to it. It is not advisable to leave a Cavalier's collar on all day if you intend to show her as this will detract from the lovely ruff she should have round the front of her neck when she grows up. Once Puppy is happy

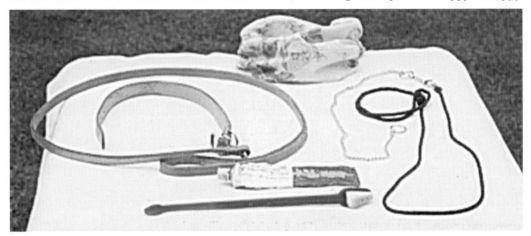

Necessary items: (from left, anti-clockwise) collar and lead for everyday use, toothbrush and toothpaste, show lead with light chain collar, hood to keep ears out of the food bowl.

wearing her collar, then attach a small, light lead to it and try to walk her round with it on. She may accept it quite happily, but she is equally likely to refuse to move when wearing it. In this case, just leave it hanging while she walks around on her own and she should gradually become used to it. Remember if you do this that she may well chew up the lead, so use an old cheap one. You may find she walks for a short while on the lead and then refuses to go on, but usually stopping and petting her will start things up again. Remember, as with house training, all pups walk on the lead in the end. During this in-house period she can also learn a few basic things, like coming when she is called – and the word 'No!'

When Puppy first goes out, be sure to keep her on her lead unless you are in a completely safe place and are quite sure she will come back to you when you want her. You can train her to come when you call her by praising her when she does so and giving her a little titbit like a chocolate drop. When she begins to grow up, this method may not always work quite as well as you had hoped, especially when something really exciting crops up, like a rabbit. Cavaliers are basically hunters, some more than others, and a really good scent can blind them to all else. So always be watchful – accidents happen very quickly.

An adult Cavalier needs a minimum of half an hour's walk a day including, if possible, some time off the lead. Once or twice a week, or more if it can be done, he will love a really long walk over the hills (but watch out for livestock) or on the beach or by the river. As I said earlier, a Cavalier will make do with a short walk some of the time, but also makes an excellent companion on a long walk and is much the better for it.

Grooming

Adult Cavaliers have long, soft feathering and even the flatter parts of their coats are 2–3cm long. This means that they need regular grooming, if possible every day. When you first get your puppy, the coat will be much much shorter, and she will probably not have any feathering at all; none the less, she will need to be brushed gently every day, partly to keep her looking nice, but also to get her used to being groomed. Cavaliers are supposed to be natural little dogs, not trimmed in any way. The only trimming that is permissible is the removal of excess hair from between the toes or beneath the foot. This does not include the small bunches of hair on top of and just between the toes; these are an essential part of the Cavalier's coat and should not be trimmed especially if you are planning to show your dog.

When you first brush your puppy, hold her gently as you do it, using a small medium-soft brush. She will soon let you stand her on a chair or low table (covered with a towel so that she does not slip off it) and brush her there. After three or four weeks, use a small comb as well; not too finely-toothed or she may take a dislike to it. As the feathering on the ears comes in, the ears especially need careful brushing and combing.

When your puppy has got most of her coat and is really no longer a puppy you will need the following grooming equipment:

*   *Two combs*, one with quite widely spaced teeth, the other with teeth closely spaced. These are illustrated in the photograph. The black finish on the finer comb means it will go through the coat more easily.
*   *A good quality brush*. The best ones are the Fortnum and Mason brushes, made with real bristle on a pneumatic base. They are very expensive but are probably worth it in the end. It is also possible to buy similar brushes made by other firms which do not cost so much but are still effective. I have used the brush in thephotograph below, with real bristle and a small oval of strong nylon to keep the bristles firm, for the last 20 years.

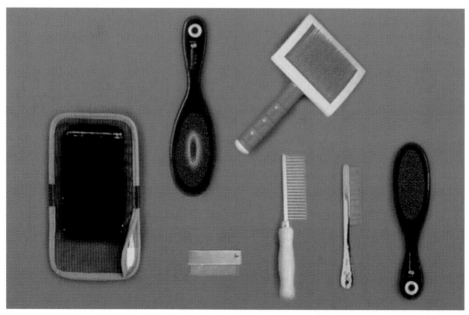

Grooming items: (from left, anti-clockwise) horsehair hand glove, fine flea comb, less fine comb, fine black coated comb, small show brush, wire slicker brush, large bristle brush.

- *Small show brush.* The one in the photograph is an old Fortnum and Mason brush.
- *Hand glove* with horse hair on one side and velvet on the other.
- *Very fine-toothed flea comb;* one hopes this will not often be needed!
- *Wire slicker brush.* I do not always use this as some of my dogs are not very happy with it and I can often manage without it. Many breeders use them a lot; perhaps their dogs have a slightly different coat texture. Recently a special slicker brush for more sensitive skins has been marketed.

When you groom your dog, place him on a non-slip surface and begin by combing his ears gently with the wider comb. First comb forward and down, then turn the ears over and back (against the neck) and comb again. If you find any knots, gently tease them out. Do not cut them out, especially if you intend to show your dog. If you groom regularly, there should be very few knots. When the ears are completely combed out with both combs, the finer one after you have used the wider one, brush them well (with the larger brush – the small brush is for use in the show ring), first downwards, then laid back as above. Next comb and then brush the front, making sure you go well up beneath the ears and round just behind them. Comb and brush the feathers on the legs, then the tail and rear. Do this latter particularly gently as Cavaliers do not always like having anything done to their rear ends. Finally, comb over the body, and then give it a really good brush. Finish off with the horse-hair hand glove. Last of all, wipe under your dog's eyes with a piece of cotton wool soaked in tepid water, possibly two or three times. If your dog is stained under the eyes, it is possible to use a stain removing lotion, with care.

Beanie being groomed.

It should not be necessary to spray your dog to get a shine. If she has been kept clean and regularly groomed and is in tip-top condition, her coat should shine anyway. A good diet and regular exercise both help to give her a gleaming, healthy appearance.

Baths

Cavaliers need the occasional bath to keep them clean and fresh. They are also always bathed before a dog show. Numerous dog shampoos are available, or you can use one of the many 'human' shampoos. Everyone has his or her own favourite dog shampoo. For everyday use, I always use a well-known shampoo called JDS, which stands for Jeyes' Disinfectant Shampoo, although now it is produced by Phillips. It is a good insecticide and also gets the coat shiny and clean. For shows, I use a good quality 'human' shampoo with oil in it.

After her bath, your Cavalier needs to be dried. It is possible to do this by giving her a good rub with a towel and then putting her by the fire while you brush her. However, you will get a smoother finish if you use a dryer. If you use a power dryer on a stand, you can use both hands for grooming and results can be excellent. It is possible to use a hand dryer, but try to get a fairly powerful one. Dry all the different areas of the coat in the direction in which the coat will lie anyway. To keep the coat on the body flat, I use the straight-ended nozzle attached to my hand dryer. Some people use old tights cut and put over the body for this, but I feel the coat loses some of its shine that way. Do not allow a puppy you have bathed to go out until it is completely dry.

Nails

Cavaliers are active little dogs, so they normally keep their nails down by the amount of exercise they take. If they exercise mainly on grass, their nails will not be worn down so much as if they use pavements or run on concrete. The nail should grow to about 3mm beyond the quick, or be cut to this length if need be. If a dog has white (well, whitish!) nails, it is easy to see the quick as a fine, red line (actually a vein) but if the nails are black it is much more difficult. A Cavalier's nails must be cut very carefully in case the quick is cut and they bleed. There are two kinds of nail clipper, both of which are equally effective: the guillotine type and the clipper type.

Teeth

A Cavalier's teeth should be inspected carefully every month and cleaned every week. It is possible to buy a 'doggy' toothbrush and deliciously flavoured 'doggy' toothpaste, so this can be done quite easily. I found my brush and toothpaste pack, bought from the vet, remarkably expensive, but it has lasted well and been very effective. The toothpaste is malt flavoured, so the dogs actually enjoy having their teeth cleaned. Some Cavaliers' teeth have a tendency to develop tartar, which in the end will loosen the teeth; if there is any sign of this, try to remove it with your fingernail or a scraper. Usually this is easier said than done so, if you are really worried about the amount of tartar on your dog's teeth, it might be as well to have a word with your vet about it. Companies such as Nylabone produce products designed to help to prevent the build-up of tartar.

Chamanic Shannon (ruby): a well cared for, well groomed dog owned by Jocelyn Inman.

Aust/NZ Ch Elvenhome Buckthorn (blen): another example of how a Cavalier should look.
Owned and bred by Mrs Jeanie Montford. Photo: Cabal

Travel in the car

When he is still quite young, Puppy should be taken for short runs in the car, to get him used to it and to check that he does not become car-sick. The best place for a pup (or a larger dog for that matter) to travel is in a comfortable cage in the back of the car. It is not really safe to have a young dog travelling loose in a moving vehicle, though many older dogs behave perfectly well loose in the car. If your pup becomes car-sick, it might be as well to let him travel in the front of the car on someone's knee with a towel beneath him until he becomes more used to driving. Most dogs settle down in the end, however. There are pictures of various kinds of cage on pages 94, 95 and 97.

General Comments

Do not leave your Cavalier alone for too long; Cavaliers like company and are very unhappy if alone for more than two or three hours. If you have more than one Cavalier the situation is very much improved, as the dogs have each other for company.

The most important thing of all that you can do for your little Cavalier friend is to make him feel really loved and part of your family; in return, he will give you unquestioning devotion to the end of his life.

Chapter Four

The evolution of the Cavalier King Charles Spaniel

Early history

At present, the lovely little Cavalier King Charles Spaniel is about the seventh most popular breed (see appendix A) in Great Britain – yet in 1928, The Kennel Club was not prepared to recognise it as a breed at all. In this chapter I will attempt to show how the breed evolved over the centuries. This means that it is also an account of the evolution of the King Charles Spaniel, as until the 20th century there was no recognised difference between the two.

A very small dog existed in Malta as long ago as 1000 BC. This was the original Maltese, called in those days the *Melitaeus*. By about 500 BC, two types of Maltese seem to have developed. One was similar to today's Maltese, which has changed relatively little over the centuries. The other was a dog more like a Pomeranian, sometimes known as the *Shock Dog* (though this name is unreliable as it has been used for other small, hairy dogs). A number of these little dogs were taken to Italy, though the Maltese islanders were jealous of allowing their own Maltese type to leave the island. The Italian dog continued to be called the Melitaeus, and some pictures of it could be found in classical times.

Later on again, a number of small reddish and white oriental dogs were brought to Italy from the Middle East. This oriental breed was crossed with the Italian Melitaeus and the final result was the little red and white toy spaniel that we know today from its appearance in the works of several of the most famous Italian painters. One such work is Titian's well known *Venus Couchée*, which hangs in the Uffizi Gallery in Florence, in which a lovely red and white spaniel lies curled beside her. This was painted around 1500, as was another picture showing one of these spaniels painted by Palma Vecchio. Veronese depicted these dogs in some of his works a few years later. These little spaniels had pointed noses and fairly short faces with high skulls, and they were very small. Although most spaniels originated in Spain (hence the name) there is no record of these toy spaniels being found there at this period.

Towards the mid-16th century, some of these little spaniels were sent from Italy to France, where they immediately became very popular at court. Mary Queen of Scots is said to have kept small dogs sent over from France. Certainly, she corresponded constantly with her Guise relations, who were still in France, throughout her long years of imprisonment in England. From this, it looks as if the little dog who was with her when she was executed could have been a toy spaniel. After her death in 1587, no more of these little spaniels came to Britain until 1660, when Charles II came to the throne at the Restoration. His sister Henrietta brought some over with her from France, and he already had some of his own. Soon there were several of these dogs at court, Charles II sensibly maintaining that he much preferred them to his courtiers. It is said that he made a decree saying that his little Cavalier-type dogs had royal status and could go anywhere; I am planning to take three of my Cavaliers to the Ritz some time to put this to the test! Henrietta also had some small black and white spaniels which she had brought over from France (Holland type, see on). None of them was black and tan at this time, but there were a few curly-coated black spaniels, related to the Spanish Truffle dog imported into England during the first half of the century. Yet the old names for these dogs during the 19th century are *King Charles* for the black and tan, *Prince Charles* for the tricolour and *Blenheim* for the red and white spaniel. The last of these is still used today.

Charles I had spaniels at court as well, but these were much bigger sporting or Springer types obtained from the Duke of Marlborough. Van Dyck's picture of *The Three*

Plush and needlework picture of tricolour Cavalier with puppy, dated c 1850.

Eldest Children of Charles I painted in 1630 shows two of these larger spaniels, although one is smaller than the other. It is said that some of the Charles II toy spaniels were crossed with these larger spaniels and from this cross the prized lozenge mark came; though there is a painting by the French artist Metsys showing a lozenge and dated around 1550. It was said that, when the Duke of Marlborough was away fighting the Battle of Blenheim, his wife the Duchess was so worried that she kept pressing her thumb on the head of one of her spaniel bitches who was on her knee. This bitch was about to have puppies and, when the pups arrived, they all had red thumb prints on their heads.

A black and white toy spaniel was also bred in Italy at the end of the 14th century. It came from an Eastern import, crossed with the Pom-type Maltese. In due course, some of these reached Holland and France. Largillière painted a picture of Louis XIV and his heirs, clearly showing one of these little black and white spaniels. This painting is to be found in the Wallace Collection in London, and the spaniel in it had a more pointed nose than the red and white spaniels and less stop (indentation where the nasal bone and skull meet). These spaniels are also ancestors of the Papillon, and have been referred to as Papillon Spaniels. Charles II had some of these little black and white spaniels and others were brought to England by William of Orange at the end of the 17th century. The Princes of Orange had these dogs for many years, having presumably acquired them from Italy round about the year 1600.

After the Stuarts (from 1688 onwards) the House of Orange ruled in Britain. They too had toy spaniels, mainly black and white, and some of the red and white type were still to be found in the highest circles also. This situation applied both in Britain and on the Continent right through the 18th century, and a number of well-known pictures show these dogs. There is Watteau's *A Lady at her Toilet,* painted about 1715 and showing a delightful little red and white spaniel, and also his *Embarcation for the Island of Cythera*, which seems to show the same dog. Fragonard's *The Souvenir*, dated about 1785, also shows a small spaniel, a little larger than the two previous ones. All these paintings are in the Wallace Collection. During this period, some of the very small red and white spaniels were crossed with some of the heavier Marlborough red and whites, so that toy spaniels were tending to become larger here.

So far little mention has been made of black or black and tan toy spaniels. The first black spaniel to be painted seems to be Mignard's spaniel, found in his picture of the Dauphin dated 1650. Its head is remarkably like the head of Mrs Lytton's Bunthorne, a curly black toy spaniel who lived around 1900. Mrs Lytton, later Baroness Wentworth, was extremely interested in toy dogs and especially in toy spaniels and their history. She did a lot of research into the subject and produced at her own expense a book of over 300 pages about the toy breeds, toy spaniels in particular.

During the period 1650–1800, there were curly-coated black spaniels, a larger curly-coated dog called the *Truffle Dog* and an elegant little smooth-coated black and tan called a *Pyramé* and found mainly in

Staffordshire pottery dogs
from the author's collection.

Europe. Greuze has a lovely painting of his wife with her 'Toy Spaniel', a charming smooth-coated Pyramé. This painting, which is in a private collection, dates to about 1770. Most of these black or black and tan spaniels were found on the Continent, though some black curly spaniels did appear in Britain during the reign of Charles I. It is said that there were not any actually at court although, as already noted, they were called King Charles Spaniels later on.

The real change during the 19th century was the introduction of the gene for black-and-tan colouring into the breed. This gene also helped to bring about the arrival of the ruby Cavalier, first shown in 1830 in one of Landseer's paintings, but not actually mentioned in print until 1875 (a Mr Garwood's 'Dandy'). Seurat shows a small red (ruby) spaniel in his well known picture *Bathers at Asnières*, painted about 1880. The introduction of the black-and-tan gene must have been brought about by crossing the little Pyramé with a black toy spaniel (such as Bunthorne) or with a curly type of toy spaniel called the *Trawler*. Both these black spaniels are probably descended from the curly black spaniel of the early 17th century. It looks as if the Pyramé had a very important influence on the future development of the breed, as it introduced both the smoother coat and the black and tan colouring.

The Miniature Toy Trawler must also have been important, as they could be either black or red (the ruby red found in Cavaliers), though never black and tan, and a Trawler litter could contain both colours. When a black and tan was crossed with a Miniature Toy Trawler, the offspring were said by Mrs Lytton to be *very like the Trawler but with black and tan markings*. Some of these offspring must have been red, but unfortunately there does not seem to be any definite evidence of this. However, Mrs Lytton states: *Black Miniature Toy Trawler mated to Black Miniature Toy Trawler: (the puppies were) always uniform in type, whole black or whole red with or without white breasts.* Hence it seems likely that the ruby originated from the red Trawler crossed with a black and tan, itself the result of a Pyramé and curly black spaniel cross. A great deal of crossing was going on among toy spaniels at this time and, as a result, to quote Mrs Lytton again, there was *utter confusion of names and colours*.

Some of the most popular pictures of toy spaniels were painted during the 19th century. Best known of all is *The Cavalier's Pets*, painted by Landseer in 1845 (see page 32–33); one is a blenheim, the other a tricolour. There are several pictures of Queen Victoria's dogs, also by Landseer, the best known being his lovely portrait of her favourite, Dash.

What really happened genetically to the toy spaniel during the 19th century will probably never be known; but by the end of the century there were blenheims, tricolours, black-and-tans, rubies, and still a few all-black toy spaniels. Nose length varied, but tended to be medium to short. Illustrations on old postcards show what some of these dogs were like (see page 34).

The Kennel Club was first set up in 1873 and, from then on, there was an ever-increasing interest in dogs and dog breeding. The toy spaniel enthusiast of that time wanted a breed of short-nosed toy spaniels and, by the 1920s, the breed known as the King Charles Spaniel had full Kennel Club recognition. The longer-nosed toy spaniel of the old pictures had disappeared.

The revival

In 1925, an American called Mr Roswell Eldridge came over to England and tried to buy a breeding pair of Cavaliers of the old type that had appeared in so many of the old pictures. He was unable to find any after looking around on several visits; but, being a man who did not give up easily, he decided to try to do something about it. He offered two £25 prizes at Crufts for the winners of two classes, one for dogs and one for bitches, for the dog most like the old spaniels, to be awarded for the next three years. The advertisement in the 1926 Crufts catalogue read:

> Blenheim Spaniels of the Old Type, as shown in the pictures of Charles II's time, long face, no stop, flat skull, not inclined to be domed, with spot in centre of skull. The 1st prizes of £25 in classes 947 and 948 are given by Roswell Eldridge Esq, New York, USA.

In fact, this prize was awarded for a further two years, making a total of five years. At that time, £25 was a lot of money, enough to encourage people to attempt to produce this type of dog; added to this, a few people were interested in taking up the challenge, quite apart from the money offered. Unfortunately, Mr Roswell Eldridge, who was nearly 70 when he put in his famous advertisment, did not live long enough to see the effects of his offer; but his name will always be remembered among Cavalier folk.

This award was first offered in 1926 and there were only two entries in each class. The winners were Mrs Treleaven's Ferdie of Monham and Mrs Raymond-Mallock's Flora. In 1927 there were three entries in each class and Mrs Hewitt Pitt (of whom more later) won first prize in the bitch class with Waif Julia. There was a big improvement in 1928, with five dogs entered and nine bitches. The dog winner was Miss K Mostyn-Walker's Ann's Son, and Mrs Pitt won the bitch class again, this time with Hentzau Sweet Nell. In 1929, there were six dogs and six bitches. Ann's Son won his class again, while the bitch winner was Flora, the winner at the first of the bitch classes (in 1926). In 1930, the last year of these special classes, there were three entries for the dog class and eight bitches. Ann's Son won the dog class for the third time.

As early as 1928, when the special classes were still going on, the Cavalier King Charles Spaniel Club was first founded. At this time, very few people were interested in this new breed, and only eight turned up at the inaugural meeting. The dog was given the name Cavalier to differentiate it from the King Charles Spaniels, the only toy spaniels to be recognised by The Kennel Club at that time.

King Charles Spaniels, or *The Cavalier's Pets*. Sir Edwin Landseer, 1845. © Tate Gallery London

Toy Spaniels on a postcard clearly marked 1905.

It was not until 1945 that The Kennel Club granted separate recognition to the 'new' type of toy spaniel. Up till then, Cavaliers had to be shown in the same classes as the King Charles except at the shows run by the Cavalier King Charles Spaniel Club, which were attended only by the new Cavaliers. The breed standard was carefully drawn up, using the old pictures, while Ann's Son was taken as the live model on whom the standard was based. The first chairman was Miss Mostyn-Walker, while Mrs Hewitt Pitt (usually known as Mrs Pitt) was the first secretary. The driving force behind the formation of the club, and hence the revival of the breed, was Mrs Pitt, perhaps known more often as Amice Pitt, who continued to be active until the early 1970s. The breed as it is today owes so much to her and to her indefatigable work in the early days.

The Cavalier Club held a show in 1930, directly after the special Cruft's class. Again, Ann's Son won three classes, all the ones for which he was eligible. Amazingly, in 1936 he was brought out of retirement and entered at Crufts, where he won again. Ann's Son was never beaten in his entire career, and produced many puppies, a number of whom are the foundation of the breed as it is today. He was described in the *Cavalier Club Bulletin* of 1955 as follows:

A toy dog of 13 lbs, short in the back, entirely flat head, streaming ears to his legs, large dark eyes wide apart, nose long with white blaze running from it right up the forehead (and) tipped with jet to match his dark eyes, thick soft silky coat like the early pictures, a lightly marked red-gold and silver Blenheim and as sound as a bell. He was supreme... It was the overall quality which this exquisite little dog had and which shines out of his face in the picture, that makes him the 'Best Ever Born'. His breeder told me of his enchanting temperament and how he was mated to lots of bitches... but alas, not many of his descendants has been his equal. All the same, he lies in the pedigrees of most kennels and perhaps one day a perfect tiny gold and silver descendant with his quality will trot into the ring. I only hope if this happens that the dog will be recognised as a paragon and not passed over!

His picture is on page 36, and he certainly looks a lovely little dog, although one can see that he has a rather narrow face, described by Mrs Pitt as *mean under the eyes*. She also said that his hindquarters were not very good. Suggestions have been made that he was closely related to a Papillon, and the fact that he was so small and graceful could bear this out. He certainly has beautiful round, dark Cavalier eyes, though.

These early breeders had many problems to overcome, not least the very small number of suitable dogs to use for breeding. This led to a lot of inbreeding. For instance, Ann's Son was

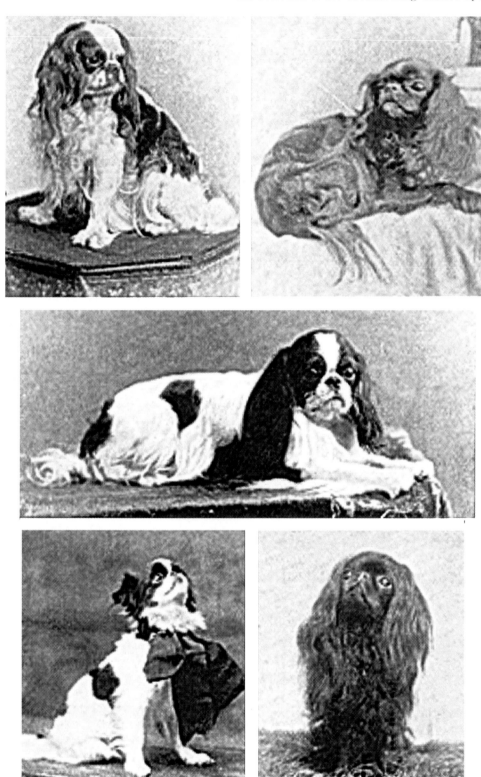

Toy Spaniels from 1893: (top left) Mrs Thompson's blenheim, Dandy;
(top right) Mrs Thompson's ruby, Ruby Princess; (centre) Mr W Phillips' Prince Charles, King of the Fancy;
(bottom left) Mrs R L Crawford Jr's Japanese, Tootsie; (bottom right) Mrs F Senn's King Charles, Romeo.

mated to his own daughter, Miss Ann's Son, one of their offspring being Daywell Nell (see page 37). The Cavalier breeders also sometimes used the long-nosed 'throw-outs' from King Charles litters as there were so few Cavalier types available. It is possible that Papillons, Cockers and Welsh Springers were used occasionally. It has also been suggested that Dachshunds were used at this time but I do not believe this. During this period, Mrs Pitt and her daughter Jane travelled to many places, showing the new Cavaliers in variety classes so that they would gradually become better known. There were few Cavaliers of the required standard in these days; many, according to Mrs Pitt herself, *fell far short of the standard and were a great deal too big*. Yet the few good Cavaliers had already found admirers.

In the *Cavalier Portrait Gallery* (pages 40–46) there are various old photographs of Cavaliers who lived between 1926 and the end of World War 2 (1945). None is a champion (or even has a stud book number) as in those days Cavaliers were not recognised by The Kennel Club. Some of

AT

STUD

FEE
3 gns.
prepaid
return
carriage
extra

" Ann's Son "

The Noted King Charles Spaniel.

NEVER BEATEN.

Winner of the £50 Trophy and £15 Special at Cruft's 1936, also winner of the £25 Special offered for Old Type King Charles Spaniels at Cruft's 1928, 1929, and 1930.

A very beautiful little dog.

Sires small stock of unmistakable type and quality

Miss Mostyn Walker,

Clova Kennels   ::   Costessey,

Norwich.

TEL: COSTESSEY 76

Ann's Son.

them (for instance, Kobba of Kuranda) have King Charles type (short-nosed) parents. A short commentary on each dog is also given. Looking carefully through these pages and studying the notes should give a much better idea of the development of the very early Cavaliers than just reading long descriptions.

The outbreak of war in 1939 was yet another set-back to the early breeders. Many kennels had to be disbanded because the owners were involved in war work and there was a serious lack of food for their animals. Mrs Pitt, who also kept Chows, had a large number of dogs, but sadly was only able to keep three bitches and one dog; the same happened to many others. The one breeder who kept going during the war was Mme J Harper Trois-Fontaines, a wealthy Belgian lady who had a school for models in London and a country home near Amersham. Because of the lack of stud dogs at this time and the shortage of petrol for travelling to those that there were, she did a lot of inbreeding (mating close relatives such as father to daughter and brother to sister).

Once the war was over, Mrs Pitt wanted to begin her Cavalier breeding all over again. She did not want a dog that was too inbred, or one that was too like the very early ones, so naturally she tried to go back to Ann's Son. Lt Col and Mrs Brierley, of Daywell Manor near Oswestry, had a little bitch called Daywell Nell. She was the daughter of Ann's Son and Miss Ann's Son, herself a daughter of Ann's Son, and she was mated to Cannonhill Richey, whose sire was Plantation Banjo. The litter arrived on 7 October 1945; and when he was old enough, Mrs Pitt and her daughter Jane drove over to fetch a little dog from this litter, although they had not previously seen him. Mrs Pitt bought him to give to Jane; his registered name was Daywell Roger, though his pet name was 'Lou'. That same year, Cavaliers were allowed Kennel Club registration, and he was the first Cavalier to gain the title of champion. He sired 11 champions, siring his last litter in his 12th year, and was a beautiful dog who would still do well in the ring today. Most Cavalier pedigrees go back to him.

The very first Cavalier championship show was held on 29 August 1946 at Stratford-on-Avon. The judge was Mrs Jennings (founder of the Plantation lines). Twenty-eight dogs and three litters were entered, making a total of 109 entries, as well as nine in the brace class and three in the team class. Note that today no puppy under six months is allowed at a show; but things were very different then. The Best of Breed (BOB) was Mrs Eldred's Belinda of Saxham, a seven-year-old Blenheim, and the dog Challenge Certificate (CC) was won by Daywell Roger, aged only 10 months. From this time onwards, The Kennel Club recognised Cavaliers as a separate breed and they were at last able to win CCs. By the end of 1949, there were seven Cavalier champions:

- **Ch Daywell Roger** (blenheim, picture page 42), breeder Lt Col and Mrs Brierley, owner Jane Pitt, born 7 October 1945
   Sire: Cannonhill Richey (ruby), son of Plantation Banjo and Plantation Dusky, both black-and-tans, half-brother and sister from Plantation Robert (blenheim)
   Dam: Daywell Nell (blenheim), daughter of Ann's Son and Miss Ann's Son (both blenheims), sire and daughter.
- **Ch Amanda Loo of Ttiweh** (black-and-tan, picture page 43), breeder Mrs Mansour, owner Mrs A Pitt, born 11 June 1946
   Sire: Bernard of Astondowns (ruby), son of Cannonhill Richey (ruby)
   Dam: Princess Anita de Fontenay (black-and-tan). Daughter of Plantation Banjo (black-and-tan)

- **Ch Katrina of Loyaltyway** (tricolour bitch), breeder Mrs Speedwell Massingham, owner Capt J Spink, born 17 August 1946
    Sire: Bouncer Rupert (tricolour), mainly Plantation breeding
    Dam: Gloria of Grenewich (blenheim), son of Rupert the Cavalier (blenheim)
- **Ch Royalist of Veren** (black-and-tan dog, picture page 43), breeder and owner Mrs Rennie, born 28 September 1945
    Sire: Cannonhill Richey (ruby)
    Dam: Rustle of Veren (tricolour), mainly Plantation breeding
- **Ch Harmony of Ttiweh** (blenheim dog, picture page 43), owner and breeder Mrs A Pitt, born 25 June 1947.
    Sire: Ch Daywell Roger (blenheim)
    Dam: Ch Little Dorrit of Ttiweh (blenheim) by Bouncer Rupert (tricolour) ex Belinda of Saxham (blenheim)
- **Ch Hillbarn Alexander of Ttiweh** (blenheim dog), breeder Mrs H Pilkington, owner Mrs A Pitt, born 26 April 1947.
    Sire: Ch Daywell Roger (blenheim)
    Dam: Cassandra of Hillbarn (tricolour), by The Young Pretender of Grenewich (Blenheim) out of a granddaughter of Cannonhill Richey (ruby)
- **Ch Mingshang Sir Roger** (blenheim dog), breeder and owner Miss P Mayhew, born 4 August 1947
    Sire: Ch Daywell Roger (blenheim)
    Dam: Mingshang Sarah (blenheim) by The Young Pretender of Grenewich (blenheim) ex Georgette de Fontenay

I have put in this list of the first champions up till the end of 1949 as a careful study of it shows several things: Daywell Roger's remarkable success as a stud dog, the importance of the ruby Cannonhill Richey, the influence of the Plantation lines, and the success of Bunty Green's Young Pretender as a stud dog. Note also the custom in those days of mixing wholecolours and particolours much more than is done today. You can see from the picture on page 41 that Plantation Robert is a blenheim, though in the past it was incorrectly stated that he was a ruby. He was the sire of both Plantation Dusky and Plantation Banjo, both black-and-tans, who have a number of particolour descendants, mainly through Daywell Nell. The *Cavalier King Charles Spaniel Club Book of Champions* gives further details of these early pedigrees and makes fascinating reading; it can be obtained from the club see **Book List** and **Useful Addresses**).

I could continue for many more pages to talk about the lovely old champions of the past, and the more recent ones. However, if I did this, the book would go on for ever! In the *Cavalier Portrait Gallery* (pages 40–46) you will find more pictures of dogs (and owners) who are part of Cavalier history. The notes by each picture attempt to explain their importance. In the rest of this chapter, I will mention a few of the many earlier breeders and their dogs who have done so much for the breed over the years.

Mrs Daphne Murray

In the early 1930s, Daphne Murray came to Mrs Pitt and her daughter Jane as a kennel pupil. She gave them a great deal of help, at the same time learning much about how to care for dogs. Jane describes Daphne as friend and helper to herself, her mother and the Ttiwehs. In due course she founded the successful Crustadele kennels, her earliest dogs being of Mrs Pitt's breeding. In 1969, her ruby bitch, Piccola of Crustadele, became the first ruby champion in the breed. I remember seeing her ruby boy, Crustadele Shumas Magic, when I came into Cavaliers.

Mrs Barbara Keswick

Mrs Keswick acquired her first Cavaliers in the late 1940s and they were mainly related to Ch Daywell Roger and the Ttiwehs. Her first champion was Ch Pargeter Jollyean of Avoncliffe, made up in 1950. He was bred by Mrs L Hitching; note that his grandsire on both sides was Cannonhill Richey. Mrs Keswick's stock was exported to a number of countries, particularly to the United States, Canada, Australia and New Zealand, and became the foundation stock of many well-known breeders in these areas (see chapter 12).

After that, Mrs Keswick bred 11 more champions before her death in 1969. The most influential of these were probably Ch Pargeter Bob-Up, Ch Pargeter Melissa, and their son, Int Ch Pargeter McBounce; they all appear in many pedigrees and McBounce won the award for Best Stud Dog in both 1973 and 1974, having produced eight champion offspring. Perhaps the best known of these is Lady Forwood's Ch Archie McMuck of Eyeworth. Helping Mrs Keswick at Cowhill was Barbara Wall, who stayed with her right up until she died in 1969, lovingly looking after all her Cavaliers literally from birth to death. She once told me that her favourite of them all was Ch Pargeter Patron. Caroline Gatheral also helped Mrs Keswick, successfully handling her dogs at many shows.

Miss Pamela Turle

Pamela Turle bought her first Cavalier in 1949 from Jane Pitt; named Lucasta of Sunninghill, she was all Ttiweh lines. Miss Turle's most famous dog was Ch Aloysius of Sunninghill, a tricolour, who won 19 CCs, his first in 1957, and sired eight British champions. He held the record for the most CCs won by one dog for 33 years, until Hall and Evans' Ch Springtide of Alansmere (a blenheim) broke it in 1993. One of Aloysius' champion offspring was Irish-bred Int Ch Sunninghill Perseus of Lochfee. Aloysius' name appears in the early pedigrees of the Crisdigs, the Alansmeres, and many others. Miss Turle continued with her Cavaliers for many years, and is now retired, living peacefully in Wales.

Lady Mary Forwood

Lady Forwood bred and showed many successful Cavaliers during the late 1950s and 1960s. Perhaps the best-known of her seven champions is Ch Archie McMuck of Eyemouth, whom I have already mentioned. She also bred and owned one of the early black-and-tan champions, Ch Cointreau of Eyemouth, whose grandsire was Ch Royalist of Veren. Lady Forwood was also a very active member of the Cavalier Club and, although now retired, she is still a top judge and continues to take an interest in the breed. She wrote a good book about the Cavalier King Charles Spaniel, first published in 1967, which I have and still sometimes use.

Others

Several people whom I originally intended to include in this section, as they were showing and breeding in the early 1970s, are still active in the breed today. For this reason I will talk about them in chapter 11, which describes the Cavalier scene in Great Britain in more recent times.

There are so many individuals over the years who have devoted themselves to our lovely breed that I will not be able to mention all of them; but I know every Cavalier owner appreciates how the work of past lovers of the breed has given us the lovely little dog we have today.

Cavalier portrait gallery

Cavaliers and their breeders 1925–1942

Hentzau Sweet Nell, born 21 March 1927, and Christopher of Ttiweh, born 14 December 1927. Bred by Mrs Brunne, owned by Mrs Pitt. Half-brother and half-sister.

Kobba of Kuranda, born 1927–1928. Owned by Mrs Rothwell Fielding. Pure-bred King Charles parents. The first good black-and-tan, and the only one to be used as a foundation sire. Grandsire of Plantation Banjo. All Cavalier pedigrees can be traced back to this really attractive dog through his great-grandson Ch Daywell Roger, and Roger's sister, Daywell Amber.

Pieter of Ttiweh (ruby), born 15 July 1928. Bred and and owned by Mrs Pitt. By Ann's Son ex a short-faced ruby King Charles. Excellent type of dog, well built, consistent winner at shows, rather big. He was also an outstanding stud dog, the sire of Rangers Bimbo, Mark of Ttiweh, Snow White of Ttiweh and Belinda of Winkwell. These are all blenheims and they all appear in many old pedigrees.

Dinah of Ttiweh, born 14 April 1927. Owned by Mrs Pitt. Typical rather 'Charlie-like' bitch used in the late 1920s.

Bridget of Ttiweh (tri), born 24 September 1929. Bred and owned by Mrs Pitt. Considered an outstanding bitch, beaten only once in six years' showing. Brother: Timon of Ttiweh, also a tricolour, who sired Timonetta of Ttiweh, dam of Snow White of Ttiweh. Sire: Wizbang Timothy (nearly black and white), litter brother to Anne's Son. Dam: Lucy of Ttiweh (ruby), litter sister to Peter of Tteweh. Dam of Freckles of Ttiweh, great-granddam of breed's first champion bitch, Ch Amanda Loo of Ttiweh (b/t).

Note long ears and long nose, unusual at this time.

Group of Mrs Pitt's dogs, early 1930s. *Left to right*: Hannah of Ttiweh (blen); Plantation Banjo (b/t), grandson of Kobba of Kuranda; Snow White of Ttiweh (blen); Judy of Ttiweh (ruby with a lot of white); Freckles of Ttiweh (blen).

Snow White of Ttiweh and Plantation Banjo, born later 1930s. Foundation stock of de Fontenay kennel, owned by Mme J Harper Trois-Fontaines. These dogs were still around just after the war (1945).

Plantation Robert (blen) born in early 1930s. Owned by Mrs Jennings.

Daphne Murray with five dogs born 1935–1936. *Left to right*: Jemima of Ttiweh, owned by D Murray; Selina of Ttiweh, owned by Mrs Pitt; Tinkle of Ttiweh (ruby), owned by Jane Pitt (now Bowdler); Rangers Bimbo, owned by Mrs Pitt; Angeline of Ttiweh, born 4 December 1936, owned by Jane Pitt.

Canonhill Richey (ruby), born 10 October 1941, owned by Mrs Stoves. Sire of Ch Daywell Roger (blen), Ch Royalist of Veren (b/t), and Ch Comfort of Ttiweh (blen). Grandsire of two black-and-tan champions, four tricolour champions, and twelve blenheim champions.

In 1950, 27 Cavaliers were entered in the stud book; of these, 21 were his children or grandchildren. He was never a champion, nor did he have a stud book number, as these were not available to Cavaliers until 1945. His owner was actually more interested in 'Charlies' than in the new breed.

Three more of Mrs Pitt's dogs. *Left to right:* Rangers Bimbo, born 1932; Bridget of Ttiweh, born 24 September 1929; Mary Ann of Ttiweh, born December 1934.

Cavaliers and their breeders 1945–1973

Ch Daywell Roger, born 7 October 1945 (Cannonhill Richey ex Daywell Nell). Bred by Col and Mrs Brierley, owned by Jane Pitt. First Cavalier champion. Sired 11 champions.

First Cavalier breed championship show, held at Stratford-on-Avon on 29 August 1946, judged by Mrs Jennings. *Bitch CC:* Mrs K Eldred's Belinda of Saxham, aged seven years. *Dog CC:* Jane Pitt's Daywell Roger, aged 10 months *(right)*. *Note:* Belinda of Saxham gained two CCs, but sadly died before becoming a champion, which she would certainly have done.

Ch Royalist of Veren, born 28 October 1945 (Cannonhill Richey (ruby) ex Rustle of Veren (tri)). Owned by Mrs Vera Rennie.

Ch Comfort of Ttiweh, born 31 March 1945 (Cannonhill Richey ex Deborah of Avoncliffe). Bred and owned by Mrs A Pitt, and probably her all-time favourite bitch.

Ch Amanda Loo of Ttiweh, born 11 June 1946, aged eight months (Bernard of Astondowns (ruby) ex Princess Anita de Fontenay (b/t)). The first Cavalier champion bitch. Owned by Mrs A Pitt.

Mrs Pitt with Ch Harmony of Ttiweh (Ch Daywell Roger ex Ch Little Dorrit of Ttiweh), winning BIS at South East Toy Dog Show in January 1951.

Ch Pargeter Jollyean of Avoncliffe, photographed 1949 (Ch Daywell Roger ex Avoncliffe Heatherbelle), bred by Mrs Louise Hitchens, owned by Mrs B Keswick. First champion owned by Mrs Keswick. Cannonhill Richey was his grandsire twice over.

Father and daughter. *Left:* Mrs B Keswick's Ch Pargeter Melissa, born 13 May 1961 (Pargeter Cedric of Ttiweh ex Ch Pargeter Polyantha of Goldicote). *Right:* Mrs A Pitt's Ch Cedric of Ttiweh, born 30 September 1959 (Pound Foolish of Ttiweh ex Britannia of Ttiweh).

Mrs Bunty Green's two dogs, 1940s. *Left:* The Young Pretender of Grenewich, bred by Mrs M Sawkins. *Right:* Avril of Astondowns, bred by Mr Vernon Green (no relation to Bunty Green).

Mrs Pitt at Broadway, Worcs, about 1950. Ch Daywell Roger under her right arm, and also accompanied by Cinderella of Turnworth, Victoria of Ttiweh, Bodkin of Ttiweh, Comfort of Ttiweh and Hamlet of Ttiweh.

Ch Pargeter Bob Up, born 7 January 1958 (Ch Abelard of Ttiweh ex Ch Pargeter Phyllida), owned and bred by Mrs B Keswick.

Barbara Wall at Cowhill with two of Mrs Keswick's dogs.

Left: Ch Pargeter Patron, born 8 November 1950 (Pargeter Athos ex Pargeter Cliquot), bred and owned by Mrs B Keswick. *Centre:* Ch Pargeter Thundercloud, born 6 June 1950 (Ch Daywell Roger ex Ch Amanda Loo of Ttiweh), bred by Mrs A Pitt. *Right:* Ch Pargeter Jollyean of Avoncliffe, born 21 May 1947.

Left: Mrs A Pitt with Ch Prologue of Ttiweh, born 31 January 1950. *Right:* Mrs B Keswick with Ch Thundercloud of Ttiweh, born 6 June 1950. Judge: Mrs Daphne Murray.

Int Ch Sunninghill Perseus of Lochfee, born 7 August 1957 (Ch Aloysius of Sunninghill ex Perle of Lenharra). Bred by Mrs Bartels, owned by Mrs Bartels and Miss P Turle.

Mrs Bunty Green with Ch Mingshang Danby and his daughter Heatherside Veronica in 1963, at Three Counties Show.

Lady Forwood's Ch Archie McMuck of Eyemouth, born 20 July 1967 (Int Ch Pargeter McBounce ex Polka of Eyeworth). Best Puppy in Show at Bath 1968, BOB at Crufts.

Mrs G Biddle's Ch Rosemullion of Ottermouth, born 20 July 1967 (Ch Vairire Osiris ex Rosette of Ottermouth).

Ch Ttiweh Roseanna, born July 1973 (Ch Rosemullion of Ottermouth ex Ttiweh Last Rose). The last Ttiweh champion, bred by Mrs Pitt and owned by Mrs Gertie Biddle.

Ch McGoogans Eideard, born 31 July 1970 (Ch Stellers Eider of Pantisa ex Ch Piccola of Crustadele), bred by Daphne Murray and owned by Mr and Mrs Gillies. Sold to an American breeder.

Mrs Janie (Evelyn) Booth with *(left to right)* Millstone Celestial (tri), Ch Millstone Beechking Tansy (b/t), Millstone Cayenne (ruby) and Mrs Reynold's Ch Leynsord Salutation (blenheim), a Rosemullion grandson.

Lady Mary Forwood's Eyeworth Cavaliers in the river Avon – Cavaliers are sporting little dogs as well as show dogs!

Chapter Five
The breed standard

Ch Craigowl Silkience;
owned and bred by Norma and Gordon Inglis.

Every breed has a standard approved by The Kennel Club that describes what characteristics it should have. These standards are carefully drawn up by the committees of the breeds concerned and then sent to The Kennel Club for consideration and final approval. The original Cavalier standard was drawn up in 1928 at Crufts by the first of all the Cavalier committees. They took as their live model Ann's Son, and also looked at many of the old pictures of small Cavalier-like dogs (see chapter 3). This early standard was short and simple since the breed was still so new, its main emphasis being on the flat head (no dome) and longer nose. The standard was revised again in 1948, this one being very similar to that used today. The present standard, drawn up in 1986, follows below. After this, the rest of the chapter discusses in more detail what the Cavalier standard actually requires and elaborates on some of the details. You can find the United States breed standards for the Cavalier King Charles Spaniel on pages 162–164.

The Cavalier King Charles Spaniel Breed Standard
(Reproduced by kind permission of The Kennel Club.)

General Appearance Active, graceful and well balanced, with gentle expression.

Characteristics Sporting, affectionate, absolutely fearless.

Temperament Gay, friendly, non-aggressive; no tendency to nervousness.

Head and Skull Skull almost flat between ears. Stop shallow. Length from base of stop to tip of nose about 3.8cm (1¹/₂in). Nostrils black and well developed without flesh marks, muzzle well tapered. Lips well developed but not pendulous. Face well filled below eyes. Any tendency to snipiness undesirable.

Eyes Large, dark, round but not prominent; spaced well apart.

Ears Long, set high, with plenty of feather.

Mouth Jaws strong, with a perfect, regular and complete scissor bite, ie upper teeth closely overlapping lower teeth and set square to the jaws.

Neck Moderate length, slightly arched.

Forequarters Chest moderate, shoulders well laid back; straight legs moderately boned.

Body Short-coupled with good spring of rib. Level back.

Hindquarters Legs with moderate bone; well turned stifle – no tendency to cow or sickle hocks.

Feet Compact, cushioned and well feathered.

Tail Length of tail in balance with body, well set on, carried happily but never much above the level of the back. Docking optional. If docked, no more than one-third to be removed.

Gait/Movement Free moving and elegant in action, plenty of drive from behind. Fore and hind legs move parallel when viewed from in front and behind.

Coat Long, silky, free from curl. Slight wave permissible. Plenty of feathering. Totally free from trimming.

Colour: Recognised colours are:

Black and Tan: Raven black with tan markings above the eyes, on cheeks, inside ears, on chest and legs and underside of tail. Tan should be bright. White marks undesirable.

Ruby: Whole coloured rich red. White markings undesirable.

Blenheim: Rich chestnut markings well broken up, on pearly white ground. Markings evenly divided on head, leaving room between ears for much valued lozenge mark or spot (a unique characteristic of the breed).

Tricolour: Black and white well spaced, broken up, with tan markings over eyes, cheeks, inside ears, inside legs, and on underside of tail.

Any other colour or combination of colours most undesirable.

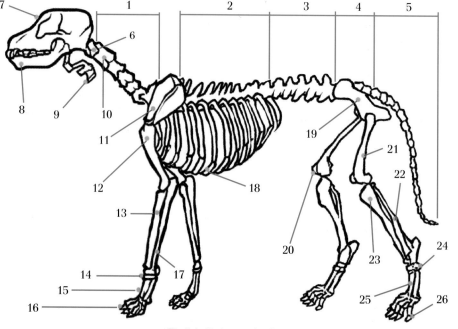

1 Cervical vertebrae
2 Dorsal vertebrae
3 Lumbar vertebrae
4 Sacral vertebrae
5 Coccygeal vertebrae
6 Atlas
7 Skull
8 Lower jaw
9 Laryngeal cartilege
10 Axis
11 Scapula
12 Humerus
13 Radius
14 Carpus
15 Metacarpus
16 Phalanges
17 Ulna
18 Ribs
19 Pelvis
20 Patella
21 Femur
22 Fibula
23 Tibia
24 Tarsus
25 Metatarsus
26 Phalanges

Fig 5.1: Skeleton of a Cavalier.

Size Weight: 5.4–8kg (12–18lb). A small, well balanced dog well within these weights desirable.

Faults Any departure from the foregoing points should be considered a fault and the seriousness with which the fault should be regarded should be in exact proportion to its degree.

Note Male animals should have two apparently normal testicles fully descended into the scrotum.

My interpretation of the breed standard

General appearance, characteristics and temperament

The first reaction on meeting a Cavalier should be to exclaim, 'Oh, what an attractive dog!' It should look happy, with big, soft round eyes and an ever-wagging tail. It should look well balanced, which means well proportioned and graceful both when standing and on the move. A Cavalier should be a little longer than it is high. Its length is measured from the withers (at the top of the shoulder blade) to the beginning of the tail, and its height is the distance from the ground to the withers (see diagram 5.1) and should be 30–32cm (12–13in). A neat, compact dog (almost square) is usually much admired, although some breeders think that bitches particularly should be a little longer, which is just as elegant and better for breeding. By this, the reader will see that, even with a breed standard, there is still some choice about which type of Cavalier a judge might prefer. The Cavalier should be bright and active, always anxious to be on the move, ready for anything. Yet with this Cavaliers should always be friendly, non-aggressive and eager to please.

The male Cavalier should be rather more heavily made than the female so that he looks more masculine; the female should look prettier and more feminine. Puppies when first shown aged six months or just over are not fully developed, so seldom have the elegance of their more mature relations; their legs may seem to be too long or their heads a little out of proportion. As they grow up, however, they gradually develop the balance they need and are (hopefully) a credit to their breeders.

Head and skull

It is the head of the Cavalier more than any other characteristic which distinguishes it from all other breeds. The skull should be wide enough for the large, round eyes to be spaced well apart and it should be almost flat. This last is important, as it defines one of the main differences between the Cavalier and the King Charles Spaniel (which from now on I will call the *Charlie*), which has a domed head. The muzzle too should be much longer than that of the Charlie (about 3.8cm as above) with a shallow stop, not the deep stop of their cousins. The ears should be set high on a flat skull; low-set ears tend to make even a flat head look domed, and low-set ears with a domed skull lose the special Cavalier look altogether. It is possible for ears to be too highly set, which also spoils the picture (fig 5.2). Cavalier owners will notice that, when their dogs are interested in something, the ears stand up very slightly on top of their heads; but when the dogs are fed up, the ears look as if they are set lower, though actually this is because they are not 'pricking up' at all at the roots.

The head should have cushioning under the eyes, giving a soft look to the face; insufficient cushioning leads to an unattractive, snipey appearance, while too much gives a certain coarseness to the face that is equally undesirable. What really matters is the balance between these characteristics; nothing should be overdone, and the final appearance should be gentle and pretty.

Fig 5.2: Head. a: Correct. b: Correct. c: Hound lips, small eyes, not enough cushioning. d: Low set ears, deep stop. e: Domed head, small, almond eyes, set obliquely.
f: Low set ears, eyes too close and rather small, white third eyelid.

Ch Crisdig Leading Seaman, said to have had one of the best Cavalier heads ever.
Photo: Peter Diment

The lips just cover the lower jaw but should not hang down like those of a hound. The nostrils should be black whatever the colour of the dog. There are numerous problems with Cavalier pigment: many, especially blenheims and rubies, may start off with good pigment but, after two or three years, the colour fades to dark brown, pinky grey or even pink and never returns. Officially, no remedy has been found to help this, but there are numerous suggestions as to possible causes (water quality, temperature, stress and so on). Herbal remedies have been tried by various people, mainly without success, though I obtained a marked improvement by using elderberry and nettle extract over a long period. Medical remedies, if there are any, are definitely undesirable because of the risk of harmful side effects. Unfortunately, there are a few people who colour their dogs noses artificially; it is almost impossible to identify this in the show ring and it is very bad for the breed. The only way to get really good pigment is to breed for it from dogs whose pigment is good; for the owner to colour the nose is seriously misleading. Bitches' pigment often varies when they come into season and when they have puppies; usually they have the better pigment when they cannot be shown!

Sometimes young dogs and puppies have small flesh marks (pink flesh-coloured patches) around their nostrils. These normally fill in and in fact dogs with this problem usually end up with very good pigment. If an older dog has a flesh mark, it counts as a fault, though not a serious one.

Eyes

It says above that the head of the Cavalier is its most important feature; but the most important part of the head itself is the eyes. The eyes should be, as it says in the standard, large, round and dark, and they should also be set wide apart. They should have a soft, loving expression, but a 'sparkle' too, and anything which spoils this effect is a fault. Light eyes (yellowy or light brown) give a harder look, as do completely black eyes. Prominent eyes give an expression of permanent surprise, which is not desirable either. Small or almond-shaped eyes also spoil the required expression. The eyes should be a very dark brown, with black rims around them, although even today some winning dogs do not have these dark rims. As the American breed standard says, they should have a *lustrous, limpid look*.

Ears

A Cavalier should have long ears covered with long silky hair. The fleshy part of the ear known as the *leather* should reach at least to the level of the mouth, and the long hair should be markedly longer than this. Ear lengths vary considerably, but very long ears are always much admired.

Ear set is very important; the ears should be set well up on the head (see fig 5.2a) as this shows up the flat skull. Low set ears emphasise the curved part of the skull and make it look domed (see fig 5.2f); high set ears give a 'surprised' look. A Cavalier's ears need considerable attention if you are to avoid tangles and matting; they also need cleaning inside to avoid ear mites and other possible problems. One of the most characteristic features of the Cavalier is its long, well-groomed, stylish ears, and every care should be taken to see that they always look their best.

Mouth

It is only since 1986 that a *perfect scissor bite* has been required; before this, a scissor bite was preferred but a level bite was still acceptable. A scissor bite is one in which the top teeth extend over the lower teeth but are *closely overlapping* them.

Adult dogs should have a set of 42 teeth: 20 in the upper jaw and 22 in the lower. In front there are 12 *incisors*, six above and six below; beside these are found the four *canine* teeth, again two above and two below. These are much the longest and strongest teeth, the ones that are sometimes called 'fangs'. Next come the *premolars*, both jaws having a total of eight, four on each side above and below. The back teeth are called the *molars*, the lower jaw having six and the upper having only four. It is the small front incisors that should overlap as described above.

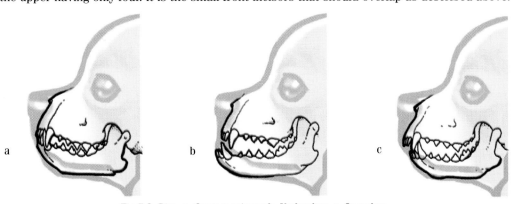

a

b

c

Fig 5.3: Bite. a: Correct scissor. b: Undershot. c: Overshot.

51

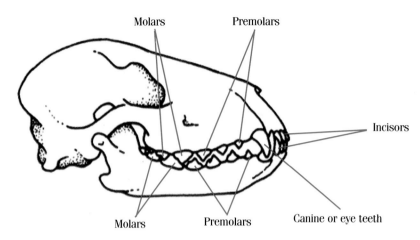

Fig 5.4: Skull, showing arrangement of teeth.

Puppies begin with milk teeth, which are gradually replaced by their full adult set; this happens from three to six months of age. A puppy aged six to nine months may have a level bite or be slightly undershot. This may come right as the pup matures, but unfortunately this does not always happen. Cavaliers are descended from the undershot Charlie, so it is not unusual to find a young – or even not so young – Cavalier with this fault. As it is one of the important differences between the two breeds, being undershot is regarded as a definite fault in the show ring.

Neck

A dog's neck runs from the base of the skull to a point just in front of the withers. A Cavalier should have a clearly visible neck, with a slight but elegant arch to it. A Cavalier with a short neck looks 'stuffy' and it often seems to carry too much weight around the shoulders. Some Cavaliers carry their heads thrown back with an almost upright neck; this can look very elegant, but it is not really desirable, as it can detract from movement.

The neck should flow smoothly into a level back; three and a half times its length should give approximately the length of the back. On the lower neck the skin should fit smoothly and not hang down to give a 'throaty' effect.

An elegant neck, in balance with the rest of the body, is another of the Cavalier's very attractive features.

Forequarters

The front legs should be straight with the feet pointed straight forward. Figs 5.5b–c show the two most common incorrect fronts, in which the elbows do not lie flat but turn out from the dog's side (known as *out at elbows*) and in which the dog's feet turn out (known as *toeing out*). A Cavalier should not have too narrow a front as it needs to have a chest wide enough to give space for good heart and lungs, but a very broad front is incorrect also.

A Cavalier should have good, firm bone, though not so heavy that it loses its graceful look. Its bone should not be what is known as *fine* (rather weak and thin).

A Cavalier's shoulder blade, otherwise known as its *scapula*, should make an angle of approximately 45° with the horizontal. This angle is made by the line joining the top of the scapula to the point where it joins the upper arm or *humerus* (point of shoulder). The upper arm should be a good length, rather longer than the lower arm, and should also make an angle of 45° with the horizontal (only in this case sloping down rather than up). This means that the

Fig 5.5: Fronts. a: Correct. b: Out at elbows. c: Toeing out.

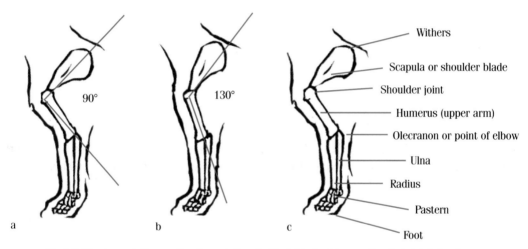

Withers

Scapula or shoulder blade

Shoulder joint

Humerus (upper arm)

Olecranon or point of elbow

Ulna

Radius

Pastern

Foot

Fig 5.6: Front angulation. a: Good angulation. b: Straight shoulders. c: Front skeletal structure.

5.7: Movement. a: Short stride and 'stuffy' neck due to stright shoulders. b: Hackney movement due to straight shoulders.

angle between the shoulder blade and the upper arm should be about 90° (45° + 45°) (see fig 5.6a). Recently there has been some dispute about this as one or two experts (among them Rachel Page Elliott) claim that the angle made by the scapula with the horizontal should be nearer 60°. Suffice to say, the shoulder should be well laid back (in other words, slope back from the point of shoulder at an angle of 45–60°) and be of a good length. It should also slope inward to the centre of the back to the point known as the *withers*. The two shoulders do not actually meet and touch at this point, but should be very close. The height of a dog is normally measured from the withers.

When a dog moves forward, both the upper and lower arm go as far forward as possible. Fig 5.7a shows how length of stride varies with angulation; with a straight shoulder, the leg cannot pivot nearly as far round as when the angle between the scapula and upper arm is smaller. Hence well laid back shoulders are important in giving good movement. A long upper arm (as mentioned above) also helps give a longer stride, although it must always be remembered that any exaggerated feature spoils the balance of the dog.

Body

Coupling in a dog really means the whole muscular band joining the chest and hindquarters, not just the section at the top known as the *loin*. However, as coupling is measured as the distance between the last rib and the hip, it is easy to see why it is so often regarded as the loin area only. This distance should be relatively short compared to the total body length.

Spring of rib means that the ribs should be seen to form a definite curve as they leave the back, leaving room for strong heart and lungs. The ribs should not come out so far that they look like part of a barrel. Flat sides over the ribs are obviously not desirable either. A

Fig 5.8: Body. a: Level back (correct). b: Roach back. c: Dipped back.

Cavalier should always be slightly wider over the rib-cage than at the hind end.

A Cavalier should have a level back both when standing and on the move (see fig 5.8a). Neither a roach back (upwardly arched) (fig 5.8b) nor a dipped back (fig 5.8c) is really what is required, although quite a number of slightly dipped backs are seen in the show ring today.

To sum up this section: a Cavalier should have a compact body, with the height from the ground to the withers almost equal to the length of the back from withers to the croup. Some breeders like Cavaliers to be almost square, while others are quite happy with a slightly longer animal. Bitches in particular are often preferred longer as this should make for easier whelping. The rib-cage should be nicely rounded, with the body narrowing slightly to a firm back end; the coupling should be short but well muscled. The elegantly arched neck should flow smoothly into the level topline. As I have said before, the overall picture should be graceful and well balanced.

Hindquarters

Fig 5.9c shows all the parts making up the *hindquarters* (or back end) of the dog. The largest bone, lying at the top of the backend, is the *pelvis*, which should be a good broad bone sloping slightly downwards. The top bone in the leg, known as the *femur*, joins the pelvis at the hip joint. The femur then joins the next part of the leg at the *stifle joint*; and at this point there is a small bone called the *patella* or kneecap. The knee joint is made up of the lower end of the femur, the patella, and the bones of the lower leg, the *tibia* and the *fibula*. At the other end of the lower leg is the *hock joint*, joining onto the *rear pastern* and then onto the foot.

It is important that the femur and the bones of the lower leg make an angle of about 90° with

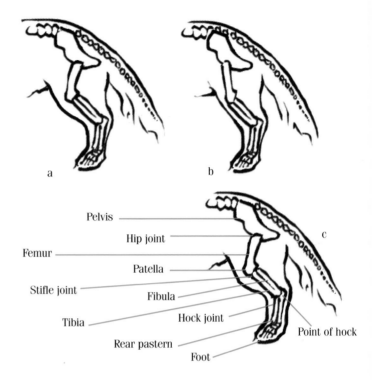

Fig 5.9: Rear angulation. a: Well angulated stifle. b: Stifle too straight. c: Rear skeletal structure.

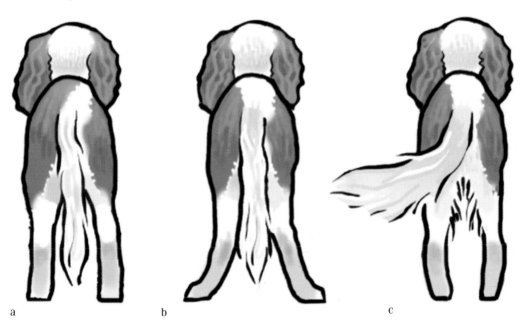

Fig 5.10: Rear ends. a: Correct. b: Cow hocked. c: Sickle hocked.

each other. This is the angle at the stifle joint, and *well turned stifle* means just this. Fig 5.9a shows the attractive curved effect at the back which results from this. If the femur and lower leg have too large an angle between them, otherwise known as *insufficient angulation*, the hind legs can look straight and stiff and movement is not as good. The thigh muscles should also be firm and well developed; note that good thighs should be the result of plenty of exercise.

Viewed from the rear, the hind legs should be straight and parallel to each other. If the hock turns either in or out, this is incorrect (see fig 5.10) giving *cow* or *sickle* hocks respectively.

I imagine that by now my observant reader will have noticed that I have mentioned in this section the *hock joint*, the *point of hock* and the *hock* itself, and will be wondering whether I am getting confused somewhere. The hock joint is a joint on the back leg between the bones of the lower leg and the group of bones making up the *metatarsus* or *rear pastern*. At the rear of the hock joint is an extension (called the *calcaneus process* technically) which is known to ordinary dog people as the *point of hock*. However, the term *hock* is often used to mean the whole rear pastern (the hock joint plus metatarsals) and this usage, though not strictly correct, is regarded as acceptable. A Cavalier's hocks should be what is known as *well let down*, which means the hocks should be fairly near the ground. They should be untrimmed and well feathered.

Feet

A dog's foot is made up of four separate toes, each of which is made up of three *phalanges*. The claws or toenails are joined onto the lowest phalanx. Each toe is joined to its neighbour by tissue, mainly consisting of skin.

A Cavalier's foot should be rounded, and the pads (soft fleshy part under the foot) should be firm and well cushioned. The foot should be well feathered and the main part of it should never be trimmed, though it is permissable to cut away some of the hair between the pads (usually for reasons of hygiene or if it grows so thickly it hampers movement).

The foot should not be splayed out (what could be called 'flat-footed'). This occurs when the Cavalier does not have enough exercise on a hard surface. For this reason, a Cavalier should always have some regular exercise on, say, a road or a hard path. Constant exercise on grass, though health giving and enjoyable, is not enough for a show dog, which needs firm, compact feet. Incidentally, 'roadwork' also strengthens the muscles, particularly at the rear.

Tail

The tail is a continuation of the backbone and should therefore join smoothly onto the back, being carried either level with it or just below (see fig 5.11). A number of tails are also carried just above the back, and the breed standard obviously accepts this as it says *never much above...* Unfortunately, far too many tails are carried much higher than this, sometimes even curling right over. I find that most Cavaliers hold their tails slightly above the level of the back when they are happy and I am not convinced that this trait can be bred out, as some people suggest. However, the tails known as *gay tails*, carried really high, are another matter, and here breeding does seem to be the answer. Persuading the dog to hold its tail down by disciplining it can lose the happy temperament so important for a Cavalier. At present, gay tails are one of the problems in the breed, although with more awareness the tails are improving already.

The breed standard still says that docked tails are permissible, but very few can be seen nowadays. Now that docked tails are officially frowned upon, the practice should cease altogether.

Gait/Movement

Free moving and elegant is as good a way as any to describe the action of the Cavalier. The dog should move smoothly, keeping a level top-line all the time. The head and neck should be held up and the tail should be wagging constantly, though not held high. The action should be rhythmic and steady; the hind legs should push firmly forward under the body and the pads should be clearly visible from behind, thus giving the required drive.

The front legs should not be lifted upwards when moving forward (*hackney action,* see fig 5.7b, page 53), and moving both legs on the same side at the same time (*pacing*) is also incorrect. The elbows should not be seen to be 'flapping'.

The legs when moving should be straight and parallel, viewed from both in front and behind. Interestingly, studies have been made which suggest that most dogs (other than those that are heavy and low to the ground) have a tendency as they move faster to single track rather than move parallel. This is because, when moving, they never have all four legs on the ground at once, so the legs need to slope slightly inwards to maintain balance, especially when moving at any speed. There may well be some truth in this, as so many Cavaliers do move slightly close behind. However, the breed standard does not allow for it and, in the show ring, that is what has to be followed.

A Cavalier on the move, then, should present a graceful and well balanced picture, moving smoothly, covering the ground effortlessly but effectively, head held up to show elegant arched neck, feathery tail gently waving – in fact, a joy to behold!

Fig 5.11: Tail carriage and movement.
a: Correct movement, correct tail. b: Incorrect movement (pacing), correct tail. c: Correct movement, incorrect tail (too high). d: Correct movement, incorrect tail (too low).

Mat (tricolour).

Coat

When a Cavalier is stroked, its coat should feel silky and smooth, whatever the colour. As the standard states, it should be long, with plenty of feathering. Puppies have quite short coats, and a full coat seldom develops before the age of 18 months. Some, particularly the whole colours, may take even longer to grow a full coat. Sometimes an older Cavalier develops a thick curly coat, although nowadays these coats are being gradually bred out. During the year, usually in the summer, a Cavalier loses its coat; that is to say, a lot of its hair gradually falls out, so the coat becomes thinner, although never bare. This is much more obvious with bitches, many losing some coat every time they come on heat. After a bitch has had a litter of puppies, she loses a great deal of coat, often having bare patches and an almost hairless tail. It could take around nine months for her to return to normal.

Quizzy (ruby).

Katie (blenheim).

Colour

Cavaliers are often divided into two groups: *particolours* and *wholecolours*. The former (blenheims and tricolours) have patches of colour on a pearly white ground, while the latter (rubies and black-and-tans) should have no white at all.

The only three colours that should be found on a Cavalier are pearly white, a rich chestnut red and raven black. As the breed standard makes clear, there are four acceptable combinations of these.

Blenheim: Blenheim Cavaliers are the most popular of the four and the ones you are most likely to meet when out for a walk.

Dora (black-and-tan).

They have chestnut red patches on a pearly white background. These patches should be quite large but there should be a lot of white between them. This is what is called *well broken up*. The ears should be red, as should the sides of the face, but ideally a white band should go up the middle of the face, broadening at the top so that there is room for the special Cavalier spot or lozenge of chestnut brown. Many of the photographs throughout the book show nice blenheim heads.

Although a lozenge is very desirable, it is not essential, and many very successful Cavaliers do not have one. Some blenheims have small coloured spots known as *ticking*. Although the standard does not mention this, many Cavalier breeders prefer their dogs not to be marked in this way, particularly when the ticking is on and around the face.

Tricolours: A tricolour has large black patches well broken up on a pearly white ground. It must have rich tan markings over the eyes, on the cheeks, inside the ears, and on the underside of the tail. If there is black inside the legs, tan should be adjacent to it there also.

Rubies: The ruby is the only Cavalier to be one colour only: a deep, rich red. Some rubies have very slightly paler hair on their fronts and at the back, but this is not a fault. Unfortunately, in some lights a ruby's coat can look paler than it really is, and this matters more to a ruby, which is only the one colour anyway.

Black-and-tans: Most of the body of the black-and-tan is a lovely raven black. It must, however, have tan markings above the eyes, on the cheeks, inside the ears, on the chest and legs, and on the underside of the tail. As it says in the standard, the tan should be bright and there should be no white. To look its best, a black-and-tan's coat needs to have a beautiful shine.

Size

The breed standard gives the weight of the Cavalier as 5.4kg– 8kg (12–18 lbs). It goes on to say that a small, well balanced dog between these weights is desirable. Ten years ago, as often as not anyone showing a Cavalier weighing around 6.7kg (15–16lb) was told it was small; at the same time, dogs weighing 9–9.5kg (20–21lb) were regular winners. This is now slowly changing, and smaller dogs and bitches are, rightly, accepted as correct according to the standard. Dogs are expected to be larger than bitches, and some quite large dogs still do well, but the smaller dogs are coming into their own.

Summary

Looking at a show ring full of Cavaliers and watching them move around, one gets a general picture of all the dogs present and an idea of which are the most striking ones. Putting together all the points made above, the dogs that stand out have a compact, almost square body, a straight back, an elegant, arched neck, a well feathered, waving tail held low, a silky coat with plenty of feathering, and correct colouring. These dogs should move smoothly and elegantly, with a good stride and legs parallel. Most important, they should have typical Cavalier heads, with round, dark eyes, long, well feathered ears, good cushioning under the eyes, black nostrils and shallow stops. They should, in fact, be true to type and balanced, both standing and on the move. They will have good conformation, since they have all or most of the points required by the standard. They should be happy and trustful, as a typical Cavalier always is.

Note The above paragraph talks of three important factors, namely conformation, type and balance. These words are often used when talking about a given dog or dogs, but sometimes one wonders just what they mean. I will attempt to summarize briefly just how each one can be defined:
Conformation refers to the actual structure of the parts of the dog (good stifle angulation; arched neck).
Type. If a dog is a good type or *typey*, it clearly has the characteristics of its breed.
Balance refers to the harmonious combination of parts, standing still and on the move.

Chapter Six
So you want to breed your own pups...

Four lovely puppies belonging to Joan Twigg of the United States: Culloden DaPinno, Donald, Drambuie and Dirk.

Breeding your own Cavalier pups is a great deal of work but none the less a very fulfilling experience when all goes well. It is very satisfying to have a puppy you have actually bred yourself, and your original bitch may have a life-long companion. The other pups will all be sold to loving homes that you have carefully selected and vetted, and you will hear all through their lives how they are getting on. This, certainly, is the ideal situation, but prospective breeders should ask themselves a number of serious questions before they go into action.

Before you start...

Why breed?
Firstly, why do you want to do this? No-one should breed puppies just to make money; Cavaliers are not commodities. Equally, owners should not have pups to 'please the children' unless they too want the puppies and are quite happy to undertake all the work involved; the adult is ultimately responsible.

Do you have the time?

Secondly, do you, the prospective breeder, have time for a litter? It is not really possible to work in a full-time job and breed puppies unless time off can be arranged when the puppies are due to arrive and it is possible to get home every lunch time to attend to the mother and, later on, the pups also. Time is needed to keep them clean (a considerable amount of time), to prepare food and then feed it to the mother and pups – and just to enjoy watching them. Breeding a litter is an almost full-time occupation for a period of about 10 weeks, so the breeder-to-be needs to be completely sure that he or she really wants to take on all this.

Are the puppies really wanted?

Thirdly, are the new puppies really wanted? There are too many unwanted dogs in the country already. However, if you as prospective breeder really want a puppy, as does one of your friends, it is very unlikely that you will be unable to find loving homes for the others.

Can you afford to breed puppies?

Finally, can the prospective breeder afford the expenses associated with the birth and rearing of the pups? If all goes well, the expenses, other than the stud fee, might not be too bad, though special milk and special puppy food has to be bought and good quality food for the mother. However, if there are serious problems, having a litter can cost a considerable amount of money. For instance, sometimes it is necessary to have a Caesarean section, which can be very expensive. Serious illnesses such as eclampsia (see chapter 7) need urgent veterinary attention and treatment. These problems do not arise in the majority of whelpings, but the breeder must be prepared to spend the money if it turns out to be necessary.

So you do want puppies...

So you have thought the matter over and decided that you are going to try to breed a litter of Cavalier puppies. I say 'try to' because, unfortunately, success is never guaranteed. Sometimes the bitch, having been mated satisfactorily, does not produce any pups or sometimes she seems to have pups at first but they disappear again. (This is called *reabsorption*.) Sometimes the pups die at or just after birth; although usually, if you and the bitch get that far, at least some of the puppies survive. However, remember that the majority of matings are very successful and that the majority of bitches have nice healthy puppies who, with adequate care and attention, all survive to maturity. Having said this, it is not unusual for one poor little pup to die in the first few days, possibly because it is too small or has something wrong which no-one can identify.

About your bitch

First of all, make sure that your bitch is suitable to be bred from. For a first litter, she should not be more than three years old or younger than eighteen months. She can have a second and third litter when older than three, but should not normally have more than three litters and should never be bred from after the age of seven. It is wiser to have the third litter while she is still six. There should be at least one season without a mating between each litter. Your bitch should not be overweight, as this makes conception less likely. She should be completely fit, with no heart murmur or inherited eye problems. Ideally, both her parents should also have good health records and not have developed a heart murmur before the age of five, although it is not always possible to know this for certain (see chapter 10).

Moorfields Magny Cours, a nine-week-old bundle of fluff from Ireland who subsequently became
Best Puppy In Show at the Cavalier King Charles Spaniel Club Championship Show.Bred by Mr and Mrs Lamont.

Choosing your stud dog

Like your bitch, the dog you choose to mate your bitch should be healthy, free of heart murmurs, and with no inherited eye problem. Many dogs nowadays have certificates to say they are free of these problems. His age does not matter as long as he is still siring puppies. It is as well to choose a dog whom you like and admire as he will probably pass a number of his good qualities on to his offspring. It is also advisable to use an experienced stud dog, especially if your bitch has never been mated before; if neither of them has done it previously, it is possible there may not be a satisfactory mating at all. A young stud dog who has never mated a bitch may not be too sure what to do and may need to have his confidence built up. Even if he has all the confidence in the world, he might not get it right first time. You should ask to see the dog's pedigree, making sure that he is not too inbred and that there is some connection with your bitch's pedigree. If the two pedigrees have nothing in common, this is called an *outcross*. There is nothing wrong with doing this if you wish to try, but it is usually regarded as better to have one or two common ancestors in the pedigrees (see chapter 9).

'Isn't life fun!'

The breeder who sold you your bitch will almost certainly be able to give you good advice about which stud dog to use. If you want to mate your bitch to a top winning-Cavalier, possibly a champion, you will probably have to pay a substantial stud fee and may have to travel quite a long way to go to him. If you are interested in showing your dogs, this may well be what you will do. However, if you do not intend to show them, you could go to a well-thought-of local dog who has done some winning at shows and is experienced – you should get a really nice litter from him, too.

When you have decided on the stud dog, contact the owner and tell him or her you hope to use the dog. She will want to know when your bitch is due to come into season, and will ask you to tell her as soon as the season begins. You will know this because your bitch will start to lose a little blood and her vulva will swell up although, if she is a very clean little bitch and keeps licking herself, it may be a day or two before you actually see any blood. The stud dog owner may ask you to take your bitch over to her on about the 11th day, assuming the bitch is ready by then. However, one of the main causes of not conceiving pups is mating on the wrong day.

When to mate your bitch

When a bitch is ready to be mated, she holds her tail in an unusual upright position and moves it from one side to the other. If you stroke her gently on one side near her vulva, she will move her tail accordingly. The vulva will be very swollen, although there may not be much blood by this time. If you have other bitches, she may position herself with her rear end towards them and her tail up. She is inviting them to mate her, and this is called *standing*.

The period when a bitch is in season (or on heat) is called *oestrus,* and there are four stages in the oestrus cycle:

- *Pro-oestrus* is when vaginal bleeding takes place, and there may be some behavioural changes. This lasts from 7–13 days.
- *Oestrus* is when the bitch will allow herself to be mated and when ovulation occurs. This lasts from 4–7 days.
- *Metoestrus* is when the ovary produces a hormone that keeps the uterus ready for pregnancy, even in the non-pregnant bitch. This lasts 6–10 weeks.
- *Anoestrus* when the bitch is back to normal. This lasts for about 15 weeks, until the bitch comes into season again.

It follows that there is only a short period when the bitch can be mated satisfactorily. Most Cavalier bitches make it clear when they are ready to be mated, usually on about the 11th day, and it is advisable if possible to have two matings, one 48 hours after the other.

If your bitch is doing what is expected of her, and is duly mated on the 11th and 13th days, you should get your litter about 63 days later (see whelping table). However, suppose there are no pups. This might be the fault of the dog, but you should be able to check this out fairly easily with his owner by asking if he is still siring pups. At the next mating it may perhaps be advisable to mate her later, even as late as the 15th day if her vulva is still swollen and she is still standing. If you take maximum pro-oestrus and oestrus periods, that brings you to about the 16th or 17th day. Sometimes the bitch should be mated sooner, but this is not usually the case. Some vets can arrange a test to find when the bitch has ovulated and, as soon as this happens, you take her to the stud dog.

There are other causes of infertility in a bitch. If she is suffering from stress around the time her season is due, this could inhibit conception. Sometimes a bitch may not ovulate at all. A bitch may have puppies to begin with but later on they could be reabsorbed, resulting in no pups. It is possible she could have an infection of the genital or urinary tract. She could have a physical abnormality that makes conception impossible. Your vet should be the best person to advise you if there is something of this kind wrong, particularly if an infection is involved.

Just in case you are getting rather depressed by all this, perhaps I should repeat at this point that most bitches are mated on the 11th and 13th days and have nice, normal litters at the correct time.

The male Cavalier

Although by its nature this chapter is mainly concerned with the bitch, it seems worth saying something about the male Cavalier. There are many male Cavaliers in the world but probably only about 10% of them are used for stud work. This is not because they are unable to pass on their sperm and sire puppies but because their owners choose not to let them do so. As in all breeds, there are a few Cavalier dogs who cannot produce young, but the majority certainly can. An older dog with no sexual experience might not be able to copulate even if given the opportunity, but many can.

It is usually established breeders who have stud dogs available for mating. Most bitch owners want to use a dog who is a good example of the breed and has done some winning at dog shows. They know too that it is advisable to use an experienced dog with an experienced owner if their bitch is being mated for the first time. The secretary of your local Cavalier society can give you advice about contacting suitable stud dog owners if you need it. You will also see some very nice dogs if you visit a few dog shows and you will be able to speak to the owner of any dog you particularly like. In the next section, I describe what actually happens when the dog and bitch mate, and this section will deal with the sexual organs of the dog and what problems he may have – though, as with bitches, most dogs are normal.

The descent of the testes

When the dog is born, his testes are right up in his abdomen. They descend to the scrotal area by the time he is about 14 days old, but sometimes they stay in the abdomen or in the canal leading from the abdomen. Many dogs can withdraw their testes from the scrotal area to the canal until they are about 10 months old, but after this age they can no longer do so.

By six months, most dogs have two well developed and fully descended testes, though this does vary. Sometimes the testes never descend at all, in which case the dog will not be able to mate a bitch. This condition is referred to as *cryptorchidism*. Sometimes only one testicle descends, in which case it is theoretically possible for the dog to be bred from. It is not advisable, however, and such dogs cannot be shown (see chapter 5, the note in the breed standard). This condition is referred to as *monorchidism*.

Sperm production

A young dog begins to produce sperm when he is 8–12 months old. Sperm are produced in the testes and the actual process of sperm formation takes 6–8 weeks. Sperm production is continuous; excess or unused sperm leak out in the urine.

When to use him, and how often

A young dog should not be used too frequently until he is physically mature, possibly at about 18 months old. Some dogs, particularly if they are not over-used, remain fertile until they are as much as 12 years old, while some become less fertile as they get older and may produce fewer pups. There is no rule for this; it seems to depend on the make-up of the dog.

Infertility

Infertility in the male can be assessed by having a sperm count done at a suitable veterinary centre. The best way to do this is to have an on-heat bitch with him and, once ejaculation begins, the vet can collect the fluid in a special container. From this, the number of sperm in the sample (calculated as a percentage) is measured, as well as the rate and direction of movement of the sperm, and its quality can be seen under the microscope. A stud dog needs an adequate quantity of sperm, and they need to move fast in the right direction (towards the ova) and must not be mutilated or deformed. To get a reasonable estimate of the dog's fertility, several sperm counts need to be done at several two-monthly intervals. This is because a bad infection, for example, can damage the sperm, but all can be well two to three months later.

Fertility can be affected by infection when a high temperature occurs, by drugs (especially steroids), very hot weather (possibly), environmental factors and psychological stress. Some dogs are fertile for two or three years, after which fertility gradually decreases until the dog finally becomes infertile. No-one knows exactly why this occurs, but it may be inherited or due to an auto-immune reaction to the dog's own sperm that has built up over the years.

Timing

Immature eggs are released from the bitch's ovaries one to three days after oestrus begins and they mature over a period of three to four days (see **When to mate your bitch**). These mature eggs live for 24–36 hours. The sperm can live for about six days so, in normal circumstances, there should be no problems. It is vital to do a mating at the right time for the bitch, as sperm production is an on-going process, while the mature eggs are only there for a short time. As I have said before, it is better to do more than one mating to make sure of fertilisation. If the timing is wrong, it is possible to have a good mating between a fertile dog and a fertile bitch and for conception still not to occur.

The stud dog at home

Dogs used at stud are just as affectionate towards their owners as other Cavaliers. My present stud dog, Toby, is just a big baby. The only problem that might occur is that they are not always as tolerant of other male Cavaliers as they could be (or any other male dogs, for that matter – as long as they're not too big to argue with!). However, males not used at stud can also behave like this. Having dogs and bitches in the house can cause problems when the bitch is on heat, especially if there are children about who forget to shut doors. If you have kennels, the problems do not arise to the same extent, but you still need to be careful.

The mating

Provided that you get your bitch to the sire at the correct time, the responsibility for the actual mating lies with the stud dog owner. However, it is reassuring for your bitch if you can stay with her during the mating, and the stud dog owner may be happy for you to hold your bitch's head and front while the dog gets on with the job. The stud dog owner (SDO) will look at your bitch to check that she seems to be ready for mating and will then bring in her dog and let them quietly get to know each other. The dog will sniff gently at the bitch and lick her ears, and she will be happy with these preliminary attentions. After a few minutes, the SDO will gently turn the bitch so that her back end is towards the dog, and allow him to climb on top of her and insert his penis into her vulva. A bitch ready to be mated will usually allow this without much fuss. Once inside her, the dog's penis swells up and he is unable to get it out again until it returns to its normal size. This stage, when the two dogs are unable to separate from each other, is called a *tie*. It is always a good sign if you get a tie, but it is possible to have a satisfactory mating without a tie, just as it is possible to have a good tie and still no puppies.

What the dog is actually doing is pumping semen into her vagina via his penis. This semen is in three parts. The first part, which is watery and contains no sperm, comes early on. This is followed by the sperm-bearing fluid, which is much cloudier than the first part. The third part is prostatic fluid, which is ejaculated intermittently right through the tie; it helps to sweep the sperm through to the waiting ova. Some of this liquid will drip out when the tie is finished, but this is nothing to worry about; it does not contain sperm.

When the dog's penis first swells, this may hurt the bitch, and she may cry, sometimes quite loudly. This does not normally last for long, although bitches do vary. A tie can last for over an hour, but 20–30 minutes is more normal. The dog's penis comes out when it is no longer swollen and, after this, your bitch should rest quietly. The SDO will take her dog away and he will rest, too.

After the final mating, there just remains the business side of the affair. You will pay the stud fee, and the SDO will give you a dated receipt with details on it of the dog's registered name and when the pups should be due. When the pups arrive, she will send you a Kennel Club form confirming that the mating really took place on the given day; this is essential before you can register the pups. Sometimes the SDO will give you this form at the time of the mating.

So now you take the proud mother-to-be home again and look after her while awaiting the safe arrival of the pups.

Pregnancy diagnosis and stages of pregnancy

The pregnancy of a Cavalier usually lasts 59–63 days. Cavaliers can deliver their pups after the 63rd day, but this is not very common; they are more liable to have their puppies early.

Pregnancy diagnosis can be done in various ways. The tiny pups, the size of peas, can be felt by a vet between the 21st and 31st days; after that it is much more difficult to feel them until later on. It is not a good idea for owners to try to feel three-week-old embryos unless they themselves are vets; they might accidentally harm them or upset the bitch. At around the 32nd day or later, there may well be a sticky, clear mucous secretion from the vagina. The teats should

Four blenheims belonging to Prue Raffan of Sydney, Australia.
Toraylac Elizabeth (left, sitting) is heavily in whelp.

enlarge and redden from about day 28 onwards and, in a maiden bitch, the teats may redden, with little or no swelling up, a week or two earlier than this. After six weeks, it normally becomes obvious that the bitch is pregnant as her flanks swell so that her whole outline from above gradually changes. She will become hungrier and needs some extra food (see next section). By the end of the seventh week, the unborn pups can be seen to move slightly while the mother lies at rest. Again, it is not a good idea to poke about in order to feel the pups.

It is possible to use ultrasound equipment to see if the bitch is in whelp. This can be done from about day 28 onwards, and will also show how many pups there are at the time of scanning, although some or all may be reabsorbed later. There is no need to use this method if everything goes according to plan, although occasionally a bitch may have only one puppy lying high up in the rib cage where it cannot be felt or seen, and it is then more difficult to tell what is happening, particularly if the nipples do not swell up much either. A word of warning here, however: if during the fourth week, the vet is unable to feel any puppies, he may say that there might be a puppy which he cannot find. In this situation, the vet is nearly always right and there are no pups so, if this happens, do not build up your hopes too much – but keep watching for enlarging teats and discharge, just in case.

From day 21, the puppies' main organ systems begin to develop and, during the sixth week, rapid growth begins and the bones begin to calcify (become solid). Note that this is the period mentioned above when her flanks swell and she needs extra food. From day 56 onwards, the pups may be born and should be able to survive if everything else goes well.

Looking after the pregnant bitch

Diet and supplements
During the first five weeks of pregnancy, the bitch does not need any special attention and her life should carry on as before. She should not be given extra food until the beginning of the sixth week. It is as well, however, to take such obvious precautions as not taking her to places where she may pick up infections or letting her get into a stressful situation. Although her usual regular walks are good for her, an excessively long or energetic walk is not advisable at this time.

The bitch should not have any special pills or medication during her pregnancy unless prescribed by her vet. She should have been wormed if necessary several weeks before she was mated; if worming during pregnancy seems to be required, get your vet's advice.

At all times, a good quality balanced diet is desirable for a dog, and this is particularly important during pregnancy. A good proprietary food should be adequate, but I prefer at least some of her intake to be fresh food such as cooked beef or chicken with a suitable biscuit mixer, cheese, fish and eggs. At the beginning of the sixth week, she should gradually be getting more food, including a saucer of milk. If she already drinks milk, give her a little more. However, there are bitches who cannot tolerate milk. By the beginning of the seventh week she could have two meals (but both smaller than the previous single meal), so that her intake is about 15% more than it was. A dessertspoonful of corn oil daily is also helpful. Fresh drinking water should always be available.

If she is getting an adequate diet, there should not be any need for vitamin and mineral supplements. I have always given a large pinch of a calcium product such as Stress daily in my pregnant bitches' main meals with no ill effects. However, modern veterinary thinking does not believe in this. It is certainly true that too many supplements can cause harm.

Exercise
From the sixth week onwards, your bitch's walks should not be too energetic and she should not be encouraged to jump about, especially towards the end of her pregnancy. During her last week, she may do a certain amount of digging – perhaps on the best settee, in a bed or, even worse, in the garden. Digging outside should not be encouraged, and she needs careful watching during the last few days in case she decides to have her pups under the garden shed. This has actually happened and, at the time, is not funny at all.

Whelping quarters

The whelping box should be prepared at the beginning of the seventh week and she should be encouraged to lie quietly in it so that she will produce her pups there when the time comes. This sounds so sensible and practical, doesn't it? Unfortunately, bitches have a way of choosing their own special place (the back of the airing cupboard, the guest room bed, underneath a large, low double bed where they cannot be reached, in the bottom of a wardrobe...), so they really need careful watching during their last week. However, the new breeder need not be too depressed as, once the pups are born, the proud mother will stay in her 'official' bed with them and all should be well.

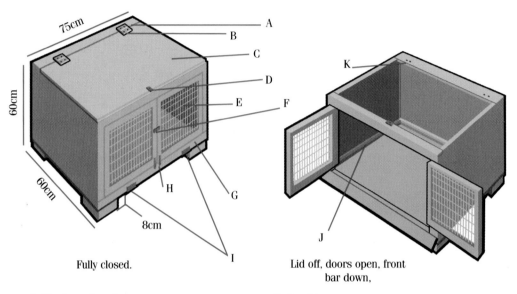

Fully closed.

Lid off, doors open, front bar down,

A: Fixed rear board
B: Hinge that can be either lifted or unscrewed
C: Lid that can be either removed or lifted up
D: Rotating catch for lid
E: Wired-fronted door
F: Rotating catch for front

G: Front bar
H: Bolts for doors
I: Hinges for front base bar
J: Wooden rail 8cm above base level
K: Hinges unscrewed and removed with lid

Diagram of whelping box.

The drawing shows an ideal whelping box for a Cavalier. It is 75cm across, 60cm high and 60cm deep (2ft 6in x 2ft x 2ft) so that it is large enough for the mother to stretch out fully and suckle her pups but not so large that it ceases to be cosy. It is high enough for her to stand up easily and there is room for her to move about without crushing the pups. A small wooden rail is fitted on three sides coming about 8cm (3in) out and 8cm above the floor. This will prevent the bitch from crushing the pups accidentally against the side of the box.

The top of the box is covered for warmth and protection but the lid can either be lifted up or removed altogether. The mother likes the privacy the lid gives. In front are two doors with wired fronts, and either or both can be opened. One open is good for the dam getting in and out when the pups are very small; both open is better when the pups can clamber in and out themselves. Beneath the doors is a front lower bar. This keeps the pups from falling out when they are very small; later on it can be put down to ground level so that it helps the pups to climb in and out of their box. It is also easier to clean the box if the front bar is put down while this is being done.

Cavalier pups need a lot of warmth and the ideal temperature should be around 24°C (75°F) for at least the first few days. This means the pups should be kept in a heated room. I use a small room with a gas fire which is kept on all the time but turned up or down as required. I keep a thermometer in the room at all times to check the actual temperature. They also have an electric heating pad covering about

The whelping box. Note wire door and hinged front, which goes down when the pups are older. Top can be lifted right off.

The whelping box, occupied, with front bar down.

half the floor area of the box and placed under the bedding. If the mother (or the pups) are too warm, they can move off the pad into the cooler part of the box. The pad I use does not get particularly hot and, if not lain on, it hardly seems warm at all. Pressure brings out the warmth in it. Some breeders use an overhead infra-red heater, but this seems to make the bitch too hot, although the pups are quite happy with it. It is important to ensure that the wire carrying the electric current to the pad goes into the box through a specially drilled hole so that it is not accessible for the pups to chew as they get older.

The box floor can be covered with vinyl tiles for easy cleaning; this also avoids splinters. The whelping box must be kept very clean and, as the lid comes off, the doors open wide and the front bar goes down, it is very accessible for scrubbing and disinfecting. The pad should have several towelling covers so that they can be washed regularly.

The best bedding to use is fluffy white Vet-bed. This allows any urine to go straight through it, while apparently keeping clean and dry itself. Some newspaper is advisable under the bedding to absorb the liquid passing through. The Vet-bed needs to be washed frequently even if it does look clean, so it is as well to have at least four pieces, each large enough to cover the floor of the box. Best quality Vet-bed is quite expensive but, as it is machine washable and lasts for ever, it is well worth getting some for your new litter.

Equipment needed for whelping

The items listed overleaf will be needed during whelping. Further explanation of their use will be found in the next section.

- Pair of clean, round-ended scissors standing in jar containing a dilute solution of TCP or similar.
- Large shoe-box containing hot-water-bottle with cover and a small, clean blanket to fit in the box and over the bottle. A second small blanket might be needed later on. This is to give a warm safe place for the first puppy (puppies) while the others are being born. Sometimes it is not needed, but it is as well to have it all ready. Fill the hot water bottle shortly after the birth of the first puppy.
- A pile of newspaper.
- Glucose (or glucose tablets) and milk (or Lactol) in case the mother needs a reviving drink.
- A bowl of water (for bitch).
- Some clean old cloths and towels to wipe up the mess.
- A pair of scales.
- Notebook and pencil for keeping record of birth times, weights and so on.

You should plan to let your bitch whelp in a quiet place with which she is familiar and where she will be able to relax. Do not let the room become too hot – just pleasantly warm. Stay with her while she is whelping and, if you have a friend whom your bitch trusts and who knows something about whelping, ask her to join you. Do not allow unnecessary visitors to come in just to watch; the arrival of your puppies is a serious and private matter, not a spectator sport!

The whelping

There are three recognisable stages of whelping, as follows:

- *Stage 1:*   Progressive relaxation and dilatation of the cervix.
- *Stage 2:*   Strong uterine contractions and delivery of puppy.
- *Stage 3:*   Expulsion of placenta (or afterbirth).

Stage 1

About 24 hours before stage 1 begins, there is a temporary drop in body temperature. A Cavalier's normal temperature is 38.3–38.8°C (101–102°F), but at this point it will drop to 36.1–37.2°C (97–99°F). The changes occurring in the cervix during stage 1 are not visible but the bitch's behaviour changes. She may start panting and become restless, trying to dig up her bed or any newspaper lying around. She might even slip up into the bedroom and try to dig up your bed. I stress again: watch that she does not do unsuitable digging in the garden, particularly under the garden hut or in an invisible corner at the back of the greenhouse. She may begin to shiver and will very probably refuse all food. These signs get progressively more marked as the actual birth gets nearer. This can go on for up to 48 hours but, if nothing has happened after 24 hours or the signs become less obvious rather than increasing, it is as well to get advice from your vet.

Stage 2

Once the cervix is fully dilated, the pups begin to arrive. It is not possible to tell the condition of the cervix by feeling, so the first visible sign of the birth is a contraction. This is rather like an extended shudder going almost the full length of the body while the bitch is otherwise motionless. There may be 10–15 minutes before the next contraction, but gradually they come more frequently and are stronger. There is some fluid loss during this period, so the bitch may keep cleaning herself. In due course, sometimes quite early on, the water bag appears in the vagina. This is a soft, shiny greyish-blue bag containing a greenish fluid; sometimes it may burst quite early on. Inexperienced breeders may well think that this is the first puppy, but it just contains some liquid and helps prepare the way out for the pups that are to follow. Contractions continue more frequently and, as the puppy moves down from the cervix towards the vagina, there should soon be a bulge in the vagina; this *is* the puppy. There will also be straining, the bitch throwing back her head, arching her back, pushing, and possibly giving a scream. This often happens just before the birth. Soon the puppy will be seen emerging and, after the next contraction, it should finally arrive.

Each puppy leaves the womb in a sac, and may or may not be born with the sac still surrounding it. If it arrives in its sac, this should be removed immediately or the pup will suffocate. The bitch will often break open the sac herself and lick the puppy to remove the mucus from the nostrils and mouth but, if she does not do this at once, the owner will need to help. The pup will have a soft cord attaching it to its mother, and this also has to be broken. The mother will probably do this herself but, if she does not seem interested in biting through it or seems excessively rough, the owner can cut it 2–3cm from the navel with the scissors, which have been left ready.

If the bitch has been straining for over two hours and no puppy has appeared, you should contact your vet. Most pups arrive head first, but sometimes they come backwards, the hind legs appearing first. Usually the bitch can deal with this satisfactorily, but sometimes the hind end does not open the passage enough for the head to come through and the puppy seems to be stuck. In this case, it might be necessary for the owner or an experienced friend to help the bitch expel the puppy by very gently putting a clean finger (coated with vaseline or KY jelly) into the opening around the puppy and carefully trying to ease the puppy out with each contraction. The other hand should gently pull the puppy downwards at an angle of about 45° as each contraction occurs. The bitch might need to be held still while this is going on, and it is important that at least one of the people present knows exactly what is going on or there could be problems.

When the pup first arrives it will not be breathing, having so far got all it needs from its mother, so it is essential that it draws its first breath as soon as possible. The mother, or perhaps the owner, removes the mucus from around the nose and mouth and, by her energetic licking, the mother will soon bring the puppy to life and its first cry will be heard. This happens quickly with most pups, but sometimes the mother will not bother to lick properly and the pup does not seem to be breathing. In this case, the owner should pick it up and rub it briskly with a rough towel. If it still does not breathe, it can be held vertically, head down, and the rubbing with the towel should be continued until, hopefully, it finally breathes. This can go on for up to half an hour and the puppy may revive; so do not give up too soon.

After a normal birth, most puppies make their own way to a teat but, if the pup has had some breathing difficulties to begin with, it may need to be put on to a teat by the owner and encouraged to begin sucking.

Stage 3

An afterbirth or placenta comes with each puppy. Sometimes it comes attached to the pup just after it is born, but often it comes separately a few minutes later. Sometimes it does not seem to appear at all although, in these cases, it actually comes rather late, seems broken up, and may not be noticed. Sometimes it comes with the next puppy.

The mother may want to eat the placenta, which is a good thing as it contains minerals and hormones that stimulate the uterus and help the production of milk. If there are four or five puppies, it is as well not to let the bitch eat all the afterbirths, and the last ones should be cleared up and disposed of.

Subsequent puppies

The second and third stages described above are repeated until there are no more pups to be delivered. The puppies may arrive within half an hour of each other or even less, but there may be a long rest between deliveries, sometimes even as long as four hours. If your bitch goes more than four hours without anything happening, and there are still more pups to come, you should contact your vet. You should also contact your vet if she strains for two hours without delivering anything. When all the pups have finally arrived, your bitch will relax and seem quite happy just to go to sleep.

When the second and later pups arrive, you should have your cardboard box with its hot-water-bottle and small blanket all prepared for the pups that have already arrived. They should lie quietly in this box until the birth is over, after which they can go back to mother until the next one arrives. Some breeders do not use a box but put the pups gently to one side during the subsequent births but, if the bitch moves about a lot and gets excited, she might unintentionally harm the pups; they might also get wet and messy from the afterbirth of the next pup.

After each puppy is born and is breathing without difficulty (as happens with most puppies), encourage it to get to a teat to suck. Most of them suck quite happily at once but, if there is rather a small one who does not seem too sure about what to do, you need to help it to get to a teat and perhaps hold it on while it sucks. It is very important that the pups are kept warm (around 24°C) but an enclosed bed with a heating pad and bedding on top will be fine. They will also get warmth from their mother's body.

When whelping is over

Take your bitch outside to relieve herself and stay with her just in case she decides to produce yet another puppy. This is unlikely but you need to be careful. Before she is allowed back to her pups you will need to clear up all the mess around the whelping box, put down clean paper and, if necessary, a clean piece of Vet-bed. You can perhaps get your helpful companion to do this or shut your bitch in the kitchen for a few minutes while the cleaning is going on. Let her return to her puppies as soon as possible (but just watch she does not squash any of them as she rushes back in) and she will lick them all then settle down quietly for a well-earned rest. Offer her a drink of Lactol with glucose, which she will almost certainly be happy to take.

If you have not already done so, weigh all the pups and keep a record of their weights. During the whelping, you should keep a record of when the bitch started the first stage and when she began straining. Record when each puppy was born, the time between contractions and any other relevant points. If you do have to call your vet, he or she will want to know all these details about what exactly has happened during the birth.

Feeding your nursing bitch

Your bitch will now need plenty of good nourishing food as she not only has to build herself up after producing perhaps four or five pups, but also has to feed the pups, who will probably double their weight within 10 days or less – all on food that your bitch gives them. Directly after the delivery she should just have a drink of milk with glucose, as mentioned already. Cow's milk is not the same as a dog's milk, so some breeders give specially prepared milk such as Lactol or Whelpi. Many bitches do well if given ordinary cow's milk (full cream). Goat's milk is also good for dogs and pups but I would not give it quite as early as this. A few hours after the whelping, the bitch should take a light meal of fish or chicken, and more milk a bit later on. After the first 24 hours or so, her diet should be more or less as follows:

- *First thing:* Drink of milk with a little glucose.
- *Breakfast:* Chicken or fish with some rice, or scrambled egg if it agrees with her.
- *Lunch (first few days):* As breakfast.
- *Lunch (subsequently):* Good quality beef with mixer.
- *Supper:* Light meal such as fish and milk.
- *Last thing:* Milk and some biscuit.

It is also possible to feed the bitch on proprietary dog food, but in increased amounts, feeding three or four times daily. Keep a good eye on her body condition while she is nursing her litter; do not allow her to get too thin (or fat). She may eat up to four times her diet before the pregnancy, depending on the litter size and her needs.

As the puppies get larger and hungrier, your bitch will need larger meals, but do not give her more than 140g (5oz) food at any one time as this could give her indigestion. When the pups are three to four weeks old they can begin eating independently (see next section). As they gradually eat more and more, their mother will not need so much food and, by the time the pups are six weeks old, her diet may well be almost back to normal. At eight weeks the pups should be completely weaned and ready to go to their new homes. Their mother may be a little thin and could do with nourishing extras like milk and a small rice meal midday (or evening, as suits) to fatten her up a bit. In general, rice and pasta are fattening so are not particularly good for dogs, but they are useful for dogs who have got very thin or are poor feeders.

Looking after your new puppies

One to three weeks

Your new puppies should be firm and rounded and they should spend their time either feeding or sleeping. They should not cry much or whimper; nor should they constantly be moving about. You will notice that, when they suck, their little tails go up. It is such a pleasure to look at a line of your own little pups, all contentedly sucking, tiny tails held aloft.

During the first three weeks, the pups do not need much done for them as they are getting all their food from mother. Their box needs to be cleaned out regularly and they need to be watched carefully in case one becomes ill or their mother accidentally lies on one of them. You might have a smaller, weaker pup who gets pushed off the teats by his bigger brothers and sisters. In this case you will need regularly to put him on the best teat and see, possibly by holding him there, that he is not pushed off again. This can be a time-consuming and exhausting task, as you may have to help him both day and night. If his mother continues to accept him, and he seems to have a will to live in spite of his problems, it is well worth persevering. After a few days, he will be able to cope for himself, and then all your efforts will seem worthwhile; though sadly some of these little pups do not survive. Always make sure your pups are warm enough – a puppy can die of hypothermia very easily.

Check your pups' weights regularly. They should have doubled their weight by the time they are about ten days old. If you have a small pup you are anxious about, as long as he is putting on weight you do not need to worry too much. Do not get over-anxious about weights and weigh twice a day! I usually weigh the pups weekly after the first two or three days, unless there is reason for concern, but many breeders do weigh daily. Keep a record of these weights.

When they are 12–15 days old, their eyes will open. At first, all you will see is tiny slits where once there was nothing but closed eyelids; then gradually they open completely. They look bluish at first, but this is perfectly normal. The puppies begin to be able to hear at around 17 days old. By this time, the temperature can be a little less, about 21°C (70°F).

Kerri with pups aged about one week. Eyes still shut. Note raised tails. The litter (Kippilaw Kindred Spirit ex Costara Kerri) belongs to Mrs Clare Campbell.

Three to four weeks

By three weeks, the pups are beginning to be aware of what is going on around them. They also begin to stagger about and to take some interest in their surroundings. At this age, they should be wormed for the first time. Ask your vet what you should use – make it clear to him or her that you are worming three-week-old pups.

At the beginning of the fourth week (day 28) you can also begin to feed them on food other than their mother's milk. The first food I give them is a piece of scraped frying steak the size of a pea; you buy a good quality steak and scrape it with a very sharp knife (old-fashioned steel knives are excellent for this). Then roll up one tiny ball for each pup. Now take the pups one at a time and put a little ball into each mouth in turn. Do not try to push it down their throats, just put it far enough in the mouth for them to get the taste and feel of it. On the first occasion, you may well find that, out of five pups, two seem to like it, two suck it for a bit with some interest and then spit it out, and one refuses to have anything to do with it. After a few days, you should find they all take it, and you can make the balls slightly larger and give more than one each. Word of warning, by the way; watch that Mother does not steal all your carefully prepared meat balls while you are concentrating on feeding Pup No 1 – it can happen!

Kerri's pups aged about two weeks. Eyes now open, but still blue.

At this stage, the pups will begin to play with each other. All you see at first is a little paw waving about for no apparent reason; then later on an unsteady little jump. Gradually these aimless movements turn into puppy play, and it is fascinating to watch.

When they are a few days older you can introduce them to liquid food. I usually start with Lactol, made carefully as per instructions and mixed with a little Farex, a very fine cereal made for babies. The result is a creamy, rather sticky, liquid. Put a saucer down in the pups' run and introduce them to this new item in their lives. To be honest, they will almost certainly walk in it and the mess will be awful. But help is at hand – bring Mother back and she will clean up everything and enjoy doing so. It will be good for her, too. If the pups do not attempt to lap it as well as paddle about in it, pick them up one at a time, put their faces by the bowl and put a little of the cereal on their tongues. After a day or two, they will soon get the hang of this and so, by about the end of the fourth week or early in the fifth week, they will be having two feeds daily: the small steak feed and the cereal feed.

Six lovely blenheim pups in their box.

Some breeders introduce the milk feed before they offer the meat. I prefer to do it the other way round, but I do not think it matters all that much which way you do it.

During this time, they are still feeding from mother as well, though by now she will appreciate some time away from them. Their teeth will be starting to come through and it may be necessary to trim their nails. This

The same puppies, showing surrounding cage, which folds up in sections. Bedding is Vet-bed.

has to be done very carefully, never cutting into the quick, and, with a small wriggly pup to handle, it would be advisable to get an experienced friend to help you.

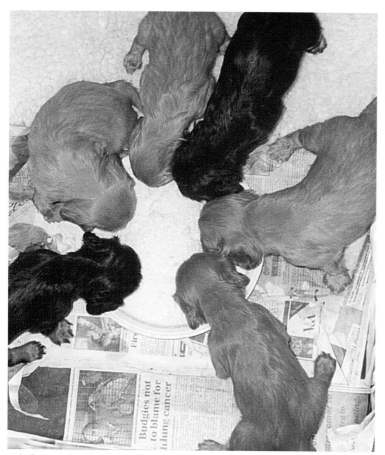

At four weeks, Kerri's pups are beginning to feed independently.

Five to eight weeks

The pups should be introduced to a much wider variety of food now, since it will not be long before they are old enough to be completely independent of mother. They can be given a small feed of (good quality) minced chicken with rice, all soaked in the chicken stock; fish, a flaky cereal (such as Weetabix) instead of the Farex with milk (Lactol of course), egg if it agrees with them... but not all at once! From day 35, gradually build up to a diet such as:

- *First thing:* Drink of milk, at start of period from Mother, then later on from bowl.
- *Breakfast:* Cereal and milk.
- *Noon:* Chicken (or fish) with rice.
- *Mid afternoon:* Drink of milk and biscuit or rusk.
- *Supper:* Best mince with biscuit (puppy meal, not *complete* food) all soaked in stock. It is in order to buy good quality mince now instead of steak and it should be lightly cooked.
- *Last thing:* Milk (from mother, later from bowl), a little biscuit.

If this diet sheet seems familiar, it is because it is very similar to the one given for the eight-week-old puppy that the new purchaser takes home (see chapter 3). As the pups grow older and larger, the meals become bigger also. After the pups are about seven weeks old, their mother should be kept away from them most of the time. After all, in a few days they will be leaving her to go to their new homes.

78

Kerri's pups at seven weeks, nearly ready to go to their new homes.

There are also various proprietary puppy foods on the market, and these should be fed according to the manufacturers' instructions.

If it is sunny and warm, from five weeks old onwards the pups can go outside for a short while to play and get some fresh air. As long as they are warm enough they will love it, and you will love watching them. One can spend a long time just watching little pups having fun together. This is the period when your puppies learn to socialise, so you and your family should pet them and play with them (very gently) as much as you can. Pups who do not get used to people at this age often are nervous and lack confidence, so it is important for their future happiness that you and your family build up a good relationship with them.

At five weeks, the pups should be wormed for the second time, and then again at seven weeks.

Eight weeks

This is when the pups who are not staying with their breeder go to a new home. By this time all your available puppies should be booked, and the new owners will call for them by arrangement.

When the new owner takes the puppy, you give her a signed copy of the pedigree, a diet sheet, and a list of the dates wormed and the wormer used. You give her the registration certificate if you have it, but, as often happens, it may not have arrived from The Kennel Club by this time, so you arrange to send it on as soon as possible. She will pay you for the puppy and

Head study of Joan Twigg's Culloden Drambuie (USA).

you give her a receipt on which there is a section for 'conditions'. I always put in the following three conditions:

1 The new owner should take the pup to his or her vet for a check-up within 72 hours. If the vet is not satisfied that the pup is in good condition, it can be returned.

2 The new owner is to keep in touch with the breeder regarding the progress of the puppy and later the adult dog.

3 If the puppy is no longer wanted and is to be sold or given away, probably when it is older, the breeder should be informed and given the option to buy it back if she is not satisfied with the new arrangements made for the dog.

Other conditions can be put on if you wish, but numbers 2 and 3 are to ensure that in future all will be well with the puppy; a caring new owner should understand this.

Summary

• Remember that the well-being of the bitch and puppies must come first.
• It is extremely important to provide a good, balanced diet, particularly for the bitch, but later for the pups.
• Do not give unnecessary vitamin and mineral supplements as these do more harm than good.
• Be available at all times and monitor all stages of whelping.
• If there are problems, contact your vet sooner rather than later.
• Remember that the majority of whelpings are normal.

Chapter Seven
Problems associated with whelping

A pair of tricolour pups: Culloden Donald and Dirk, owned by Joan Twigg (USA).

This chapter concerns various important groups of problems. First come problems with the bitch, both during whelping and after it. Then there are the problems with the puppies, before birth, during whelping and after birth, and some guidelines on how to hand rear puppies, in case you find yourself in the unfortunate situation of having to do this. Most whelpings are trouble-free, but it is as well to have some idea of what might go wrong and why; however, there are times when you never find out why.

Whelping problems due to the bitch

Uterine inertia

When a bitch has *primary uterine inertia*, the uterus does not contract at all and there is no sign of second stage labour. There is not normally anything that can be done about this and a

Caesarean section is usually required. It might be an inherited condition, or due to a hormonal lack. If the bitch is in poor condition, particularly if she is too fat, this also could cause uterine failure. Perhaps one of the most common causes is an over-large litter where there is so much crammed into the uterus that it cannot contract properly. A very small litter can also cause this problem.

Secondary uterine inertia occurs after the delivery of one or more puppies, or sometimes after there have been a number of contractions that have stopped without anything happening. It can be associated with low levels of blood calcium and glucose. After three or four pups have arrived, fatigue can set in, which also can lead to uterine inertia. The problem can often be treated with a hormone injection, but another may be needed for each subsequent puppy.

A promising blenheim pup at three-and-a-half months.

I experienced this inertia problem a few years ago with Paula, my older ruby bitch, who was nearly six at the time. She was enormous with pups and very restless. Then at 3.00 pm (on a Sunday afternoon), we saw that her water bag was visible, though there were no contractions. From 4.00–4.45 pm there were a few small contractions, but nothing really happened. At 5.00 pm the vet came and gave her oxyticin; shortly after this she had a number of contractions but nothing further happened and the contractions diminished again. At about 6.00 pm she was taken to the vet in the car and he decided she should have a Caesarean section. She was lying on the table looking huge and exhausted, really pathetic. I said good-bye and good luck to her and went outside, naturally very anxious. About two minutes later, in came the vet, all smiles. 'She's just had a puppy!' he said. After that, we took her home to see if she could produce the rest herself, and she did just that, giving us a total of six lovely pups who all survived. Later, friends suggested that it was the 10-minute run in the car that helped; maybe it was.

Physical problems
The pelvis may be formed in such a way that the puppy cannot be passed out from it. The vagina may be an abnormal shape or unable to open up enough; the vulva may be wrongly shaped or positioned. In all these situations, a Caesarean will be needed.

Whelping problems due to the puppy

Oversized puppy
A bitch may have one very large pup only, or a very large one among a few normal ones. When this happens, the pup is too large to be pushed out in the normal way. Occasionally a vet can get the pup out, although under these circumstances it seldom survives. Usually a Caesarean is required.

Abnormal puppy

If the pup has a very large head or body it cannot be born normally and, as in the above case, a Caesarean section is needed.

Abnormal presentation, position or posture

If the pup does not work its way down the vagina head first or possibly back legs first, it is liable to get jammed in the narrow passage. A vet, or possibly a very experienced breeder, can deal with this, but an inexperienced person can easily do more harm than good. As I have said already, get help if there is a problem.

A veterinary text book on whelping shows illustrations of some of the ways a puppy can get stuck on its way out. It is also possible for two puppies, one from each horn of the womb, to reach the point where the horns join at the same moment.

Lindsay with four-and-a-half-month-old Polly.

A litter of tricolours and blenheims. Note the puppy enclosure.

I will not elaborate further on these very unfortunate developments. Suffice to say, they do not happen very often.

Problems that can affect the bitch after whelping

Excessive bleeding

After whelping, a bitch will always have a slight reddish brown discharge, which may go on for two or three days. However, if she loses blood or has a copious discharge, you should contact your vet.

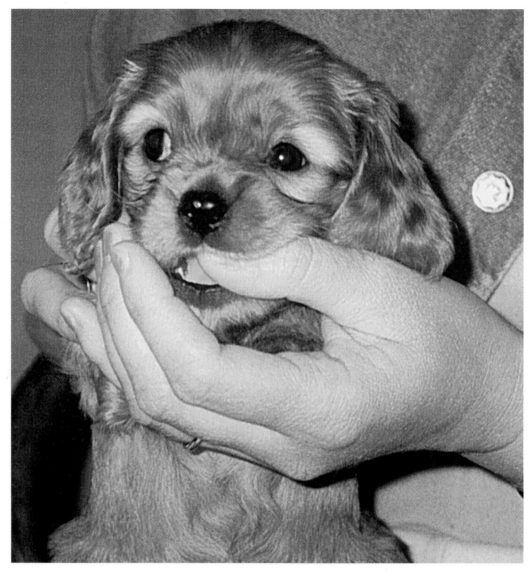

'Humans taste nice!' However, he's not biting – just thumb sucking!

Infection of uterus

This can mean a very minor infection or a much more serious one. It is best to talk to your vet, who will give you suitable medication.

Mammary congestion

This is when the teats swell up and get red and hard; it can be very sore. It is sometimes seen on the big back teats if they get very full and the pups insist on sucking from the smaller teats nearer the front. You can help with this problem by gently putting hot and cold compresses alternately on the affected teats. It helps if the pups will suck these teats, but often you will not be able to get them to do this. If you are not making any progress with improving matters, your vet will be helpful. (See also Chapter 10.)

Mastitis

This is an infection of the mammary glands themselves. Your vet should be consulted.

Eclampsia

This extremely serious illness requires immediate attention from your vet (and I mean *immediate*) or your bitch will die. It is due to a fall in the level of calcium in the blood. You should always be on the look-out for eclampsia when you have a litter, especially a week or two after the birth.

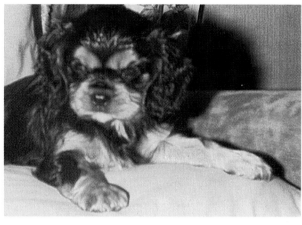

A black-and-tan at eight weeks – just about ready to go to his new home.

Connie at four to five months.

A bitch developing eclampsia begins by being very restless. She seems nervous and her behaviour does not seem normal; she is worried and over-anxious. She will pant a lot and dribble saliva. She soon loses interest in the puppies, and you may notice muscle tremors and shivering. Convulsions will occur, followed by complete collapse and then death. Obviously, you will have to get her to the vet before this occurs. The vet will give her an intravenous calcium injection, and she should recover as quickly as she went downhill. Always be on the watch for this dangerous condition until the pups are feeding independently.

Calcium is needed for many body processes, including the adequate functioning of the nerves and muscles. This calcium should be obtained from the diet, but there is a mechanism in the body whereby the bones can transfer calcium to the body's calcium pool. When a bitch has pups, she uses some calcium to build up the skeleton of each foetus. After birth, she needs a lot of calcium for the milk the pups take from her. It is at this time that the bones are able to provide calcium as required. If a great deal of calcium has been provided in the diet in the form of calcium tablets, this may inhibit the body's ability to get calcium from the bones and hence do more harm than good.

Older breeders like myself have always given supplements, especially calcium, though never too much. See, for instance, Janie Booth's very well thought of book, *All about the Cavalier King Charles Spaniel*, sadly no longer obtainable. Now modern veterinary research tells us that we should no longer do this, and certainly never in excess. What is vital is a good, well balanced diet containing all the calcium and vitamins required without the use of additives.

What a lovely handful!

Problems affecting puppies after whelping

Fading puppies

These pups seem healthy at birth but gradually weaken and die about two weeks later. Sometimes a whole litter can be lost this way, sometimes just one or two pups. There are various possible causes such as hypothermia, a congenital defect (a problem they are born with), poor mothering or an inadequately-fed mother, a difficult birth or too many worms. They may have an infection brought in, perhaps by the owner, from outside; hence many owners insist that all visitors to the pups take off their shoes before going to see them. Often no-one knows for sure what causes the pups to fade. It is very sad and upsetting when it happens, and I have every sympathy for anyone who loses a litter in this way.

Death shortly after birth

I have already mentioned this and said that it is not always known why the pups die. There are many possible reasons, some which at this stage cannot be identified. It is always very satisfying if a weaker pup can be saved.

Loss of puppies before birth

A bitch can be known to have several puppies when she is three to four weeks pregnant but, by the time they are due to be born, there may be none at all or perhaps just one or two. This has already been mentioned in the previous chapter. When this happens, the pups have either been reabsorbed (resorption) or aborted, probably with no one noticing anything.

Whole litters can be lost in this way due to a variety of causes, for instance:

- Overcrowding (too many pups)
- Hormone imbalance
- Infection
- Injury
- Stress
- Lethal genes, in other words something in the genes making up the pups that causes pre-natal death
- Poor or inadequate diet given to the bitch

Reading this list carefully will indicate various important ways in which you should give your pregnant bitch special care, right from when she is first mated:

- Do not let her come into contact with infection; this includes not taking her to dog shows.
- Do not let her indulge in wild play with other dogs or people.
- See that she gets a good, wholesome diet.
- Avoid stressful situations such as putting her in kennels.

Orphan puppies

Occasionally, the bitch cannot rear her puppies and they have to be reared by other means. The first and best possibility is to find a foster mother for them. This is not always easy, and there is also the possibility that the foster mother you find will reject the new pups. A bitch with only one or two pups might accept orphan pups. The bitch should be taken away for a few minutes and the new pups rubbed thoroughly with soiled bedding and the bitch's own puppy; this is so that they will smell familiar to the mother when she returns. The bitch will usually accept the pups in this situation, although I doubt if it would be successful with more than two pups. The two lots of puppies should be more or less the same age. Very occasionally a bitch who has lost all her own pups might be available, or possibly a bitch with a phantom pregnancy might be pursuaded to take over.

However, it is not usually possible to find a bitch who can take over. Where there is none, the owner has to take on the major task of rearing the pups herself. For one person alone, this is almost impossible, as they need feeding day and night: for the first week every two hours, then every three hours for the next two weeks. If there are other people in the house who can take a turn at feeding, the situation is not quite so bad.

Orphan puppies need to be kept very warm, at first at a temperature of 30°C (85°F). They should be fed every two hours with a premature baby feeder or special puppy feeder if you can get one. Use Lactol or a similar milk powder, carefully made up as directed on the tin. After a week, feed every three hours and, after they are two weeks old, leave out the feed in the middle of the night. At three weeks old, try to pursuade them to lap; bottle-fed pups often lap more readily than normally reared ones. Continue with the bottle as well, though. If they lap really well, they might manage without the bottle from about four weeks onwards. Try little balls of steak and so on, as listed for bitch-reared pups in chapter 8.

After every feed, the pups' ano-genital area should be gently but vigorously rubbed with warm cotton wool to stimulate bodily functions. The mother always does this by licking so, if there is no mother, it has to be done by the owner. Their eyes and mouths should also be wiped.

Bottle-reared puppies need to be weighed daily. Be especially careful not to expose them to infection, as they may not have had the early bitch's milk containing colostrum, which protects against infection.

Fortunately, Cavalier puppies seldom need to be hand reared. However, it is certainly a rewarding, if exhausting, experience if you do manage to rear a healthy litter in this way.

Conclusion

Every pregnancy and every whelping is unique, and there is no guaranteed formula for success. The majority of litters arrive as expected with no serious problems. Rearing your own litter is a uniquely satisfying experience.

A family snapshot of Anne Crossgrove with Heidi (left) and Lindsay Gow with Polly.

Chapter Eight
Showing your Cavalier

As well as having your Cavalier as a much-loved pet, you may feel you would like to take him to dog shows to let other Cavalier folk see him and to see how he compares with the other Cavaliers. This can be good fun; you see many other dogs and meet many people, all with a similar interest in dogs. The only thing you need to watch is that you do not take it all too seriously. Dog showing should be a pleasurable and social hobby; it should not become some sort of obsession. Winning does not really matter, although getting a card (prize) is always satisfying; what is more important is that you and your dog enjoy your day out.

There is actually quite a lot to find out about the different kinds of show, the different classes and what it is possible to win. The best a dog can do is to become a champion (other than being Best in Show at a major Championship show); and I will explain all this in subsequent sections of this chapter.

Marion wiggins' top-winning tricolour Whyteplace Apollo (above) at four months and (below) at one year.

Getting a show dog

The only way to buy a show dog is to find a breeder who is selling a young dog who has already been to a few dog shows and has won one or two cards (though not necessarily firsts). This dog will very probably be expensive, often very expensive, and as he has been brought up by someone else he will not be used to your ways.

Most people go to a reputable breeder whose dogs they have seen in the ring and really liked. They ask him or her to let them have a puppy (usually giving sex and colour, for example blenheim bitch) when she has a suitable one available. No breeder can sell an eight-week-old puppy as a future show dog; all she can say is that she thinks it is a promising puppy that could turn out well. You always have to take a chance, but often the breeder is right. Remember though what I pointed out in chapter 2, that a breeder will always keep the best one for herself; unless she does not keep males, in which case a male might be the pick of the litter. If you buy a really attractive bitch puppy, she may do quite well, possibly even very well, in the ring and, when she is between two and three years old, you can mate her to a top-winning dog you really like and breed your own litter of lovely pups.

When you are choosing the puppy you hope to show, look for all the qualities I mentioned in chapter 2 – outgoing temperament, solid body, shiny coat and so on. However, there are some other things you should look for that relate to pups aged eight to nine weeks old.

Bumble, a promising blenheim puppy, at seven to eight weeks.

Colour

If you are looking at particolours (blenheims and tricolours), the patches of red or black should be well spread out on the white coat. The pup should not be be too white, and neither should the coloured patches cover an area much greater than the white (this is called *heavily marked*). It is relatively simple to assess coat colour in a young particolour, although you have to remember that the coloured patches get larger as the puppy grows up. There are many photographs in this book of well marked particolours.

The red colour in the mature blenheim should not be pale. The deeper it is the better, as long as it is not a brown or liver colour; it should always be rich and bright. Most blenheim puppies start off rather pale, but darken as they grow up, though a pup with a deeper coat will probably end up with a deeper colour than a paler one. A *lozenge* mark in the centre of the head is always desirable when it occurs. In a tricolour puppy, as well as the coloured patches being well broken up, there should be tan markings over the eyes, inside the ears, on the cheeks, on the underside of the tail and inside the legs if the black reaches down to the leg. Some tricolours have black down their back legs or, worse, one black leg. This is not actually a fault, but it is undesirable.

Bumble at four to five months.

Wholecolours (rubies and black-and-tans) should not have any white markings at all. If you are looking at a six-week-old pup, it may have a thin line of white on top of its head or on its chest. The breeder will tell you this will disappear as the puppy gets older and the coloured part of the coat spreads, and this is almost certainly true. On the other hand, a large patch of white on the front will not go, and nor will a white foot. Many wholecolour pups these days have no white markings at all.

A black-and-tan should have definite tan markings above the

eyes, on the cheeks, inside the ears, on the chest and legs and on the underside of the tail. Sometimes the tan on the legs and feet is rather muddy looking; this will often improve as the pup grows up, though not always. Ruby pups are born paler than they will be when they finally mature, though again, the deeper the better.

Head study of six-week-old puppy, showing muzzle *neither too long nor too short.*

The puppy's head

The top of the head should be flat or very nearly flat. This is the main area of difference from the King Charles Spaniel, which should have a rounded top to its head. However, most Cavalier pups have this head shape so it is seldom a problem. One of the first things to look for in choosing a puppy with show potential is big, round eyes, dark and set fairly far apart. The ear flaps, when pulled forward, should reach the tip of the nose, even though at this age there will be no ear feathers, or only very few. The muzzle is difficult to describe, but it should be neither too long nor too short. A Cavalier should have cushioning under the eyes, but this does not

Ch Maibee A Cameo – one of my favourite champion bitches. Photo: Russell Fine Arts

always develop at this age. Nose pigment should be completely black. It is better if a particolour has a white blaze down the middle of the head, though not essential. Freckles round the face, although not mentioned as a fault in the breed standard, do rather spoil the pearly white ground that is asked for. The same goes for ticking on the coat itself.

Teeth

An adult Cavalier that is undershot will not win in the show ring. If a puppy is undershot, it might be forgiven because it is young and might come right. Usually, it is not forgiven, and the puppy is not placed. Therefore, if you are hoping that you may be able to show your puppy later on, make sure that it has a correct scissor bite. Unfortunately, it is possible to buy a puppy at eight weeks that is not undershot and then, when its second teeth come in, they may not be correct. Sometimes they right themselves in the end, but quite often they do not. When this happens, it is nobody's fault; it is just very bad luck and very discouraging. However, it does not happen so very often.

I once had a dog with a perfectly correct mouth but, if he took a dislike to the judge, he pushed out his lower jaw and, of course, the judge thought he was undershot. Fortunately, he did not take a dislike to many judges. When he did, they were always forceful males – I wonder what this proves!

Tail

All puppies hold their tails up when they are playing with each other and running around. If, on the other hand, a puppy's tail is held straight up or curls right over its back, this could mean that the mature dog will have what is known as a *gay tail*, which is a fault.

Structure and body shape

Most young pups will, if held and encouraged, stand on a table in some sort of show stance. From this, you can look for a number of qualities.
- The shoulders should be well laid back.
- The neck should be of reasonable length, not short and stuffy. It is a bonus if it is slightly arched. The head should be held high.
- The front legs should be firm and straight.
- The back should be fairly short; hence the pup should be almost square.
- The back should be level (parallel with the ground).
- The back legs should have good stifle angulation and be firmly placed.
- The overall effect should be well-balanced and harmonious.
- The puppy should move well with its legs parallel. It is not always possible to assess movement at this age, but usually you can get some idea.
- It is as well not to choose a pup that is either very large or very small compared to the others in the litter. Sometimes, though, the relative sizes change as the pups mature.

Summary

Look for an outgoing puppy who is happy to welcome you and play with you; temperament is extremely important. Look for a neat, compact shape and a good head with big, shining eyes. Try to find a pup who is stylish and well balanced, with that little extra indefinable 'something' which makes him a winner. Actually, easier said than done... but good luck to you and your pup!

Training your show dog

A dog who is to be shown needs to learn to walk steadily on his lead, staying beside his owner and not pulling forwards, backwards, or sideways. He also needs to stand up straight on a table (in practice, often wobbly), and finally he needs to stand steadily and in the correct position possibly for 5–10 minutes while the judge is choosing her final winners. He must not bark at the dogs standing near him or try to play with them.

Much of this can be taught at home, but doing these thing in the unfamiliar company of many other dogs and strange people is a different matter. Once at a show, he may do things all wrong: sitting down, pulling on his lead or even trying to jump off the table – no, they don't do this often! If possible, then, it is a good plan to take your young dog to a ringcraft training class. There are also obedience training classes, but these are quite different. For one thing, the dogs are taught to sit, and this is not what you want your future champion to do! At the ringcraft class, they learn to do all the things they need to do at a show and, very importantly, they get used to being with other dogs. You, the owner, will meet a lot of other doggy people, probably make a number of new friends, get help and advice about showing your dog and find out when and where the shows are to be held.

Travelling with your show dog

Exhibitors travelling to shows, sometimes a long distance, put their dogs in specially-made dog cages or plastic travelling boxes. The cage will fold down flat (see page 97) but the box will not (see below). Do not feel that it is unkind to put your dog in a cage; a dog feels very safe in its

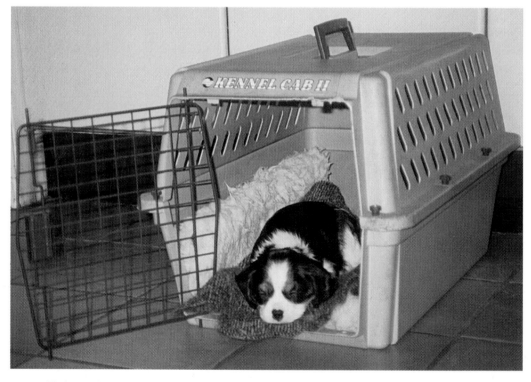

'You're not leaving me behind!' This tricolour puppy has taken up residence in his travelling box.

Cage in the car, with pretty blenheim occupant.

cage and will often go in there from choice. When I first arrive at a show and am getting the cage ready, putting in the cushion and so on, it is quite difficult to keep the dogs out while this is being done. They are anxious to be safe and cosy in their own sheltered place. The same is true when travelling on a long journey. I do not mean that a dog should be shut up in a cage for a long time every day; that is quite a different matter. If you leave your cage in a corner of the kitchen, open, you will probably find your dog sleeps in it from choice anyway, but in a home situation he should feel free to go in and out of it as he wishes.

Different kinds of dog show in the United Kingdom

Championship shows

These are the highest grade of show, the only kind where Challenge Certificates (CCs) can be won. A CC is awarded to the best dog and the best bitch in the breed. With Cavaliers, there can be over 200 dogs and 200 bitches present at one of these shows. Because of these large entries, there are nearly always two judges: one for dogs and one for bitches. Some of these shows are what is known as *All-Breed* shows, in which there are classes for almost every breed; other shows, run by the breed club concerned, are for one breed only. For Cavaliers in the United Kingdom, each of the 10 breed clubs runs its own Championship show and the remaining 26 are big All-Breed shows.

At these shows, there are usually 8–10 classes for each sex, making a total of 16–20. First there are the puppy classes: *Minor Puppy* for puppies aged 6–9 months and *Puppy* for pups aged 6–12 months. No puppy under 6 months old can be shown in any class. Then there is *Junior* for young Cavaliers up to 18 months of age. After that the classes are mostly based, not on age, but on what your dog has won previously: the more your dog has won, the higher the class he has to enter and the hotter the competition. The schedule you receive before the show tells you what classes there are and the conditions for entering them; a list defining them can be found at appendix B. You can obtain a schedule by sending for it to the address given in the dog papers, or you often find them available at other shows. Dog training clubs often have them too.

After all the dog classes are finished, all unbeaten dogs (by which I mean males) are lined up, and the judge chooses the one he or she thinks is the best; this is the CC winner. She also chooses the runner-up, and he is awarded a Reserve CC. These awards are very much sought after and, as I have already pointed out, can only be won at Championship shows. Then the bitch CC and Reserve CC are awarded in the same way. Finally, the Best of Breed (BOB) is selected – a great honour for whoever wins it.

When a dog (or bitch) has won three CCs (all under different judges), he (or she) becomes a champion. This is not easy for a Cavalier, as there is considerable high-powered competition.

Newcomers to the breed and to dog showing would be well advised to go to the smaller shows at first. Championship show entries are very expensive, averaging about £15 for each entry. There is fierce competition from among the top dogs in Great Britain, so the inexperienced dog and handler can be at a disadvantage. Details of other types of shows follow below.

Open shows

These are held all over the United Kingdom at all times of the year. Any dog registered by The Kennel Club can enter, champions included, but usually the entries come from nearby, up to an hour's drive away perhaps. For this reason, they can be very friendly shows, as you may recognise several people in your own breed or from your dog training club.

There are fewer classes for any given breed than at a Championship show, but they have to be chosen from the same range of classes as before – Puppy, Junior, and so on. They also have a few variety classes where different breeds compete with each other. Each Cavalier breed club also runs its own Open show once a year, and at this there are many classes. Dog and bitch classes are again separate, and there are colour classes such as *Open Wholecolour*, a special class called *Maiden* for dogs which have never won a first, and so on. Again, you will meet many people and dogs that you know, and you may get to know some more.

Limit shows

Limit shows are like Open shows except that no champions can compete and entry is restricted to members of the club running the show. They are run at venues all over the country and, as with the Open shows, the Cavalier clubs each hold one annually. The class qualifications are higher, to give dogs starting out more of a chance; for instance, at an Open show, a dog cannot go into a class called *Post Graduate* if it has won *a Challenge Certificate or five or more first prizes at Championship Shows, in Post Graduate or above*; at a Limit show, the qualification reads, *five or more first prizes at Championship or Open shows...* This keeps more dogs out of the class, as quite a few win at Open shows who do not go to Championship shows.

Exemption shows

These are shows run for charity but, like all the others, they have to be licensed by The Kennel Club. They usually have 4–6 classes for pedigree dogs and 9–10 fun classes, with title like *The Dog with the Waggiest Tail*, *The Dog the Judge would most like to Take Home* or *The Greediest Dog*. They are good fun and you know that any money you spend will be going to a good cause

Cage containing Toby.

Cage folded flat.

Cage with Toby on trolley.

such as the National Canine Defence League or the local Dog Rescue centre. Both registered and unregistered dogs can be entered in these shows, unlike the three types above.

Entering a dog show

Before you enter the show ring the following requirements must be met:

- Your dog must be at least six months old.
- Your dog must be registered with The Kennel Club (except at Exemption shows).
- Your dog must be completely fit and must not have been in contact with any infectious or contagious canine disease for the previous 21 days.
- You will need a schedule for the show and must fill in the entry form provided with it. This is sent with payment to the Secretary by the given date. The schedule also gives details of all classes, where and when the show is to be and anything else you might want to know (so don't lose it before the show!)
- You turn up on the given day with your dog, carefully prepared for the occasion.
- You buy a catalogue listing the names of all the dogs and owners in each class.
- Ask the officials where the Cavalier ring is and make your way to it.

What happens at the show

You are by now at the Cavalier ring; other Cavalier people and their dogs will be all

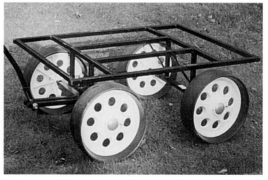

A trolley for carrying a cage at a show.

C.K.C.S.C. Championship Show   Date 9-3-91

Breed Cavalier KC Spaniel   Sex Dog

Kennel Club
Challenge Certificate

I am clearly of the opinion that

CH BARSAC THE PALIO

(Name of Exhibit)

owned by Mr KJ Town

(Name of Owner)

is of such outstanding merit as to be worthy of the title of Champion.

(Signed) R. Williams   *(Judge)*

Challenge Certificate (CC).

around, most of the dogs in their cages or being groomed. You find a suitable space for your cage, put it up and let your dog get into it. Find out how long it will be before your class so you know how much time you have to get ready. I always try to arrive in good time for a show, and the first thing I do when I have set up the cage and unpacked is take the dog or dogs as the case may be to do their business. It is usually possible to go outside for this at an Open show. If you are at a Championship show, a small area is cordoned off for this purpose, with sawdust laid down (which my bitches refuse to use, although the dog does not mind!). During the summer, most shows are out of doors, which is easier unless it pours with rain. Then everyone has to move into a huge tent where small and often damp rings have been set up and there is space set aside for the dogs who are not in the ring. I trust your first show will not involve what is known as the 'wet weather tent', as it is enough to put an inexperienced exhibitor off for life.

Toby with the author at a dog show, being 'gone over' by judge Bill Moffatt.

Toby misbehaving (he should not be sitting).

Most Championship shows have *benching* where large metal compartments are set up for every dog. Toy dogs have doors on their benches, as these compartments are called, so you do not need to set your cage up. You might, however, need to wheel in the cage on a special trolley if you do not wish your dogs to get dirty and wet walking from the car to the show. Once the dog has relieved himself, you go back to your bench or cage and brush and comb him. Then you do not take him out of the cage again until the class before your own, when you brush him up once more so that he is looking really nice and take him over to the ringside to wait for his class.

When it is time for your class, you take your boy into what is fondly known as 'the ring'; actually it is always either square or rectangular. You are given a number as you go in, which you pin on with a special clip. Then you and all the other exhibitors stand in a circle (or part of a circle if there are not many of you). The judge walks round looking closely at each dog and asks you all to move twice round the ring. Next the owner of the dog standing at the head of the queue puts her dog on a table specially set up in a corner of the ring for this purpose. The dog should be standing four square with his head up; and after looking at him for a minute from a few feet away, the judge comes up to the table and *goes over* the dog. This means he looks at the teeth, has a good look at the whole head and eyes, feels the shoulders to check that they are well laid back, feels the back, chest, stifle, checks coupling, and so on. Then he has another look at the whole dog. After this the judge asks the exhibitor to move her dog, usually in a triangle and then up and down. The exhibitor moves cross-wise over the ring, straight across the side opposite the judge and then back again, and then from the judge to the far side of the ring and back again. When she gets back to the judge, she gets her dog to stand beside her looking as nice as possible. The judge then has another good look at the dog, often walking right round him; then he smiles (usually) and says 'Thank you'. At this point the exhibitor and her dog walk away and stand at the end of the line.

When all the dogs have been looked at, the judge walks along the line of dogs looking at them again even more carefully. When he reaches the end, he will probably stand in the middle of the ring and look at them all from there. Then he will pull out the winners, first one first, and they will stand in the centre of the ring. Once the judge is quite sure that he likes what he has done, the winners' numbers are called out and they each get a card. Four cards are usually awarded, First (red), Second (blue), Third (yellow), and Reserve (green). Sometimes a fifth is awarded called *Very Highly Commended* (white). Finally, the judge writes notes on the first and second prize winners, to be published in the dog press (*Dog World* and *Our Dogs*).

If your dog wins a first prize and is not beaten in another class, he is called into the ring when the class judging is finished, together with all the other unbeaten dogs, and the judge chooses either the best dog (or bitch after the bitch classes) if it is a Championship show, or the best exhibit regardless of sex if it is an Open show. (A club Open show will have the best of each sex judged separately.) Then the Best of Breed (BOB) is chosen from the two winners. At a show where there are other breeds, the BOB will go on to compete for Best Toy (in other words, Best in Group); should he be considered the Best in Group, your dog finally competes for the Best in Show (BIS) award. It is always an honour to win this together with, probably, two or three cups.

Another award much prized by exhibitors in the United Kingdom is the Junior Warrant (JW). Every time your dog wins a first prize in a breed class at an Open show, he wins one point. When he wins a first in a breed class at a Championship show, he scores three points. If he can score 25 points between the day he is one year old and the day he is 18 months old, he is then awarded his Junior Warrant. At one time, these points could be won between the ages of 6 and 18 months, but recently it has been changed to the six-month period mentioned above. This was because it was considered that some people campaigned their puppies far too much, and this was not at all good for them at less than a year old. Certainly showing a young dog too much can cause it to get bored and lose much of its vitality and 'sparkle'.

Hints on doing well with your dog

To do really well, you need a top class dog with most of the qualities listed in the breed standard (chapter 5). If you are not too sure what this means, look at one or two champions and top winners when you are at a big Championship show. This should help to give you a picture in your mind's eye of what you want. There are many photographs of champions and other outstanding dogs in this book, so look closely at these as well. You will not win much with an indifferent dog, especially in Cavaliers where there is so much competition.

It is very important that your dog moves well. It also makes a difference if he shows himself off to advantage. Even an absolutely top class dog who pulls on the lead, sits down when the judge looks at him, hangs his head, hunches himself up because he is nervous, or perhaps even

snaps at the judge (temperament is very important) will not win anything. For this reason, it is advisable to try to accustom your dog to show conditions. Some Cavaliers seem to love showing, make the very best of themselves, and really do have that extra something that will catch the judge's eye. However, many are high quality dogs who have become used to showing and are happy to do what their owner wants of them, and these too can manage to do quite a bit of winning. In fact, there are relatively few Cavaliers who cannot be trained and encouraged to put up quite a

The future Ch Maibee a Cameo aged eight weeks.

Molly Coaker with Ch Homeranne Caption, walking him around to show his movement.

Winners at Richmond Show 1996 – (left to right) Dog CC: Ch Lymrey Royal Reflection of Ricksbury; Best Puppy: Woodstock Kerris; Bitch CC: Ch Maibee A Cameo. Judges: Joyce and Tom Boardman.

creditable performance in terms of showmanship. If your new puppy seems impossible, don't despair – he will learn to behave in the end!

Various types of show lead can be used. I use a thin leather lead with a small chain collar clipped to the end which loosens and tightens as you move. You will have seen other variations on this. Note that you never use a conventional collar and lead for a dog show, as it is too heavy and not flexible enough.

Ideally you should not attract your dog's attention with titbits to make him look up or to stop him from being a fidget. However, many people will do this if it really does improve their dog's performance and there is no rule against it.

If you are nervous and tense when showing your dog, this feeling can be transferred to the dog, who then fails to make the best of himself. Remember what I said earlier about the importance of enjoying dog showing. If you are there for a pleasant day out, everything else should fall into place too – and what's more, your lovely boy might well win something!

Points to remember

- Arrive in good time.
- Do not forget your ring number and ring number clip.
- Do not forget the titbits (if you use them).
- Remember to take a small brush to use if your dog gets rumpled while you are waiting in the ring to be seen.
- See that your dog is beautifully groomed before he enters the ring.
- Enjoy your day out... and your dog will too.

Cavalier line-up at Richmond Championship Show 1996.
(Left) Joan Reid with Ch Chantiz Alboreto (right) Kevan Berry with Ch Lymrey Royal Reflection of Ricksbury.

Cavaliers at an Open Show in Scotland, author judging.

Chapter Nine
Genetics and successful breeding

There has already been a chapter on breeding in this book, but this chapter is about becoming a consistently successful breeder of good quality puppies that go on to do well in the show ring. There are many well known breeders in the United Kingdom and overseas, many of whom I have mentioned in this book.

To be a good breeder, I consider that two main qualities are needed. Firstly, the ability to recognise a good dog and, with that, the ability to identify the really promising puppy; secondly, a knowledge and understanding of pedigrees. The good breeder also needs to develop as time passes a good idea of what his or her dogs may produce. Your aim as a breeder is to improve your stock all the time, always bearing in mind that health factors in the long run are even more important than appearance.

Methods of breeding

There are three kinds of breeding, *inbreeding*, *line-breeding* and *outcrossing*.

Inbreeding
Inbreeding means mating close relatives, such as father and daughter. If the breeder really knows what he or she is doing and has a line of dogs with no physical problems, this can sometimes be done. The earliest Cavaliers were often very inbred; for instance, Daywell Nell, Ch Daywell Roger's mother, was the daughter of Ann's Son and his daughter, Miss Ann's Son. In those days, things were very different, as there were very few Cavaliers about and hence there was a very small gene pool. You will note, however, if you look back at Roger's pedigree, that his father is not related to his mother at all; a complete outcross in fact, which is interesting. I feel that in a breed such as Cavaliers, where there can be various serious recessive problems, close inbreeding should not be undertaken (see chapter 10 concerning these problems).

Line-breeding
Line-breeding is practised by most good breeders and means mating dogs that are related, but not too closely. If a breeder has a very nice bitch with one unfortunate fault (let us say she has a gay tail) he will mate her to a dog with a well carried tail. He must be careful not to bring in new faults, however, as these can be hard to breed out again. Hence he would use a dog who has some ancestors in common with the bitch. The offspring should be of a similar type, since the stud, like the bitch, is a nice dog with few obvious faults, but *he* has a well carried tail. They should therefore produce a nice litter, quite like themselves, and in the litter there should be several pups with well carried tails, though it is not always too easy to tell this when the pups are very young. In real life, what so often happens is that the pup with the beautiful head and

An interesting litter bred in Ireland by Geoffrey Parker (Salador Celtino (b/t) ex Ir Ch Rincreevy Ring-a-Roses (ruby)). So where did the blenheim come from? Looking at the pedigrees, Salador Celtino has a blenheim sire and Ring-a-Roses a tricolour grandparent. The outcome was therefore unlikely, but possible.

Kerri's puppies. Both parents were dominant wholecolours, so there is no white on them.

compact body is also one of those whose tail stands up over its back while the two with good tails have small eyes and stuffy necks. This is known world-wide as *Sod's Law*!

Outcrossing

Outcrossing occurs when a bitch is mated to a dog who has no ancestors in common with her (though there might be one or two a number of generations back). There is sometimes a need for it, as when the bitch has been closely line-bred for several generations and some change is called for. Normally after this the breeder will continue to line-breed; but she now has a completely new set of genes in one of her lines which, if it has worked successfully, is very desirable.

You can see from these two pictures of Martha that, although she is a ruby, she has white on her feet and on the top of her head. She also has some on her front. Presumably this is because her dam's sire was a blenheim.

Four lovely Australian Cavaliers belonging to Marilyn Madigan: (left to right) Merseyport Jet Setter, Aust Ch Merseyport Aloysius, Aust Ch Upperton Lynette (UK import) and Aust Ch Casamba Chloe Bell. The blenheims only carry the recessive genes $a^ta^tees^ps^p$, but the tricolours could carry either $a^ta^tEEs^ps^p$ or $a^ta^tEes^ps^p$.

Though one can discuss how to be a good breeder as above, I have always felt that top breeders have a special gift and do not just learn this. It also needs dedication and perseverance, especially in the early days. It needs too the often talked of *eye for a dog*; this is fundamental.

Colour inheritance

The colour of a Cavalier depends on the colour genes it has received from its parents. All a dog's characteristics depend, as do ours, on what genes it has inherited, and there are several genes among dogs that determine coat colour. When Cavaliers mate, there is only one certain outcome in terms of colour: two blenheims will always result in blenheim puppies. This is because a blenheim Cavalier has only recessive genes. I shall attempt to explain this.

There are nine groups of colour genes for dogs, known to geneticists by the letters *A*, *B*, *C*, *D*, *E*, *G*, *M*, *S* and *T*. There is a note at the end of the chapter saying very briefly what each of these gene groups does. In the Cavalier, the only colour genes that vary are in groups *A*, *E*, and *S*, so these are the ones we need to think about.

The A series
The *A* series of genes affects the relative amounts of dark (black or brown) pigment in the dog and of light (tan or yellow) pigment. The Cavalier has a gene called a^t which produces what is known as tan points: *the typical tan-point pattern includes areas of tan pigment on the sides of the muzzle, throat, and belly line, inside the ears, on the chest, over each eye, on all four feet and part of the legs, around the anus, and on the underside of the tail.* This quote, from Dr Little's book *The Inheritance of Coat Colour in Dogs* may well sound familiar to my readers; it is almost the same as the description of the colouring of the black-and-tan in the breed standard, and similar in parts to the standard for the tricolour. In fact, all Cavaliers have the a^t gene but, where they also have a gene for yellow colour rather than black, the tan points effect does not show up or is *masked*. If you look closely at a ruby, the hair above the eye often seems slightly different from the rest of the ruby hair around it, since the ruby also has the a^t gene.

The E series
Next comes the *E* group of genes, which governs whether the dog has black in its coat or just tan. The *E* gene allows the formation of dark pigment evenly over the whole coat, while the *e* gene restricts all dark colour to yellow or red. This means that Cavaliers with the genes *ee* can be neither black-and-tan nor tricolour – in other words, their coats cannot have any black coloration. Hence they must be either blenheim or ruby.

The S series
Finally comes the *S* group. The *S* gene gives a completely pigmented body surface, though not necessarily in all the same colour. However, there will not be any white. The s^p gene is for piebald spotting, resulting in large patches of colour on a white ground; the blenheim and the tricolour, in fact.

To summarise...
So let us see where we are now. All Cavaliers have the a^t gene. Some Cavaliers have *ee* genes, so cannot have any black in their coats, while others have the *E* gene, so can have black. Some Cavaliers have an *S* gene, so do not have any white while others have $s^p s^p$ genes, so can have large patches of white.

At this point the reader may wonder why I seem to have been rather vague about the number of genes, ee at one point but E alone at the end of the sentence. This concerns a very important point; namely that some genes are what is called *dominant* and override the effect of others in the same group. With S and s^p, the S gene is dominant, so if both S and s^p are present (in other words, the gene pair is Ss^p) then the dog concerned will not be a particolour. Similarly, with E and e, the E gene is dominant so both EE and Ee pairs mean the black colour will be present. Conversely, the e gene and the s^p gene are what is known as *recessive,* and their influence is only seen when they are both in the pair (ee and s^ps^p). Genes always go in pairs; this is because one comes from the mother and one from the father.

Colour gene patterns

I will now put all this together and write down the variable colour gene patterns for the different coloured Cavaliers.

- Black-and-tans: a^ta^tEESS $a^ta^tEESs^p$ a^ta^tEeSS $a^ta^tEeSs^p$
- Rubies: a^ta^teeSS $a^ta^teeSs^p$
- Tricolours: $a^ta^tEEs^ps^p$ $a^ta^tEes^ps^p$
- Blenheims: $a^ta^tees^ps^p$

Note that, in the actual dog, the ee genes effectively mask the effect of the a^t genes.

At appendix C there is a list of all the possible gene patterns (45) that can occur when two Cavaliers are mated, based on the various gene combinations. Wherever there is an E, the resulting puppy will have black in it, but an ee pair gives no black. An S gives a whole colour (no white), while s^ps^p gives particolours. The pair a^ta^t is in all the patterns but does not show up if ee is there too. Here are two examples:

1: Blenheim x tricolour
The blenheim (blen) can only have the genes $a^ta^tees^ps^p$
The tricolour (tri) can have two gene patterns: $a^ta^tEEs^ps^p$ or $a^ta^tEes^ps^p$

Where the tricolour has $a^ta^tEEs^ps^p$
The tricolour parent can only give a^tEs^p
The blenheim can only give a^tes^p
Therefore the resulting pups all have $a^ta^tEes^ps^p$ and are tricolours.

Where the tricolour has $a^ta^tEes^ps^p$
The tricolour parent can give a^tEs^p or a^tes^p
The blenheim parent gives a^tes^p

(from blen parent)		a^tes^p
(from tri parent)	a^tEs^p	$a^ta^tEes^ps^p$ (tri)
	a^tes^p	$a^ta^tees^ps^p$ (blen)

It follows that the resulting pups can be blenheim or tricolour, chances equal. The probability ratio is 1:1.

2: Ruby x black-and-tan
The black-and-tan (b/t) can have four different gene patterns.
The Ruby can have two.

This means that there are eight possible combinations (see appendix C), so as an example I will consider a ruby with $a^ta^teeSs^p$ and a black-and-tan with $a^ta^tEeSs^p$.

(from b/t)		a^tES	a^tEs^p	a^teS	a^tes^p
(from ruby)	a^teS	a^ta^tEeSS (b/t)	$a^ta^tEeSs^p$ (b/t)	a^ta^teeSS (ruby)	$a^ta^teeSs^p$ (ruby)
	a^tes^p	$a^ta^tEeSs^p$ (b/t)	$a^ta^tEes^ps^p$ (tri)	$a^ta^teeSs^p$ (ruby)	$a^ta^tees^ps^p$ (blen)

It follows that the probabilities for black-and-tan, ruby, tricolour and blenheim are 3:3:1:1.

These examples demonstrate the uncertainties of Cavalier breeding as far as colour inheritance is concerned. The obvious problem is that one cannot usually tell what colour genes any given dog has, unless it is a blenheim. If a tricolour dog always throws tricolours, although frequently mated to blenheim bitches, he is almost certainly a dominant tri whose gene pattern is $a^ta^tEEs^ps^p$. The famous Homerbrent Andy Capp was one of these. Similarly, a black-and-tan who always throws black-and-tans is a dominant wholecolour with the pattern a^ta^tEESS and also a dominant black-and-tan. A ruby can be described as a dominant wholecolour if it never throws particolours; its genes will be a^ta^teeSS. It would be incorrect to describe it as a dominant ruby as, if it is mated to a tricolour or a black-and-tan, it can throw a black-and-tan, since both these colours have the dominant gene E for black. But no, it cannot throw a tricolour, as the genes SS cause it to throw wholecolours whatever it is mated to.

Colour breeding summary
- *Blenheim to blenheim* always gives blenheim.
- *Blenheim to tricolour* normally gives blenheims and tricolours.
- *Blenheim to ruby:*
  1. A ruby whose ancestors for the last two or three generations have been wholecolours (ruby type A) should give rubies only.
  2. A ruby with a particolour parent or one or two particolour grandparents (ruby type B) can give rubies and blenheims.
- *Blenheim to black-and-tan:*
  1. A black-and-tan whose ancestors for the last two or three generations have all been wholecolours (black-and-tan type A) will give black-and-tans or rubies.
  2. A black-and-tan with a particolour parent or one or two particolour grandparents (black-and-tan type B) can give all four colours.
- *Tricolour to ruby:*
  1. Tricolour to ruby type A gives rubies and black-and-tans only.
  2. Tricolour to ruby type B can give all four colours.
- *Tricolour to black-and-tan*
  1. Tricolour to black-and-tan type A will give black-and-tans and possibly rubies.
  2. Tricolour to black-and-tan type B can give all four colours.
- *Tricolour to tricolour* gives blenheims and tricolours unless a dominant tricolour is used, in which case all the pups will be tricolours.
- *Ruby to ruby* normally gives rubies although, if many particolour genes are present, some blenheims may be born also.
- *Ruby to black-and-tan* is a very common mating and, as there are many dominant

wholecolours around these days (that is, dogs carrying *SS* genes), it usually results in ruby and black-and-tan pups. If the parents share a lot of particolour genes, it is possible to have all four colours.

- *Black-and-tan to black-and-tan:* Like ruby to black-and-tan matings, this one, which is not uncommon, results in black-and-tans and rubies, sometimes all black-and-tans. With particolour genes coming down from the parents, anything can happen (well, maybe they

François Huet from France with his lovely dogs.

will not actually give birth to Chihuahuas!). Note that there are 10 possible gene combinations when you do this mating; see appendix C for details.

Note 1 Remember that, when you mate a particolour to a dominant wholecolour, you may get mismarks, for example wholecolours with white markings that last into maturity. Hence it is usually wiser not to cross wholecolours and particolours unless you are looking for some particular qualities.

Note 2 The above is a list of the possible results of the various matings, but this does not mean you will always get exactly what it says. For instance, if you mate a tricolour to a black-and-tan type B, the list says you can get all four colours. This only means all four colours are possible; you might actually get two black-and-tans and a blenheim.

Summary of colour genes found in dogs

- *A* series influences amount of dark (black or brown) and light (tan or yellow) pigment in the hair and in the coat.
- *B–b* pair produces black colour, or lighter brown pigment in its recessive form, *b*.
- *C* series is responsible for the depth of pigmentation in the dog.
- *D–d* pair: the *D* gene gives densely pigmented dogs; the *d* gene produces a blue dilution, as in the blue Greyhound.
- *E* series: *E* allows the formation of dark (black or brown) pigment evenly over the coat; the recessive *e* allows no dark pigment to be formed in the hair, leaving a shade of red or orange. There are other members of this series such as E^{br} (black mask) or e^{br} (brindle).
- *G–g* pair: the gene *G* causes a pup born of a uniform dark colour to become greyer. It is found in Kerry Blue Terriers, Poodles and some other breeds.
- *M–m* pair: the *M* gene produces merle or dappled animals.
- *S* series: gene *S* produces solid coloured coat with no white. Gene s^p gives a piebald colour pattern.
- *T–t* pair: the gene *T* gives *ticking* on the white parts of the coat: gene *tt* gives clear white areas.

Chapter Ten
The Cavalier's health

Breed-specific problems

Heart problems

Unfortunately, Cavaliers are liable to develop heart problems at an early age. What seems to happen is that the dog gradually develops a heart murmur, and this deteriorates, often very slowly but sometimes quite fast, until the dog becomes seriously ill. This heart murmur, which can easily be detected by your veterinary surgeon, is caused by an unfortunate ailment called *mitral valve disease*, but known for short as MVD. Research at Edinburgh University Veterinary School finds that a Cavalier is 21 times more likely to develop MVD than the 'average' dog. One hopes this is not typical, but one hears of so many Cavaliers with heart problems that I fear it could well be.

The heart consists of two pumps in series. The right side pumps the blood to the lungs and the left side pumps it out of the heart to go round the rest of the body. Each half is divided into two parts: an *atrium*, which is a collecting chamber, and a *ventricle*, which is a pumping chamber. Blood from the body collects in the right atrium, then passes through the valve dividing the atrium from the ventricle and is pumped via the pulmonary artery to the right and left lungs. Here carbon-dioxide is given off and the blood becomes re-oxygenated with the oxygen that has been breathed in. From here it is pumped into the left atrium and then through the mitral valve separating the left atrium and the left ventricle. It is then pumped via the aorta into the systemic circulation to supply fresh blood to all the body (see diagram opposite).

As they get older, many dogs develop chronic heart valve disease or *endocardiosis*. The valves gradually deteriorate, becoming thickened and less flexible. All the heart valves can be affected to some extent but the mitral valve, in the left side of the heart between the left atrium and the left ventricle, is the most seriously and frequently affected. As flexibility in the valve decreases, some of the blood leaks in the wrong direction. Initially, this causes no ill effects, though a heart murmur may be heard. As the condition gets worse, there is more leakage, and the heart becomes overstretched. This eventually results in serious complications whereby the lungs and abdomen may fill with fluid. This may lead to complete collapse and, in the end, death is inevitable.

Although many dogs have this problem when they are old, the trouble with Cavaliers is that they develop it much too early, often as young as four or five. The first indication is a heart murmur, which is normally found when a vet listens to the dog's heart. Later on, the dog may begin to cough and wheeze and not want to walk as far as it used to. Research has shown that male Cavaliers are more often affected than females and that, once a dog develops a murmur, there is a gradual deterioration as time passes. Some Cavaliers deteriorate very fast, while others live for many years. It has been suggested that there are two types of MVD. In one type, deterioration is fast and the dog dies one or two years after the murmur is first heard, or even sooner; in the other, a murmur may be heard when the dog is five or six, but there are no apparent ill effects and the dog concerned lives to twelve or thirteen. At a recent symposium on MVD in the Cavalier, this matter was discussed, and no firm conclusion was reached; some of the experts felt that it was all the same disease but that the rate of deterioration was very variable. (If so, why?)

Research in Sweden and elsewhere has shown that MVD is an inherited disease so, to cut down the incidence of MVD, only dogs without murmurs should be used for breeding. This is all very well, but very few dogs have murmurs at the normal breeding age (two to three) anyway. For this reason, it is now suggested that the parents and other relatives (especially male) of the dogs to be mated are checked to see if they are still

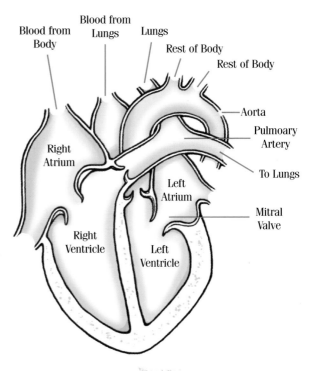

The anatomy of the heart (diagrammatic).

murmur-free. The Cavalier Club produced a book in 1996 listing Cavaliers aged five and over who still did not have a murmur, and since then it has been updated annually. Ideally, dogs to be mated should be at least two-and-a-half, not have a heart murmur, and have parents and other relatives who by the age of five still had no murmur either.

Treating a Cavalier with heart problems This is an indication of the stages of this condition, but *all treatment should be carried out in consultation with your vet*.

- When a murmur is first detected by your vet but your dog is otherwise perfectly fit, no treatment is required. Your dog just needs its usual good food and exercise and may well carry on as happily as before for many years. Do not allow it to become overweight.
- The first symptoms are usually breathlessness with probably a slight cough and less inclination to go for energetic walks. In fact, these early symptoms can be almost negligible. If you feel your dog is not as fit as it was, it is as well to visit your vet for a check-up. Your vet may find that the murmur you knew was present has become a little worse and advise treatment. Two well-known types of drug are used for these problems: one, known as a *diuretic*, clears fluid from the lungs and, in later stages, helps to clear it from the chest and abdomen; the other type helps to prevent fluid retention in the first place. These drugs increase quality of life for a dog with heart problems and may help it to carry on with few further ill effects for several years.
- As the heart problem gets worse, the dog experiences increasing difficulty in breathing; sometimes it cannot breathe properly lying down and sits up all night gasping for breath. If this happens, contact your vet. At this stage, it is essential to keep in touch with your vet and to give the recommended treatment.

Final comments It is sad to think that such a lovable and active breed as the Cavalier should have this problem. However, more is being done now to try to improve the situation. Research is taking place in various parts of the world, and many breeders are trying to ensure that their dogs are murmur-free and have ancestors with a good heart record. Many Cavaliers have lived for many years, sometimes up to as much as 15 or 16, and it is obviously a good plan to try to breed from their descendants. Some of these long-lived Cavaliers may have had a heart murmur for some years, but it cannot have been of the type that causes an early death. It is up to all lovers of the breed to do what they can to decrease the frequency of these heart problems by careful breeding.

Eye problems

Retinal dysplasia This congenital problem varies from small folds on the retina to complete non-attachment of the retina to the rest of the eye (*total retinal dysplasia*). Puppies with this latter condition are born blind but, as far as is known, this problem does not affect Cavaliers. However, a number of Cavaliers have been found to have *multifocal retinal dysplasia*. In a mild form this makes little or no difference to the dog concerned but, in its more severe form, it can affect the sight to some extent and may give rise to some pain, though this has seldom if ever happened with Cavaliers. This condition can be seen in a very young puppy but may then disappear altogether, so recently eyes have not been tested until the young dog is about 15 months old. Recent research suggests that the condition will not have disappeared but is just masked – hence puppies should be tested at about eight weeks after all. This is still being discussed by the eye specialists, but all members of the Cavalier Club (English) have been notified of what is going on. This problem may be hereditary.

'No, we don't want our photographs taken!'

Cataract Cataracts affect only a small number of Cavaliers at present. There were problems with this in the past but careful testing under the British Veterinary Association/Kennel Club (BVA/KC) Scheme over a period of years has kept the occurrence of this defect down to a minimum.

Lee and Ollie playing together.

Other ailments

Abscess

An abscess is a septic region caused by bacterial infection, consisting of a pool of pus surrounded by a wall of fibrous tissue. It can occur anywhere. The swelling gradually gets larger and more painful and finally bursts, discharging blood and pus.

For an accessible abscess, the best treatment, as with humans, is to bathe the swelling gently with warm water and then hold a warm damp pad over it until it bursts. Continue to bathe the wound and do not allow it to heal up too quickly or another abscess may appear. Unless the abscess is very superficial, an antibiotic will be required, so consult your vet.

One of the more common abscesses a Cavalier owner will meet is a tooth abscess, often the result of infection at the root of one of the large molars. The cheek may swell just below the eye; the abscess will burst but will reform. The only cure is to ask your vet to remove the affected tooth.

Sometimes an abscess occurs in one of the anal glands (see **Anal glands**).

Allergies

An allergy is a hypersensitivity to some substance which may cause the skin to come up in raised blotches and can cause sickness and/or diarrhoea. Once the *allergen* (the substance causing the allergy) is removed, the dog recovers quite quickly. It is often very difficult to know what has brought on the allergic reaction; one of the more usual is reaction to a wasp or bee sting (see **Stings**).

If the allergy keeps recurring, then you should consult your vet. It is possible for a dog to

117

develop a long term allergy that causes constant itching and scratching. A complete change of diet sometimes helps, and some people have found homeopathic remedies particularly helpful for this kind of problem. Fortunately, the problem is not found very often among Cavaliers.

Hilary with a puppy pal.

Anal glands

The anal glands are situated on either side of the anus and are large enough to hold a broad bean. They contain a sickly-smelling fluid which acts as a scent marker and should be passed out whenever the dog has a motion. This could be useful in the wild, but has little real use in today's restricted conditions. Sometimes these anal glands fail to empty adequately and cause the dog some discomfort and irritation. The dog will slide its tail and back end along the ground or keep licking and biting under the tail. Your vet will empty these glands quite easily (without any anaesthetic) by gently squeezing them. The owner can do this with care if he has been shown what to do by his vet or a knowledgeable person who has had experience of doing this with a number of dogs. If the anal gland has become infected, it may continue to pass a smelly unpleasant discharge even after emptying. In this case, your vet should be consulted and antibiotics may well be prescribed.

Sometimes, an anal gland abscess forms. The duct leading from the gland blocks up and the gland fills with septic matter, causing a painful red swelling at one side of the tail. Your vet should be consulted as soon as possible if this happens.

Note 1 The anal glands should not be emptied unnecessarily; if emptied too often, they will fill up more quickly.

Note 2 It is sometimes said that a dog who pulls its back end along the ground has worms. It is much more likely to be an anal gland problem, but worms can sometimes be the cause.

Arthritis and rheumatism

As in humans, arthritis affects the joints, particularly in older dogs. There is no certain cure but many modern drugs can be helpful. Rheumatic muscular pain, possibly due to over-exertion, will pass in due course and is often helped by a mild pain-killing drug. Elderly dogs are more likely to get rheumatic pains after too much exertion, but they still need adequate exercise.

Bad breath

This is often caused by bad teeth or inflammation of the gums due to tartar deposits. A visit to the vet is indicated, and he or she will extract decayed teeth and remove tartar. The dog will feel much better after this has been done. A dog's teeth should be cleaned regularly with a special canine toothpaste to avoid this problem (see chapter 3). Companies such as Nylabone manufacture products designed to help keep dogs' teeth free of tartar as they play with them.

A dog's breath will smell after eating very fishy foods or unsuitable substances such as horse manure, and an old dog may have bad breath because of serious disease such as kidney failure. However in the latter case there will be a number of other symptoms.

Coughs and snorting

The Cavalier may give an odd cough very occasionally, and it does not mean anything at all. Loud barking or very active play might cause this.

Many Cavaliers will sometimes lower their heads and make a loud snorting noise, which will go on intermittently for some time. This can be stopped easily by either holding the dog's mouth firmly shut and pushing the head down, or holding the dog's back legs up high so that its body makes an angle of about 70° with the ground. This snorting is said to be due to the soft palate at the back of the throat temporarily restricting breathing. I have had one or two Cavaliers who always snorted when they pulled on the lead!

A continuous cough should always be taken seriously. It could be due to:

* *Kennel Cough*, which is very infectious and can be picked up easily at dog shows or boarding kennels. If it is picked up by a fit and mature dog, it is unlikely to give rise to any ill effects other than the actual coughing. However, young puppies and very old dogs can be seriously affected by it, so no dog with kennel cough should be allowed to mix with other dogs. If the cough does not seem to be clearing up, your vet should be able to advise you. Do not sit with a coughing dog in a vet's waiting room; it is always possible to slip out and fetch your dog from the car when your vet is ready to see you.
* Heart trouble (see **Heart problems** earlier), particularly in an old dog. When a dog suffers from MVD the excess fluid from the heart that may be squeezed into the lungs will cause the dog to cough. This is often the first symptom noticed when a dog develops MVD.
* Canine distemper, a very serious illness, is not seen so much these days, as nearly all dogs are protected from it by vaccination. A young puppy might pick it up if it comes into contact with infection on, say, the sole of someone's shoe. One of the symptoms is coughing so, if a young pup starts to cough, your vet should always be consulted.
* Coughing can indicate an obstruction in the throat such as a bone (or piece of bone). Even grass that 'goes down the wrong way' can cause coughing.

* Puppies may cough if they are seriously infected with worms as the larvae have to migrate through the lungs.
* Respiratory disease.
* Tonsillitis, pharyngitis and laryngitis.
* Inhaling of irritants such as aerosol sprays.
* Poisons such as paraquat or warfarin.

Note Dogs do not develop coughs and colds like humans do.

Drowning in a sea of dogs.

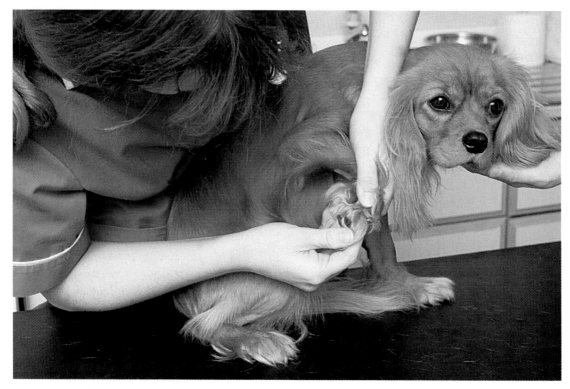

Cavalier having its nails examined at a routine veterinary check-up. Photo: Frank Naylor

Diarrhoea and constipation

Diarrhoea is the frequent passage of abnormally soft motions. It is an indication of a number of illnesses, some relatively trivial, some serious.

Diarrhoea is caused most frequently by digestive problems and the condition should improve when the offending food or other unsuitable substance has passed through the system or is withdrawn from the diet. If your dog has diarrhoea, do not give it any food for at least 12 hours. Water should be made available, but do not allow the dog to drink excessively. When you begin to feed it again, give light foods such as fish, egg or plain boiled rice, in small quantities at first.

If the diarrhoea does not clear up or there are other symptoms, contact your vet. It is particularly important to talk to your vet if a litter of very young puppies gets diarrhoea, as they become dehydrated very quickly and diarrhoea can be one of the symptoms of distemper. It occurs with several other viral and bacterial infections affecting adult dogs as well as puppies, so can be a serious matter.

Other causes of diarrhoea may be:

- Overfeeding, especially with young pups.
- Feeding too much liver or kidney or over-rich foods.
- Too much milk. Some dogs cannot tolerate milk at all.
- Putrid or decaying food.
- Scavenging.
- Sudden change of diet.

Marion Wiggins with Mat and friends.

- Stress can cause diarrhoea in some dogs. Many situations, such as changing home, a dog show, boarding kennels, can cause stress in a sensitive dog and this could lead to diarrhoea. However, most dogs accept these situations philosophically without any apparent ill effects.

Constipation in the dog is not common and is usually due to an unsuitable diet such as too many bones or a low-residue, all-meat diet, both of which result in small, hard faeces that can be difficult to pass. If this happens, cut right down on the bones (and on no account give bones like chicken bones or any others that can splinter) and add some carbohydrate, such as dog biscuit or rusk, to the meat diet. Some liquid paraffin is helpful; give about one dessertspoonful for every 13.6kg (30lb) of dog.

Mechanical obstruction can be caused by an enlarged prostate gland (found in the older male dog) or a narrowing of the rectum (either congenital or caused by too much straining). It is as well to seek veterinary advice if these situations occur.

Straining to pass motions is not always due to constipation. If a dog has passed a very runny motion, it may continue straining to get rid of the last of it, but in fact does not pass anything – not because it is constipated but because it has nothing left to pass.

A dog who does not get sufficient exercise and is confined too much to the house may well become constipated. A dog may also be slow to pass a motion after being shut for a long time in a car, perhaps travelling to a dog show. A dog should have a good walk every day and the opportunity to run around, have fun – and also relieve itself.

Deafness

Cavaliers often become slightly deaf as they get older; although I'm afraid there are those who are only deaf because they do not want to hear! You can be sure a dog is deaf if you come into the house, having been out for a while, and your dog does not lift its head or acknowledge your return in any way, although when you wake it, it is as bright as an (old but well polished) button and delighted to see you.

Some puppies are born deaf but it is very difficult to spot this as they copy all the other puppies and run around just as they do. Cavalier puppies, as far as one can tell, are seldom born deaf. However, some Cavaliers become deaf as they get older. By this time, they know what their owner wants of them and seem to lead a perfectly normal life, but owners must remember that their dogs will not answer a call if they cannot hear it.

Ear care

Dogs with long ears, such as Cavaliers, need special care, as the ear canal is not as open to the air as it is with the breeds with shorter ears and less hair on them. A Cavalier's ears should be groomed daily, both on top and underneath, and the inside of the ear should be looked at frequently to make sure that it is not too waxy or sore in any way. A little waxy secretion is quite normal.

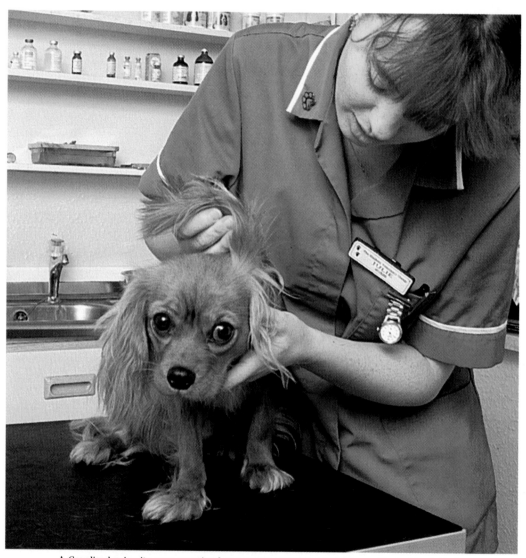

A Cavalier having its ears examined at a routine veterinary check-up. Photo: Frank Naylor

If your dog keeps shaking its head, scratching its ears or both, you should ask your vet for advice rather than trying to deal with the problem yourself, as the ear is very sensitive and it is easy to do more harm to it. Your vet will almost certainly give you some eardrops, which should help a lot. I prefer oily drops, which can be warmed slightly by standing the whole bottle in warm water, to drops that contain some sort of spirit and can sometimes sting.

Grass seeds or spikes can get caught on the ear and work their way into the ear canal, causing sudden, dramatic head shaking. If this happens, the seeds will need to be removed by your vet, possibly under sedation or even under a general anaesthetic.

The term *canker* used to be used for inflammation of the ear (*otitis externa*). It is very probably some form of this that causes your dog to scratch and shake its head. One reason for this is could be the presence of ear mites, very small white mites that hide in the dark part of the ear canal. They are found more often in cats than dogs but it is not uncommon for a dog to have a few. They cannot be seen with the naked eye, but your vet will be able to see them with an auroscope (a long illuminated cone that enables the vet to see what is happening) and he or she will give you a product that should solve the problem quite quickly.

Some breeders suggest using various kind of powder to help dogs' ear problems. Although these may work if administered very carefully and removed completely after use, the veterinary profession in general does not like this method, as a cake of powder stuck solidly in the ear can do a lot of harm. Remember that the ear is a very sensitive organ and it is much wiser to consult your vet rather than run risks with home remedies.

Epilepsy
See section on **Fits**.

Eye care
The Cavalier's beautiful, dark, round eyes are among its most striking features. The two major problems that can occur, retinal dysplasia and cataract, have already been discussed under the heading **Breed-specific problems** (page 129).

Wipe under your dog's eyes regularly, using cotton wool dipped in clean, tepid water, one piece for each eye. Some Cavaliers have permanently runny eyes, which means continual wiping and the use of special cleaning liquid bought from your vet or a pet shop. It might be worth asking your vet if anything can be done about this problem. In my experience, after careful tests with my pup at the age of about six months, the specialist said nothing could be done except a very unpleasant operation, which I would not consider; a couple of months later, the problem had gone away of its own accord. So do not give up hope too early of this clearing itself.

If your Cavalier's eyes look red and inflamed, consult your vet, who will give you some eyedrops which should soon bring your dog's eyes back to normal. You should consult your vet immediately if there seems to be a serious problem, such as an ulcer or a foreign body embedded in the eye, or if the dog keeps rubbing its eye and seems to be in pain.

False pregnancy
This occurs when a bitch who has not been mated, or has been mated and failed to conceive, shows many of the signs of being in whelp, such as lactating, digging up a bed (or a series of beds), panting, or carrying toys around as if they were puppies. She may even get fatter like a pregnant bitch would. This happens between eight and nine weeks after her season, when the pups would have been due.

The best way of dealing with this is not to take it too seriously; give her other things to think about such as extra walks, take away the toys, and cut down slightly on fluid intake to dry up the milk. It might be necessary to cut down the food slightly as well. If she seems very upset, your vet might give her a sedative to calm her down and possibly hormone or diuretic tablets to help take the milk away.

Paula (left) and Beanie. Photo: Alan V Walker

Once a bitch has had a false pregnancy, she will probably have one every time she has a season. It may decrease in intensity each time, but this is not inevitable. While not a serious problem, it is a worry for the owner and it upsets the poor little bitch. Also, continuing false pregnancies can increase the chance of a **pyometra** (womb infection, see page 129) later in life.

Fleas and other external parasites

Fleas During a warm summer, it is very easy for even the cleanest dog to pick up a flea when it is out, either from its surroundings or another dog, or even a cat, if it gets near enough. Fleas are small, brown insects, easily visible to the naked eye, and can be seen running about on the dog's underside if you look quite carefully. They are blood-suckers, living on the blood they suck from their host (the dog). They lay their eggs in the dog's bedding or other upholstery. These hatch into small larvae, which pupate until conditions are suitable for hatching. They emerge and attach themselves to the nearest dog; then the cycle begins again.

A dog with fleas will scratch, sometimes a lot, and may bite its coat in an attempt to catch the flea. A flea leaves black, hard flea droppings the size of grains of sand. If you put one or two of these in a few drops of water, you will see that very soon the water becomes red with the blood from the droppings. This is a sure sign that fleas are present.

A dog with fleas can be bathed with an anti-flea shampoo, but these are not always effective.

Unfortunately, some earlier shampoos and dips that seemed to work wonders have now been banned as unsafe. Nowadays, it is best to use a powerful flea spray prescribed by your vet, being very careful to follow the instructions and not allow any of it to get into your dog's eyes. This should solve the problem if your dog just has one or two fleas. It is also advisable to wash the bedding with disinfectant and spray the bed, its surroundings and the clean bedding before the dog re-uses it. If you have several dogs, and the infestation seems quite bad, they should be sprayed every two weeks for about six weeks. It is also important to get a special spray for use in the house after vacuuming and cleaning everything. This may sound to you a major operation

Three of Sheila Gauld's Craigbet Cavaliers: (left to right) Craigbet Bossy Boots, Busy Bee and Hoi Polloi.
Photo: Jays Photography

– you're dead right, it is! But it only needs to be done after the first treatment, not three times.

Nowadays there are new products available where drops are applied to the skin on the back of the neck once a month. These kill fleas by dispersion through the coat and not by being absorbed into the dog's system.

Clean, well groomed dogs do not usually have fleas, but there are years when they are very hard to avoid. Dog fleas do not live on human beings. Hedgehog fleas can trouble a dog for a short while but will not stay on it for long. Cat fleas can be passed on to dogs but will not stay on people.

Ken Town with his friend Richard
(Ch Barsac The Palio).

Lice Lice lay their eggs (nits) on the dog and the nits are attached firmly to the dog's hair. The louse itself will stay on a dog for a few days only and it then moves on. Lice can be got rid of by the use of a good insecticide. Bathing, followed by combing, is also called for to get rid of the nits. I have never come across lice on a Cavalier, but they are sometimes picked up in unlucky situations.

Ticks Any dog can pick up a tick when walking through fields or bushes, especially dogs like Cavaliers whose bodies are fairly near to the ground. A tick is a round, grey creature, at first about the size of a pearl of barley but, after it has sucked its fill of blood from its host, it can be the size of a large pea. The presence of a tick does not seem to bother a dog very much and, after a few days, the tick just falls off and waits for another host (preferably a sheep). However, they are best removed. The important point to remember is that it will cause a localised skin infection if the tick's head is not removed with the body, and this can be quite difficult to achieve. One method is to soak the tick with ether or surgical spirit, using a pad of cotton wool. It gradually loosens its grip and can be removed complete. People who have spent some time in the Far East seem to learn the knack of removing ticks correctly by hand. A friend of my husband taught him how to do it; so, if one of our dogs gets a tick, my husband is always summoned.

Cheyletiella This small parasite is barely visible to the naked eye. It does, however, cause some dandruff, which can be seen if the coat is rubbed up the wrong way or after combing with a fine comb. If you examine the dandruff with a magnifying glass, you can sometimes see adult mites moving through it, which has led to the condition being described as *walking dandruff*. This dandruff is usually found on the back. Several treatments with a really good spray should eliminate it in due course although, as the mite is long-lived, perseverance may be needed.

Fits

A fit is a convulsive seizure followed by a period of unconsciousness, which may last from a few seconds up to several minutes. At first the body seems stiff, and then the dog starts to twitch and the legs thrash about in a paddling movement; it may well froth at the mouth. The dog may recover consciousness very quickly and seem almost its normal self again, or it may seem dazed and exhausted for quite a while. In either case, it should be kept quiet in a darkened or shady room for at least an hour. Do not touch the dog during a fit unless it is essential to move it to a safer place, such as away from the top of the stairs.

There are several causes of fits. One isolated fit might be caused by various things such as poisoning, pain, stress – sometimes it is impossible to tell. A little bitch of mine had a fit at about one year old because she thought she could not get back to me as a wall was dividing us (she only had to turn back and run round it) and, 15 minutes later, she was accidentally banged quite hard by a door. Her fit followed immediately. Now aged nine, she has never had another one – touch wood!

Many fits are due to epilepsy and, if a Cavalier is suffering from epilepsy, the fits are liable to begin when it is about three. Several weeks may elapse before the next fit, but an epileptic dog (or human) will go on having fits all its life unless treated. These days, excellent drugs are available, which the epileptic dog takes regularly and often never has any more trouble. Epilepsy could be inherited, though this has not been proved, so an epileptic dog should not be bred from.

If your dog has a fit, it is always as well to tell your vet, though if it is a 'one-off' fit with apparently a reason for it, he may well say, as mine did in the case mentioned above, that I should keep her quiet for the rest of the day and then, if all is well, not bother about it unless another one follows. Always remember that there is no point in giving medication unnecessarily.

Fractures

If your dog breaks a bone, usually in one of its legs, there is considerable pain, the dog will not be able to put any weight on the leg and the leg may look deformed where the break has occurred. Immediate veterinary advice is called for, but the prognosis is usually good.

Heat stroke

A Cavalier suffering from heat stroke looks distressed, has difficulty breathing and its tongue may turn blue. In the end it will collapse completely. The commonest cause of this is leaving a dog shut in a car on a hot day.

If this should happen, cool the dog as much as you can, sponging it with cold water, especially over the head, or putting ice packs round it, or both. Remove the dog at once from the overheated car if this is the cause. If there has been a complete collapse, get veterinary advice as soon as possible, but cool the dog while you are waiting. Completely plunging it into cold water would be too much of a shock to the system.

Never leave a dog shut in a car on a hot day, even with the window open.

Hernia

A hernia is a swelling resulting from the abdominal organs or fat pushing through a weak area in the surrounding muscle. It is often quite small and comes and goes according to the position the dog is in. Cavaliers are liable to get two kinds of hernia:

- *Umbilical hernias* are formed at birth when the abdominal wall does not heal over completely at the navel after the breaking of the umbilical cord. They are often very small and heal over quickly. If an umbilical hernia is large, it might need a minor operation to contain it; but wait until the pup is about five or six months before having this done – it may go of its own accord.
- *Inguinal hernias* occur at either side of the lower abdomen and are also found, but not very often, in young pups. If you stand your pup on its hind legs, holding up the front ones, a small swelling may be visible in one or both groins. They may disappear of their own accord but are a risk if the bitch is bred from – the extra weight can enlarge the hernia opening.

It is not known for certain whether these hernias are inherited, but it seems likely they are.

Interdigital cysts

Cavaliers are liable to develop small cysts between the toes known as *interdigital cysts*. There is a fair amount of space between the pads (as in all spaniels, but not all breeds of dog) but also a lot of hair, so mud and dirt can collect there and, if a particle of grit or a grass seed should penetrate the skin, a cyst may form. Sometimes the cyst becomes infected.

You may remember that a Cavalier should be *free from all trimming except between the pads* (breed standard) – this is why. A cyst can be quite sore and the Cavalier will keep chewing at it. The best thing to do is hold the paw in warm water to which you have added some Epsom salts for about five minutes; often the cyst will burst. Then dry the paw and apply an antiseptic powder. If the cyst is infected, it will probably be necessary to get an antibiotic from your vet.

Be sure to keep the hair under the pads short and do not allow your dog's feet to become excessively muddy and dirty, especially if it is prone to these cysts.

Mastitis and mammary congestion

Mastitis (see also chapter 7) is an inflammation of the milk glands and is most often found when a bitch is feeding her pups. The teats may become abscessed and tender, and the bitch may develop a temperature and seem depressed and sickly. This condition is dangerous for both the mother and the pups. Immediate veterinary advice is required and the pups may need to be hand reared. This condition can also occur in young maiden bitches. However, it is not common in any breed of dog and is seldom encountered in Cavaliers.

Mammary congestion (see also chapter 7) can often occur when your bitch has a litter. Pups tend to go to the smaller, softer teats nearer the front of Mum's body and the big teats at the back get too full of milk and become red, hard and swollen. Holding a damp, warm towel over them can often help. If the condition persists and the bitch seems to be in some distress, your vet might help. Many vets do not like to give antibiotics to a nursing bitch as the pups may receive some of it through their mother's milk, which is not a desirable outcome. Insist that the biggest, strongest pups suck from the big teats to soften and partially empty them. Sounds easy – but they can actually be very naughty about this! You, the owner, can also draw off some of the unwanted milk. As the pups get older, this problem will usually right itself.

Poisons

If your Cavalier begins to vomit, often violently, foams at the mouth, possibly has diarrhoea and begins to stagger about and show signs of complete collapse, this may be due to a poison it has found and eaten, although it could also be due to other very serious conditions. In either case, you will require immediate help from your vet.

All poisonous substances should be kept well out of the way of your Cavalier, just as such things are kept well out of the way of small children, locked safely in a cupboard. Here is a list of some of the substances you should keep well away from the dogs:

*   Warfarin, strychnine and cyanide, often used to keep down rats and other vermin, also wasps.
*   Garden sprays and weedkillers, containing such things as arsenic, sodium chlorate, paraquat, and organo-phosphate compounds.
*   Slug pellets are very poisonous to dogs.
*   Anti-freeze (ethylene glycol). This can sometimes be found on the ground or by the roadside

and drunk by the dog. It seriously damages the internal organs and there does not seem to be any cure. My son's dog Dunbar died this way. Everything possible was tried over a period of weeks, but the end was inevitable; it was so very sad. We think he found the antifreeze in a puddle in the gutter, so always be very careful with such products.

- Old paint and paint remover.
- Tar and creosote.
- Putty. Old putty should be carefully disposed of in the dust-bin as, if a dog eats this, it can die. We also experienced this recently when a neighbour's Labrador became ill and died and it turned out that workmen had dumped old, unused putty at the end of his garden; sadly, Burra ate it.
- Laburnum can be poisonous to dogs and other animals.
- Some berries and bulbs and some fungi can be poisonous.

So be very careful – it may seem unlikely, but it could happen!

Pyometra

This is an accumulation of pus in the womb of a bitch, usually occurring about five weeks after a season. A pale, yellowish discharge may be seen. The bitch will be very thirsty and seem rather quiet and lethargic. Sometimes the pus cannot come away as the neck of the womb is closed, so the condition is not so obvious, though in due course the abdomen becomes very swollen.

Pyometra requires immediate veterinary attention or your bitch may be completely poisoned by this infection. With a young bitch, it is sometimes possible to cure the condition by the use of antibiotics; this is seldom possible with an older bitch, and the only permanent solution is to allow your vet to carry out a hysterectomy (complete removal of the womb). It is surprising how quickly a dog will recover from this; particularly if she was not too physically 'down' when the operation was performed.

Skin and coat problems

Cavaliers do not often have skin problems other than those caused by parasites, which have been covered earlier in this chapter. The best known skin diseases in the canine world are *eczema*, *mange* and *ringworm*; if you suspect your dog has any of these, contact your vet.

Good feeding and condition have a considerable bearing on the quality of your Cavalier's coat. It is good for general condition and hence the coat if you give half a dessertspoonful of vegetable oil daily and a large pinch of garlic. I add garlic granules bought at the local supermarket, with the oil, to the main meal. I also add a large pinch of seaweed powder.

Plenty of exercise also improves general, and hence coat, condition. Regular grooming is also very important.

Stings

Cavaliers have a regrettable tendency to chase wasps, bees and other insects, so are liable to be stung by them. If possible, remove the sting and gently apply a mild antiseptic solution. As long as there is no allergy, all should be well quite quickly.

However, if the sting is in the mouth or throat, this may cause swelling, pain and difficulty in breathing. In this case, contact your vet as soon as possible. An antihistamine injection should give relief quite soon.

Ch Craigowl Hopscotch of Homerbrent, owned by Norma and Gordon Inglis.

Strains and sprains

A strain is a torn or overstretched muscle, while a sprain is a torn or overstretched ligament or tendon. Both can be caused by sudden wrenching and twisting movements. Your dog is playing quite happily when it gets a sudden pain and can no longer use the leg properly. There may be a swelling around the injured area.

A cold compress placed over the injured area may bring down the swelling and reduce pain. If the injury does not clear up quickly, it is as well to refer the matter to your vet to find out how much damage has been done and what has been injured.

Swellings and lumps

See previous sections for causes of various swellings.

Vomiting

It is quite usual for a dog to be sick once or twice and then carry on as if nothing had happened. Cavaliers often eat some grass deliberately to make themselves sick and clear their stomachs. They may sick up their dinner if they have eaten it too quickly – and will then proceed to eat it again.

Persistent vomiting may last for a few hours and then clear itself. A dog that is being sick may want to drink a lot but must only be allowed very small quantities of water; otherwise it will be even sicker and will soon become dehydrated. The dog can have a little glucose in its water but must not be allowed any food for 24 hours. If the vomiting seems to be getting worse and particularly if it contains blood, you should contact your vet at once.

Vomiting can be a sign of several very serious diseases such as parvovirus, gastroenteritis or kidney disease. It may also be caused by eating a poisonous substance. If an object such as a stone, a small toy or a piece of bone sticks in your dog's throat or gullet, you will again have constant vomiting and retching, often accompanied by a frothy foam. In all these situations, veterinary help is needed immediately.

Sometimes it can be difficult to decide how serious the sickness is, since most of the occasions when a dog is sick are not serious at all. If your dog seems ill in itself, will not eat, tries to drink a lot, has diarrhoea, and particularly if it vomits blood, there is obviously something very wrong and your vet should be contacted as soon as possible.

Warts

Warts are quite common especially in the older dog but do not do any real damage. They can be removed by your vet if they seem to be a nuisance.

Worms

Roundworms These are white worms about 10cm (4in) long and both young and adult dogs can acquire them. Your Cavalier should be wormed twice a year as a precaution; it is better to get advice from your vet about what remedy to use, as he knows the good ones available.

During pregnancy, the release of hormones activates roundworm larvae that are lying dormant in the bitch. Some will pass into the developing pups and others will remain in the bitch herself. This means that all puppies will have worms and it is essential to worm them. A pup badly affected by worms will have a staring coat (dry, harsh and open) and a distended belly, but will otherwise look thin. It may vomit or have some diarrhoea. In fact, it will not be seen to be thriving.

Pups should be wormed for the first time at three weeks old and then at fortnightly intervals until they are three months old. They should be wormed again at six months and then every six months for the rest of their lives. Mum should also be wormed.

The most common roundworm is *Toxocara canis* and it is particularly important to see that all faeces are removed and that the pups' area is kept very clean, as these worms can be picked up by humans. It is known these worms have caused damage (though never complete blindness) to children's eyes, although the number of cases recorded is minimal. Once again, regular worming is very important.

Tapeworms These are flat, white, segmented worms which can be as much as half a metre (20in) long. They attach themselves by the head to the dog's intestine and every now and then one or two segments break off and can be found in the faeces. These contain tapeworm eggs. These eggs may be swallowed by flea larvae and in due course pass into the body of the dog should he catch and eat a flea. So once again, it is very important to keep your dog free of fleas. If you do find evidence of tapeworms, ask your vet's advice regarding the best product to use to eliminate them. They are not very common among Cavaliers so you may never have a problem with them.

A different kind of tapeworm can be picked up if your dog eats raw liver from a dead rabbit or even a dead sheep.

Heartworms This dangerous worm is found in warmer countries, including parts of America and most of Australia. All dogs in these countries are given a heart worm tablet daily, which seems to be both safe and effective. Fortunately, heartworms are very rare in Britain.

Wounds, cuts and abrasions

Minor wounds and cuts These normally heal quickly in a normal, healthy dog. Wipe the area carefully with a weak saline solution, dry carefully then sprinkle with an antiseptic powder. If your dog insists on licking the wound, a little licking may not do any harm, although it is really better if you can stop this altogether. If hair is getting into the wound, it is as well to trim some of it off in the adjacent area.

Punctures Watch that this kind of wound (possibly the result of a fight with a cat) does not heal too quickly, as there may well be infection left in the wound, which could cause an abscess to form.

Deep cuts over 2.5cm long will probably need stitching, so a visit to your vet is called for. The wound can be covered temporarily with a pad of lint or clean gauze, then with a layer of cotton wool. Finally, bandage with a woven cotton or a crêpe bandage, making sure it is not too tight. A few bands of adhesive plaster may help to keep the bandage in position.

Conclusion

This long list of possible problems may seem alarming but do not let it worry you. Cavaliers are very healthy little dogs and so are seldom ill. This chapter has been put in just in case you need it – you probably won't.

Good luck to you and all your dogs over the years ahead.

The Scottish team at the Amice Pitt Rally held at Chacombe Priory.

Chapter Eleven
Crufts 1973 and afterwards

Ch Alansmere Aquarius winning BIS at Crufts 1973.

Crufts 1973

Everyone who has had anything to do with Cavaliers knows what happened in 1973. This was the year when a Cavalier became Best in Show (BIS) at Crufts, and thus finally put this relatively new breed right into the public eye. In total, 7581 dogs were entered for Crufts that day. Alansmere Aquarius, aged 17 months, won the Junior Dog class under judge Mr Viv Bennett, who finally chose him out of all the class winners as his Best of Breed (BOB). He then went into the Big Ring to compete for Best Toy, which was awarded to him by Mrs Judy de Casembroot. Finally, the well-known judge Owen Grindey gave him the highest award any dog in the show world can get: Best in Show at Crufts.

In 1973, there were 5071 Cavalier registrations; in 1997 there were 13,022 registrations and, out of nearly 200 breeds, Cavaliers came seventh (see appendix A). The registration figures below show how rapidly the popularity of the Cavalier has increased since it became a breed in 1945, but particularly since 1973:

1946	1951	1962	1973	1980	1987	1991	1993	1995	1996	1997
134	310	1595	5071	8898	9110	15514	13705	14449	13941	13022

In some ways, this is regrettable as the very popularity of the Cavalier has led to the breeding of puppies just for commercial gain and to the increase in the number of puppy farms to be found today. However, as shown above, the registration totals have decreased slightly overall since 1991, as breeders today are less inclined to breed unless they really want one or two out of the litter for themselves.

Ch Alansmere Aquarius with his friend Ch I'ma Blossom of Amcross.
Photo: Diana Pearce

Leading kennels

There have been many beautiful Cavaliers during the last 25 years, and they have remained true to type throughout. There have been a few changes; for instance, a level bite is now frowned upon. Winning Cavaliers are getting smaller as more notice is being taken of the 8kg (18lb) maximum weight asked for in the breed standard. Gay tails are seen less often than they used to be. Yet overall the Cavalier has remained the same super little dog he always was. In this chapter, I shall mention a few of the kennels of which I have thought highly over the years, in alphabetical order. As it happens, Alansmere comes first, so I can begin by saying more about Alansmere Aquarius, his breeders and some of their other dogs.

Alansmere

Alan Hall and John Evans began their Alansmere kennel in the 1960s, and they are still around today. Aquarius, known to his many friends as 'Chirpy', was born in 1971. His sire was Ch Vairire Osiris, a son of Ch Cerdric of Ttiweh, and his dam was Ch Alansmere McGoogans Maggie May, bred by Caroline Gillies-Compston. At that time, Maggie May was the bitch breed record holder for the number of Challenge Certificates (CCs) won (15). Chirpy was also a great-great-grandson of Ch Daywell Roger. He was an outgoing, friendly dog with great stamina and ring presence, one of the most famous Cavaliers of all time.

Another record-breaker from this kennel was Ch Spring Tide at Alansmere (right), who until 1996

Ch Spring Tide of Alansmere winning Group at Crufts 1994.
Photo: David Dalton

held the record for the highest number of CCs won (28). He won his first CC in May 1991; he was BIS at the Cavalier Club Show in 1993. He was finally retired in 1995, after again winning BIS at the Cavalier Club Show held in March that year. His breeder was Roger Calladine, his sire was Homerbrent Jeremy at Cottismeer and his dam Alansmere Angel Song. Among his ancestors are Ch Vairire Osiris and his son, Ch Rosemullion of Ottermouth. During his show career, Spring Tide won four Toy Groups including the Toy Group at Crufts in 1994.

Alan and John have bred many lovely Cavaliers and several champions other than the three

mentioned above. A number of their dogs have been exported overseas. They are invariably helpful to those interested in the breed and Cavalier folk owe them a great deal.

Amantra

The Amantra kennel belongs to Diane Fry and her daughter Tracey, now Mrs Jackson. They have produced several well-known champions, including Ch Amantra Anchors Away (blenheim dog), Ch Amantra Bohemian Image (tricolour) and Ch Amantra

Ch Amantra Bohemian Image. Photo: Thomas Fall

Bohemian Rhapsody (tricolour dog). Rhapsody was later exported to Australia, where he did a lot for the breed. The Frys have exported their dogs to many countries and hence have had a considerable influence overseas.

Ch Barsac The Palio: BIS at the CKCSC Championship Show 1990.

Barsac

The photograph shows Ken Town's Ch Barsac The Palio (Richard), a lovely tricolour dog and great friend of mine. His particular claim to fame was that he was Best Dog at the Cavalier Club Championship Show not once, but twice, in 1990 and 1991. In 1990, he was BIS as well. His sire was Ch Salador Corrigan and his dam Ch Barsac Touch and Go, both of whom are descended from Ch Rosemullion of Ottermouth. Richard is still around today, giving great pleasure to all the people he meets.

Ch Chacombe Camilla. Photo: Thomas Fall

Chacombe

Mrs Schilizzi is one of the breeders who could have appeared in chapter 4, as two of her champions were born in the late 1960s (Ch Ivan The Terrible and Ch Cordelia, both 'of Chacombe' and both wholecolours, black-and-tan and ruby respectively). Her best known tricolour champion was Ch Chacombe Alexis, born in 1973. Perhaps her most famous champion was Chacombe Camilla, a lovely ruby bitch by Ch Edgebourne Red Rake of Caplode out of Ch Cordelia. Camilla was the first ruby to be BOB at Crufts (in 1978, under judge A J Chandler).

(Back row left to right) Ch Cordelia of Chacombe, Ch Ivan the Terrible of Chacombe, Amelia of Chacombe and (front) Ch Chacombe Venetia. The three wholecolours are litter-mates. Photo: Thomas Fall

A year or two before this, in my very early days, I was at a big outdoor show when I saw the most beautiful Cavalier I had ever seen just walking along beside her owner, elegant, beautifully balanced, with a graceful, feminine head; to me, in my very early days, a dream come true. So I decided at once to find out who her sire was and mate my bitch to him. The bitch I saw was Camilla, and my own bitch was a black-and-tan called Tara, so at least the idea was feasible. In fact, it soon became a reality, and all my dogs since are descended from my own much-loved Ruaridh, one of the puppies from that litter. So, looking back, Camilla is, to me, the most 'special' of all the lovely dogs of the past.

Diana Schilizzi is still breeding and showing Cavaliers today. She is also very prominent in the world of dogs as well as the world of Cavaliers as she is an active member of The Kennel Club. She is as much part of the Cavalier scene today as she must have been way back in 1970 and will be for many more years.

Chamanic

The Chamanic Cavaliers belong to Jocelyn Inman and her husband, Hugh. The best-known among their dogs are their wholecolours, although there are also some good Chamanic particolours. Their first champion, the bitch Ch Chamanic Finistère, was by Salador Charlock (see page 145). Her brother Trafalgar (one CC and a JW) also sired some nice offspring, including my own little 'Beanie' who you will see once or twice in the pages of this book. Ch Chamanic Lucasta, a really beautiful ruby bitch, was by their ruby bitch Chamanic Bell Rock, a daughter of Finistère and Sorata Llewellyn (see page 145). Lucasta went on to win nine CCs, a record for a ruby. Her sister

Ch Chamanic Lucasta.

Leonie, mated to Ch Rheingold Ringold Von Salador, a black-and-tan by Salador Charlock, produced Ch Buckny Mellowman of Chamanic and his sister Ebony, not to mention their other sister Cinderella, dam to my own little Dora.

Chantiz

For a number of years now, when looking at dogs in the ring and seeing one I specially like, as often as not it turns to be one of Joan Reid's Chantiz dogs. My favourite one of all is Ch Chantiz Alboreto, who became a champion in 1996. His sire was

Ch Chantiz Alboreto. Photo: Carole Ann Johnson

the famous Ch Alberto of Kindrum, his dam Chantiz Moonflorin. As the photograph makes clear, he is a lovely blenheim dog, and an ideal size (which of course a photograph cannot show); he must weigh around 7.7kg (17lb). There is another photograph of him with his owner, Joan Reid, on page 102.

Craigowl

Norma and Gordon Inglis began breeding Cavaliers way back in the early 1970s, a year or two before I did. They have bred many memorable dogs, including six champions, all of them blenheims. Their first champion, made up in 1984, was Ch Craigowl Cashmere, by the famous Ch Homeranne Caption (see page 141). Her dam was a granddaughter of Ch Rosemullion of Ottermouth. Next (1985) was Craigowl Storm of Homerbrent, another blenheim bitch by Caption. Then in 1988 came Craigowl Replica; her parents, Craigowl Hoodwink and Ch Craigowl Cashmere, were both by the famous Caption. In 1990 and 1991, first Craigowl Hoodwink and then Craigowl Hopscotch at Homerbrent became champions. They were litter brothers, and they too were by Caption. Finally, in 1993, came the pretty bitch Craigowl Silkience, also descended from Caption.

Ch Craigowl Cashmere (lying down) and Ch Craigowl Storm of Homerbrent.

Ch Crisdig Leading Seaman. Photo: Peter Diment

Crisdig

Mrs Susan Burgess and her husband Brigadier Jack Burgess bred Cavaliers under this affix as far back as 1962 and Mrs Burgess still has Cavaliers today, though sadly her husband died a few years ago. During this long period of time there have been over 20 Crisdig champions, the last being Crisdig Angelique, a great-granddaughter of Leading Seaman on both sides of her pedigree. Ch Crisdig Leading Seaman (see left) was born in 1973 and was made up in 1976. Many Cavalier breeders consider that he has the perfect head. The Crisdig lines began with two half-sisters bred by Mrs Burroughes, who had the well-known Vairire kennel. This affix appears in many of the older pedigrees, as does the famous Crisdig affix. Susan Burgess is at present Chairman of the Cavalier King Charles Spaniel Club (UK).

Fontelania

Maurene and Jim Milton began to breed Cavaliers during the 1970s. Their first champion was Fontelania Capricious, a tricolour. Her sire was Farne Silver Shadow of McGoogans, whose sire in turn was Ch Rosemullion of Ottermouth. The Miltons' special claim to fame is that they are the first breeders to have bred and owned champions in all four colours. Their black-and-tan champion was Fontelania Burnt Toast (Salador Charlock ex Volney Miss Molasses of Fontelania); he was an extremely handsome dog, magnificently structured, a favourite of mine. His ruby brother Burnt Almond was exported to Finland, where he became a Finnish champion. Maurene

and Jim bred three ruby champions: Fontelania Burnt Honey (born 1986), Fontelania Dancing Brave (born 1988) and his son Fontelania Dancing Sunset (born in 1990). Burnt Honey was a daughter of the Finnish dog mentioned above and her dam was Fontelania Capricious. Dancing Brave was a grandson of another very famous dog, Ch Sorata Fissical (see page 145), and his other grandsire was Burnt Toast.

Ch Fontelania Dancing Brave.

Ch Fontelania Dancing Sunset.

Harana Too Darn Hot. Photo: David Dalton

Sunset's grandsire on his dam's side was also Burnt Toast. Dancing Brave is used quite a lot at stud and many of his offspring are around today, the best known being the ruby Ch Harana Too Darn Hot who was BOB at Crufts in 1995. My own special boy Roderick (Toby to his friends) is also a son of Dancing Brave. Finally, there are the Miltons' two blenheim champions, Fontelania Domingo and Fontelania Silver Momento. Domingo is sired by Alberto of Kindrum and Caption is his great-grandsire. Momento has Alberto as her grandsire on both sides.

Molly Coaker with Ch Homeranne Caption when he won his first CC and Toy Group in 1978 in Scotland.

Harana

Lucy and her mother, Mrs Diana Koster, have during the last 12 years or so bred a number of really beautiful wholecolours. In 1995, their ruby Ch Harana Too Darn Hot won BOB at Crufts, an outstanding achievement. His sire was Fontelania Dancing Brave (see page 139), and his dam Harana Making Whoopee. He has many winning offspring all over the United Kingdom and he seems to throw very much his own type. Lucy's first champion was Knight Magic at Harana, a striking black-and-tan mainly of Sorata breeding; tragically, he was run over when quite young.

Homerbrent and Homeranne

These two affixes belong to Molly Coaker and her daughter Anne (now Mrs Kennoway) and are among the best known of all affixes, both in the United Kingdom and

140

overseas. Molly has bred so many lovely champions that it is difficult to know which to mention. However, I can already hear my reader say, 'What about Ch Homeranne Caption, the dog mentioned earlier?' and he is indeed the most outstanding of all the Coaker dogs. He was born in 1976 and lived until he was 15, dying in 1991. His breeder was Anne Coaker, but he was owned by Molly. He won 13 CCs, including three Toy groups. He also

Ch Homeranne Caption at home in the garden, aged six-and-a-half.

sired 16 champions and many other top winning dogs, both at home and overseas, passing on his type to his descendants. Note he lived to a ripe old age, as did a number of his progeny. This is important when we know of all too many Cavaliers who have died young. As he has had such an influence on the breed, I give his pedigree in full.

Aust Ch Homerbrent Henry (blen)	Ch Bredonvale Bernard (blen)	Ch Rosemullion of Ottermouth (blen)
		Bredonvale Ttiweh Lavengro (blen)
	Homerbrent Dolly Gray (blen)	Int Ch Tnegun Charivari (blen)
		Crisdig Betsy (blen)
Ch Homerbrent Captivation (tri)	Homerbrent Crisdig Reflection	Ch Crisdig Merry Matelot (blen)
		Crisdig Genevieve (blen)
	Homerbrent Nolana (tri)	Crisdig Mr Patch (tri)
		Belmont Nell (blen)

Note that his pedigree includes Ch Rosemullion of Ottermouth (see pages 46 and 149), whom I have already mentioned several times, Ch Crisdig Merry Matelot and other Crisdig dogs, and even a Ttiweh (Mrs Pitt's affix).

I have included several photographs of Homerbrent dogs and I explain under each picture who it is and some relevant details. I particularly like the three photographs of Homerbrent Bewitched at different ages (overleaf) and the four-generation picture with that lovely 'disapproving' expression on Carson's face!

Four generations of Homerbrent champions: (left to right) Ch Caption, Ch Carson (looking disapproving), Ch Carnival (misbehaving) and Ch Festival.

Ch Homerbrent Bewitched at four weeks (centre left),
10 weeks (centre right) and as an adult (bottom).
Photos: J K & E A McFarlane

Kindrum

Mrs Pam Thornhill and her daughter have been breeding Cavaliers at least since the late 1960s. Their first stud dog, Kindrum Roulette, was by Rosemullion (yes, again!) and one of their earliest bitches was a Pargeter, Pargeter Fuji of Kindrum (Ch Cerdric of Ttiweh ex Pargeter Catriona). Pam Thornhill has bred many beautiful Cavaliers who bear all the characteristics of her kennel; many have been exported overseas, especially to the United States and Canada. She bred among others

142

Ch Kindrum Sylvia, made up in 1978, (twice great-granddaughter of Rosemullion), but perhaps her most famous Cavalier is Ch Alberto of Kindrum, who won his title in 1988. He is by Harry of Kindrum, son of Kindrum Sylvia, and his maternal grandsire is Ch Salador Crismark, so we have a good Salador line coming in here too. Alberto has sired many top winning dogs such as Ch Chantiz Alboreto and Ch Emsmere Royalist, and the well-known Lymrey/Ricksbury dogs also go back to him. In fact, Ch Lymrey Royal Reflection of Ricksbury is Alberto's grandson.

Ch Alberto of Kindrum

Ch Lymney Top of the Pops, aged six years. Photo: David Dalton

Lymrey

Sylvia Lymer has bred many good Cavaliers but her best known is Ch Lymrey Top of the Pops, a lovely blenheim bitch (see photograph) by Cinola Motown of Sukev and Lymrey Rambling Rose (a Caption granddaughter). She also was one of the outstanding dogs who were twice BIS at the Cavalier Club Show, in both 1991 and 1994.

Maibee

Shealagh Waters has been breeding Cavaliers for a number of years and her dogs are in many of the pedigrees of winning Cavaliers in the Northeast. Her latest champion, Maibee A Cameo, was made up during 1996 when she won seven CCs. A blenheim bitch born on 26 August 1994, she is by Ch Lymrey Royal Scandal at Ricksbury and Maibee Peggylee. As the photographs show, she is small and pretty with a very special expression and super conformation – one of my absolute favourites.

Ch Maibee A Cameo. Photo: Russell Fine Arts

McGoogans

Caroline Gillies Compston (known in earlier days as Caroline Gillies) was breeding during the 1960s. Her first champion, McGoogan's Ruari, a blenheim dog, was a grandson of Ch Pargeter Bob Up and a granddaughter of one of Susan Burgess's first bitches, Ch Vairire Charmaine of Crisdig; all of which takes us well back into Cavalier history. Ruari was the sire of Ch Alansmere McGoogans Maggie May, also bred by Caroline, winner of 15 CCs and dam of the famous Alansmere Aquarius. Caroline bred other champions also, including McGoogans Eideard (see page 46), a ruby sired by Ch Steller's Eider of Pantisa, another well-known ruby whom she also owned. He in turn was sired by a famous black-and-tan going back to the days of Mrs Pitt, namely, Ttiweh Black Prince of Cockpen.

Ricksbury

Kevan Berry and Brian Rix, like Shealagh Waters, come from Northeast England and have been breeding Cavaliers since the 1970s. Their first champion, Ricksbury Only Charm, was sired by Caption while her dam, Ricksbury Cool Charm, was a granddaughter of Rosemullion and Crisdig Leading Seaman. Recently, they have come very much into the limelight, as their outstanding dog Ch Lymrey Royal Reflection of Ricksbury has become the breed record holder, winning a grand total of 32 CCs. His litter brother, Ch Lymrey Royal Scandal at Ricksbury, has also done

Ch Lymney Royal Reflection of Ricksbury.
Photo: Russell Fine Arts

extremely well, though it was his brother who usually was shown and who hence broke the record. Both were excellent studs. Reflection has sired Ch Peakdowns Fantasia and Ch Ricksbury Royal Review at Brymarden and many other youngsters who have won Best Puppy and BIS awards. Scandal has done as well, if not better, as a stud dog, siring the lovely little Cameo. He also sired the new young champion, Ricksbury Royal Mistic, and his litter brother, Royal Emblem, also doing very well. Many other youngsters by him are winning well at championship and open shows. Reflection and Scandal are by Ch Emsmere Royalist (son of Ch Alberto of Kindrum) out of Ch Lymrey Top of The Pops.

Salador

In 1972, Sheila Smith acquired her first Cavalier, Pantisa Christmas Carol, whose pedigree went back to one of Mrs Burgess' first two Cavaliers, Ch Vairire Charmaine of Crisdig. Since then, she has bred many Cavaliers, including 16 British champions, but all are descended from this original bitch. Sheila has bred all four colours successfully, and was the first breeder in Britain

Salador Charlock. Photo: Diane Pearce

to make up champions in all four colours, though she only bred three of them. One of her most famous dogs was the tricolour Ch Salador Celtic Prince, made up in 1982. He was an outstanding sire, as was another of Sheila's dogs, Ch Salador Crismark.

Sheila also did a great deal for wholecolours. Her most famous , though he never became a champion, was Salador Charlock (left). Although not used a great deal at stud, he sired many winning dogs including the Inman's Ch Chamanic Finistère and Aust Ch Chamanic Centaurus, both black-and-tans. As late as 1987, he sired a litter to Rheinvelt Celtic Lass, which included the black-and-tan Ch Rheinvelt Ringold von Salador, made up at 16 months. Charlock was a striking dog to see, one I was proud to have met towards the end of his life.

Sorata

Joan Pagan and her Sorata Cavaliers have had a great influence on wholecolours in the breed, and her dog of whom everyone thinks first is Ch Sorata Fissical, an 'utterly stunning' (to quote Sheila Smith) ruby dog. His photograph shows just how exceptional he was. His sire was Sorata Llewellyn, a grandson of Charlock, and his dam was Sorata Isabella. He did not sire a large number of offspring, but several of today's top winning wholecolours are descended from him. Molly Coaker used him at stud and kept two dogs, Homerbrent Apache and Homerbrent Comanche. Comanche was mated to Maurene Milton's tricolour Fontelania Sierra Sadie, and Ch

Fontelania Dancing Brave was one of this litter. Dancing Brave in turn was the sire of Ch Harana Too Darn Hot and, as I have said earlier, Too Darn Hot has had a number of very successful pups. My present wholecolours are all descended from Fissical and I still have a 'Fissy' daughter, now aged nearly 12. (Note to anyone interested: she is the 'large dog in small basket' in a much earlier photograph!) My most successful youngster (Dora) goes back to 'Fissy' twice, as she is a Dancing Brave granddaughter.

Ch Sorata Fissical. Photo: David Dalton

Fissical's father, Sorata Llewellyn, was one of a very successful litter, the other two being Sorata Lawrence and Sorata Lucilla. Lawrence sired Sorata Linda and Sorata Lynette, both black-and-tan bitches. Linda was the dam of Ch Harana Knight Magic and Lynette was the granddam of Ch Rheinvelt Ringold Von Salador. Meanwhile, Lucilla was owned by the well known breeder Mick Shinnick (affix *Leelyn*) and many of his lovely wholecolours are descended from her.

Joan Pagan has exported a number of Soratas overseas, and is still breeding. She also, to her great credit, gives up a lot of her time and energy to running the Cavalier Club's Rescue service.

Top: Ch Volney Cheerleader, known to her friends as Deborah.
Below: (left to right) Ch Volney Cheerleader, Volney By Jove Jeeves (puppy) and Volney Shenanigan.
Photos: David Warne

Volney

Joyce and Tom Boardman have been breeding their Volney Cavaliers for a number of years and their first champion was a Crisdig Leading Seaman daughter, Crisdig Peace of Volney, a blenheim. Their most recent champion is Volney Cheerleader, another really attractive blenheim (Hillyacres Cotton On to Keyingham ex Volney Skylark). The top photograph on the opposite page is of Ch Volney Cheerleader by herself and below you can see her with her brother, Volney Shenanigan, and her son, Volney By Jove Jeeves. Together like this, they make a lovely 'family album' picture.

Whyteplace

Marion Wiggins' tricolour Whyteplace Apollo (Mardler Norman at Tonnew ex Whyteplace Titania) has a well-deserved place in Cavalier history; in 1990 he not only won BOB at Crufts under Mrs Joan Winters but also went on to win the Toy Group under Tom Horner.

Others

There are many other excellent breeders and affixes in the United Kingdom today that I have not mentioned. Among these are Ellie Mordecai's Millhills, Caroline Ackroyd's Toraylacs, Anne Rennard's Deranmars, Barbara Stanley's Astraddles, Virginia Barwell's Charlottetowns (which

Homerbrent Charlatan (see pages 140–142).

Whyteplace Apollo (Mat).

Ch Toraylac Joshua. Photo: David Dalton

The late Mrs Peggy Talbot with four of her tricolours, all placed in the first three of their classes at Crufts 1988. (Left to right) Maxholt Love Story, Charlottetown Wader, Ch Maxholt Jack in the Box and Maxholt Victoria's Hope.

include some lovely tricolours), the Fox's Pamednas, Loraine Hughes' Lorankas, Mick Shinnick's Leelyns, the late Peggy Talbot's Maxholts, Hilary McQuaid's Hilarny dogs and many others. All these breeders and the others mentioned earlier are carrying on the traditions of those who came before them, ensuring that the Cavalier remains the very special little dog it has always been.

Pedigrees

Any reader seriously interested in pedigrees and how they all link up will realise that there are many gaps in the above, which is no more than an indication of how dogs are bred. The *Cavalier King Charles Spaniel Club Book of Champions 1928–1988* and the second one, *1988–1994*, give the pedigrees of all the champions since Daywell Roger, together with a picture of each one, its date of birth, colour, owner and breeder. It also gives the colours of each dog mentioned in the pedigree. So if you want more of this fascinating information, get hold of these books; the club secretary should be able to help you obtain one if you have a problem. These and other books about Cavalier King Charles Spaniels are listed in the **Book list** on page 200.

I am concluding by giving the pedigree of Rosemullion of Ottermouth (see page 46), as he appears in so many pedigrees and was such an influential sire.

Ch Vairire Osiris (blen)	Ch Cerdric of Ttiweh (blen)	Pound Foolish of Ttiweh (blen)
		Britannia of Ttiweh (blen)
	Vairire Isis (ruby)	Vairire Spencer of Santander (tri)
		Vairire Cleopatra (b/t)
Rosette of Ottermouth (blen)	Ch Crisdig Geordie of Ottermouth (blen)	Ch Pargeter Bob Up (blen)
		Ch Vairire Charmaine of Crisdig (blen)
	Ch Roulette of Temple Hill (blen)	Ch Raoul of Ttiweh (blen)
		Rhea of Eyeworth (b/t)

Chapter Twelve
The Cavalier world-wide

North America
A brief history of the Cavalier in the United States of America

This article was contributed by Mrs Joan Twigg of Cambridge, Maryland. Joan Twigg is the owner of the Culloden *Cavaliers and had her first Cavalier in 1974; she joined the Cavalier Club the next day and for many years has been an extremely active Committee Member (called a Director in the United States), being Trophy Chairman for 22 years. Her husband was Secretary for five years.*

It is thought that the first two Cavaliers to set foot onto American shores were Robrull of Veren and Bertie of Rookerynook; both of these were males, the former coming to Mrs Harold Whitman in 1946, the latter to Mrs John Schiff in 1947. Although both of these dogs arrived to live their lives in the State of New York (as have so many famous immigrants), the real beginnings of this Club occurred in 1952 when Lady Mary Forwood sent a gift, in the form of a black-and-tan bitch puppy, to her friend Mrs W L Lyons Brown of Harrods Creek, Kentucky. Sally Brown and her Psyche of Eyeworth were the foundation of Cavaliers in America, as Mrs Brown was so enchanted with her little gift that she tirelessly set about trying to find other Cavalier owners in the United States. Fairly soon, through her efforts, she had not only found some other Cavalier people in North America but also established an active little nucleus of Cavalier enthusiasts among her family and friends in the Louisville area. The Cavalier King Charles Spaniel Club, United States of America (CKCSC,USA) was founded in 1954 and incorporated in 1956. Sally Brown is owed a tremendous debt of gratitude, as it was she who started the stud book, bred the first litters of Cavaliers in America, was the first President from 1956–1962, and involved two other extremely important ladies in the foundations of the CKCSC,USA: her sister-in-law Gertrude Polk Brown Albrecht and Elizabeth Spalding.

Within a few years there were enough pioneers to hold the first CKCSC,USA Annual Specialty (Breed Championship show). By 1962 there were 72 members of the Club and a total registration of 76 Cavaliers, so on 13 October 1962, with a famous American Spaniel judge Colonel Joseph C Quirk doing the honours, the Louisville contingent hosted the American Cavalier World at Sutherland (in Prospect, in the suburbs of Louisville), the lovely home of Mr and Mrs George Garvin Brown. At this first show there were 26 exhibitors, with 41 entries and a total of 35 Cavaliers in competition (14 dogs and 21 bitches). It may possibly be of some interest to note that on that momentous day at Sutherland there were 17 blenheims, 8 tricolours, 4 rubies and 6 black-and-tans. The young Miss Spalding from Maine had a superb outing in that her Pargeter Mermaid was Reserve Best In Show (RBIS) and Best Opposite Sex (BOS) to her Pargeter Lotus of Kilspindie, who was Best in Show (BIS). Not a bad day either for Mrs Keswick of the famous Scottish Pargeter affix. In perusing the pedigrees of the top winners from those early days, not very surprisingly the two affixes most often seen are those of Pargeter and Ttiweh, although Kilspindie (Miss Spalding's affix) is certainly very consistent on the honour

Four super Culloden pups: (left to right) Donald, Drambuie, Dirk and DePinna, owned by Joan and Oliver Twigg.

roll from the very first show and for many years thereafter. At the end of the show, everyone was invited to enjoy the hospitality of Mr and Mrs W L Lyons Brown and to attend the Club's first Annual General Meeting. It was at this meeting that Sally Brown retired as President after all her years of hard work and passed over the reins to her sister-in-law, Trudy (Gertrude Polk Brown Albrecht), who was to be the President for the next six years. Trudy had also taken over the chore of Recording Secretary from the very early years and continued it until her untimely and much-mourned death in 1983. Liz Spalding was then elected to her first tenure as President from 1968–1972 and then again from 1987–1989. It may have become clear by now that Trudy and Liz were the strong backbone of the CKCSC,USA, and that without their leadership, it would not be the solid Club it is today.

This was the first of many memorable shows to be held at Sutherland, a site that will ever linger in the memory of anyone who was privileged to visit there and enjoy Trudy's graciousness. The first five annual National Specialty shows were all held in the autumn but then, in 1967, the date of the show was moved to the third weekend in May, where it remains to this day. It is vaguely comforting that, when one is hunting for dogsitters, one can tell them that they are needed for that third week-end in May for perpetuity. Although the judge for that first show was an American, we have had very few of those since, the great majority being British breeder judges whose names read like a partial list of a British Hall of Fame of Cavalierdom: Mrs Barbara Keswick, Sir Dudley and Lady Mary Forwood, Miss Beryl Sadler, Mrs Amice Pitt, Mrs Daphne Murray, Miss Barbara Palfree, Brigadier and Mrs J R Burgess, Mrs Evelyn Booth, Miss Pamela Turle, Mrs Vera Preece, Mrs Diana Schilizzi, Mrs Amy Nugent, Mr D Rainey Brown, Miss Caroline Gatheral, Mrs Molly Coaker, Mrs Jane Bowdler, Mrs Jean Kent, Mr Ken Town, Mr George Donaldson, Mrs Pam Rooney and Mrs Pam Thornhill. Several of these listed have graced the American ring on more than one occasion. In 1997, we were privileged to have Mrs Joyce Boardman, to be followed in 1998 by Mr Roger Calladine and in 1999 by Mrs Caroline Gillies.

Very early on it was decided that the CKCSC,USA Inc should remain an independent organization and not join the American Kennel Club. Although American Cavaliers were still permitted to show in Miscellaneous, few did, with the exception of those hard workers who competed in Obedience. The Club has always kept its own records and stud book, has its own shows, first only the one National Specialty in May, but now approximately one show weekend per month with each region of the United States (Northeast, South, West and Midwest) hosting at least two shows in addition to the National, which now travels from region to region each year. There was a very special Silver Jubilee Anniversary Show held on 12 October 1985, judged by Lady Forwood (with 224 Cavaliers in competition), followed by the first Gertrude Polk Brown Albrecht Memorial Rally judged by Mr George Donaldson in September 1987. It was decided in 1996 to make the Gertrude Polk Brown Albrecht Rally an annual event to honour Trudy's memory, so the Parent Club will in effect be hosting three shows a year, as we also now have the Spring Classic Show, making the National Specialty a two-show weekend.

In May 1976, a championship points system was instituted so that the top winners would be rewarded with the deserved title of champion. Under this system, to attain a championship a Cavalier must win two majors plus class points under three different judges. A major can be any of the following: Winners Dog, Reserve Winners Dog, Winners Bitch or Reserve Winners Bitch; in other words, either a CC or a reserve CC qualifies. However, as we all know, it can take several years and much travelling finally to gain a title, and sometimes it never happens; that elusive second major can be a feather in the wind. However, at the time of writing over 200 champions of the CKCSC,USA have been made up. Admittedly, while there are still some rather small shows in the United States (there are still very occasionally some with entries of under 100 in competition), others have had more respectable numbers of over 200; clearly it is not easy to make up a champion and that dog (or bitch) has to be very deserving in the eyes of at least three experts to be awarded the much sought-after title. As of 1997 we are also considering awarding Club championships in both Obedience and Agility.

And finally to the great divisive question which has haunted the CKCSC,USA, since its founding – the American Kennel Club (AKC). A large number of CKCSC,USA members felt that they did not want to join an organisation as huge as the AKC because they thought they could control the breeding, the health, the overall well-being, the quality and the standard of Cavaliers better than the AKC possibly could. They also felt that they were better able to keep them out of puppy mills and pet shops. In this regard, four ballot votes have been held over the past several years, the most recent being in May 1994. That the percentage of the membership who voted against the AKC has remained so consistent over these years, even while the people who make up the membership have changed so dramatically, is both extremely interesting and amazing:

1976	1982	1988	1994
71 pro – 244 against	84 pro – 367 against	166 pro – 760 against	117 pro – 1237 against

It was obviously the majority opinion that not joining the AKC served to protect American Cavaliers, since it seemed very frightening to think of the vast numbers that might be registered if the CKCSC,USA were to become a member of that organisation. Growth was already rapid, with the membership at approximately 2200 and over 150 dogs being registered each month; some long for the recent past when the Cavalier was almost unknown in America. However, despite these votes and the feelings of the huge majority of of the membership, the Cavalier King Charles Spaniel was officially recognised by the AKC in January 1996. There are now two Cavalier Clubs in the United States: The CKCSC,USA (which, to paraphrase Mark Twain, is still flourishing despite reports of its demise) and the American Cavalier King Charles Spaniel Club. Many members show at both the CKCSC,USA sanctioned shows and at AKC shows; at the time of writing there have been no known reports of bloodshed at any show.

It must be admitted that it helped to promote the popularity of Cavaliers in the United States when, for her 1985 Christmas gift, President Reagan gave Mrs Reagan a beautiful blenheim male named 'Rex'; in 1635 there were Cavalier-type spaniels in Charles I's Palace; 350 years later there was one in the White House; and in February 1997 they were shown for the first time at the Westminster Club Dog Show, the American equivalent of Crufts... ah, progress!?

© Mrs Joan Twigg

A brief history of the Cavalier in Canada

The Cavalier King Charles Spaniel was first recognized by the Canadian Kennel Club (CKC) in 1957. Lady Spencer-Churchill sent to her brother, Mr C Cunningham of Toronto, a Cavalier called Deanhill Panda, who was the first Cavalier to be registered in Canada. In March 1958 he was shown at the Canadian National Sportsmen's Show and thus became the first Cavalier to be shown at a Championship show in Canada. In 1959, Lady Spencer-Churchill sent a tricolour bitch, Deanhill Guenavar, to her brother as a mate for Panda, and the litter, one dog and three bitches, arrived on 28 October 1959. During this period, Heatherside Belinda (a blenheim) and Hillbarn Ulysses (a tricolour) were imported by Mrs Stibbard, while Miss Carolyn Whitehead imported Augustus of Brandynote. Hence Deanhill Guenevar was the fifth Cavalier to be registered in Canada.

Two shows in 1958 and one in 1959 had a total of four Cavaliers, and after this none was seen in the show ring for the next four years. During the six years from 1958 until 1964, six litters were registered, as well as 32 individual Cavaliers; also during this period, other Cavaliers had been imported but not registered with the CKC.

In 1964, Cavaliers began to be shown again. The Rowans of New Brunswick imported Kilspindie Snowdrift from Elizabeth Spalding in the States, and Mr C S Frew and Mrs J W Anderson both imported Pargeter stock from

Can Ch Salador Celtic Dirk, CD (see page 155)

153

Ch McGoogans Tuesdays Child of Culloden aged 13.

the United Kingdom. Cavaliers were by now being shown on both coasts and, in April, Kilspindie Snowdrift won Canada's first Cavalier group placement being awarded a Group 4th. The following year, Anderson's Pargeter Flashback became the first Canadian Cavalier champion.

Also in 1964, the question was raised of registering American-bred (that is, United States) Cavaliers at the CKC. After a great deal of negotiating by Elizabeth Spalding of the United States and Mrs J W Anderson of Canada, who was also CKC Director for British Columbia, the CKCSC,USA was recognised and its records accepted by the CKC.

Cavaliers continued to be shown all through the 1960s and into the next decade, becoming steadily more popular. In 1970, Can/Bermuda Ch Newforest Rufus, a blenheim owned and bred by Poppy Steel, was made BIS at Oakville, Ontario thus being the first Cavalier to go Best In Show (All Breeds) in Canada. The same year, he became the first Cavalier to reach the Canadian *Top Ten Toys* category. Eight years later, in 1978, Roseff's Can Ch Dijers Chandlers Snow Knight went Best in Show at Granby, Quebec. In 1979, Wayne's Ch Azores Mystiques Jolly twice went BIS in British Columbia and in 1982, Ionson's Ch Wynfield High Timer was made BIS at Sydney. Sandy Elsasser's Camlane's The Highwayman (1975) and Gingell's Homerbrent Tartan Laddie (1982) both were made Best Puppy in Show.

BIS awards at Toy Specialties have been won by Elizabeth Spalding's Ch Pargeter Fergus and Ann Benedetti's Can/Bermuda Ch Helensley Fair City of Perth, both imports, as the affixes show. In 1976 Can Ch Wilblea Cristy, bred and owned by Ev Bleaney and Nancy Wilson, won BOB at the 15th Cavalier King Charles Spaniel Club (USA) Specialty Show, becoming the first foreign Cavalier to do so. Since then, a number of Canadian Cavaliers have done outstandingly well at USA Specialty shows, including Angela Thomas' Can Ch Peatland Dasher (BIS 1981); Kendrick's Can Ch Kindrum Prince at Jasago (RBIS 1978 National); Purser's Can Ch Wilblea Darby (RBIS 1979 National); Bleaney's Can Ch Wilblea Elsa (RBIS 1979 CS); Purser's Can Ch Brookedale Shamrock of Beaverdams, (RBIS 1982 CNE.); and Penney's Ch Beaverdams Irish Melody (BOS 1982 CNE). In 1980, a Cavalier was again among the Top Ten Toys in Canada; Gloria Watkins' Ch Pixyline Ivory Coast, as well as being Number One Cavalier, was Number Three Toy.

The Cavalier King Charles Spaniel Club of Canada was formed in 1973. Henry Benedetti, a founding member, was the first president until 1977, when he was succeeded by Chuck Purser. The Club has gone from strength to strength ever since; it ran booster shows and has its own Annual Specialty show. It also has its own yearbook and a newsletter to keep all its members in touch with what is happening in the Cavalier world.

Many lovely Cavaliers are in Canada at present and are being successfully shown both at home and in the United States of America. Cavaliers there also take part in both Obedience and Agility contests, often taking top honours in their class. Mrs Brigida Reynolds' bitch 'Minnie' gained the title of Dual Ch (otherwise known as OTCH and Ch) in 1986, being at that time only the third Cavalier to achieve this. Sadly, Minnie died in 1988, but other Cavaliers have continued to do well in these fields.

Some of today's North American Cavaliers

There are many beautiful Cavaliers in North America today. This comment refers to almost all Cavaliers anywhere as our pet dogs are all beautiful to their owners – and, being Cavaliers, to everyone else too. There is a picture of Joan Twigg's Ch McGoogans Tuesdays Child of Culloden aged nearly 13 on the opposite page – a wonderful old girl. We all have treasured photographs of our beautiful oldies at home, so the word *beautiful* certainly refers to more than just superficial appearance.

I was looking through my CKCSC,USA 1996 yearbook the other day and was again very impressed by the quality of the dogs depicted. There are today many excellent breeders in North America, and as a result they have many lovely top class dogs. Unfortunately, I can mention only a very few of these, so I shall write briefly about one or two whose dogs I particularly like and where I can see some interesting breeding points.

First of all, I want to mention Brigida Reynolds of Canada. Mrs Reynolds acquired her first Cavalier (Robbie the Bruce) in the autumn of 1977 as a pet but by the next year he was doing well in the show ring. She soon had several more very successful dogs, including the imports Kindrum Emma and Salador Caroline. Then in 1986 she imported the tricolor dog Salador Celtic Dirk from Shiela Smith. He was nine months old when he arrived and became a champion after only four shows. Danny, as he was always called, was a very successful sire. In Canada, he sired

Some of the Pinecrest Cavaliers. On the extreme left is CKCSC,USA/AKC Ch Pinecrest Kiss Me Kate (see pages 156 and 159).

Pedigree of CKCSC,USA/AKC Ch Pinecrest Kiss Me Kate

Parents	Grandparents	G-Grandparents	G-G-Grandparents	G-G-G-G-Grandparents
SIRE CKCSC,USA Ch Ravenrush Gillespie	SIRE CKCSC,USA Ch Ravenrush Tartan	SIRE Can Ch Salador Celtic Dirk	SIRE Ch Salador Celtic Prince	SIRE Salador Chelsea of Loranka
				DAM Salador Cherrybird
			DAM Ch Salador Colleen	SIRE Ronnoc True Luck
				DAM Salandor Country Girl
		DAM CKCSC,USA Ch Monbarle Ceri Mair of Ravenrush	SIRE Ch Salador Corrigan	SIRE Ronnoc True Luck
				DAM Salador Country Girl
			DAM Montbarle Marie Louise	SIRE Ch Homerbrent Samson
				DAM Salador Charismas of Montbarle
	DAM Ravenrush Xacta	SIRE CKCSC,USA Ch Kindrum Archie Tee of Primrose	SIRE Ch/Can Ch Kindrum Lucifer at Rutherford	SIRE Ch Salador Corrigan
				DAM Kindrum Flame Lily
			DAM Kindrum Lily Langtree	SIRE Ch Salador Crismark
				DAM Kindrum Flame Lily
		DAM Craigowl Prudence of Ravenrush	SIRE Ch Merrylaine Made to Measure for Symra	SIRE Homerbrent Westward Sun
				DAM Merrylaine Molley Coddle
			DAM Homerbrent Honesty of Craigowl	SIRE Fame Silver Shadow of McGoogans
				DAM Ch Heidi of Homerbrent
DAM Shagbark Cayenne of Pinecrest	SIRE CKCSC,USA/Can Ch Rutherford Elliot of Shagbark	SIRE Can Ch Salador Celtic Dirk	SIRE Ch Salador Celtic Prince	SIRE Salador Chelsea of Loranka
				DAM Salador Cherrybird
			DAM Ch Salador Colleen	SIRE Ronnoc True Luck
				DAM Salador Country Girl
		DAM Can Ch Kindrum Alice at Rutherford	SIRE Kindrum Cardinal Red	SIRE Kindrum Danny the Red
				DAM Kindrum Dixie
			DAM Kindrum Matilda of Biscay	SIRE Ch Salador Crismark
				DAM Kindrum Flame Lily
	DAM CKCSC,USA Ch Crossbow Martha's Choice of Shagbark	SIRE CKCSC,USA Ch Ravenrush Tartan	SIRE Can Ch Salador Celtic Dirk	SIRE Ch Salador Celtic Prince
				DAM Ch Salador Colleen
			DAM CKCSC,USA Ch Monbarle Ceri Mair of Ravenrush	SIRE Ch Salador Corrigan
				DAM Montbarle Marie Louise
		DAM Kindrum Savanna of Crossbow	SIRE Kindrum Cardinal Red	SIRE Kindrum Danny the Red
				DAM Kindrum Dixie
			DAM Kindrum Flame Lily	SIRE Kindrum Roulette
				DAM Kindrum Rose Petal

Pedigree of CKCSC,USA Ch Ravenrush Tailor Made of Pinecrest

Parents	Grandparents	G-Grandparents	G-G-Grandparents	G-G-G-Grandparents
SIRE CKCSC,USA Ch Ravenrush Best Dressed	SIRE CKCSC,USA/Can Ch Rutherford Elliot of Shagbark	SIRE Can Ch Salador Celtic Dirk	SIRE Ch Salador Celtic Prince	SIRE Salador Chelsea of Loranka
				DAM Salador Cherrybird
			DAM Ch Salador Colleen	SIRE Ronnoc True Luck
				DAM Salador Country Girl
		DAM Can Ch Kindrum Alice at Rutherford	SIRE Kindrum Cardinal Red	SIRE Kindrum Danny the Red
				DAM Kindrum Dixie
			DAM Kindrum Matilda of Biscay	SIRE Ch Salador Crismark
				DAM Kindrum Flame Lily
	DAM Sanubray Secret Promise of Ravenrush	SIRE Ch Homeranne Caption	SIRE Homerbrent Henry	SIRE Ch Bredonvale Bernard
				DAM Homerbrent Dolly Gray
			DAM Ch Homerbrent Captivation	SIRE Homerbrent Crisdig Reflection
				DAM Homerbrent Nolana
		DAM Sanubray Saraminti	SIRE CKCSC,USA/Can Ch Sanubray Sherami	SIRE Sanubray Rufus
				DAM Sanubray Suki Sue
			DAM Sanubray Saramanda	SIRE Cobblestone Ferris of Santander
				DAM Sanubray Tarkwa
DAM Redtop Ravenrush Reflection	SIRE CKCSC,USA Ch Ravenrush Tartan	SIRE Can Ch Salador Celtic Dirk	SIRE Ch Salador Celtic Prince	SIRE Salador Chelsea of Loranka
				DAM Salador Cherrybird
			DAM Ch Salador Colleen	SIRE Ronnoc True Luck
				DAM Salador Country Girl
		DAM GKCSC, USA Ch Montbarle Geri Mair of Ravenrush	SIRE Ch Salador Corrigan	SIRE Ronnoc True Luck
				DAM Salador Country Girl
			DAM Montbarle Marie Louise	SIRE Ch Homerbrent Samson
				DAM Salador Charismas of Montbarle
	DAM Ravenrush Opry Belle	SIRE Can Ch Kindrum Jovial Joe of Biscay	SIRE Kindrum Cardinal Red	SIRE Kindrum Danny the Red
				DAM Kindrum Dixie
			DAM Kindrum Lily Langtree	SIRE Ch Salador Crismark
				DAM Kindrum Flame Lily
		DAM Salere's Rocking Betty of Ravenrush	SIRE Salere's Hey Rock 'n' Roll	SIRE Crisdig Tony of Hurleaze at Saintbrides
				DAM Hurleaze Golden Delicious
			DAM Salere's Serenade	SIRE Crisdig Tony of Hurleaze at Saintbrides
				DAM Sanubray Trecarrack of Salere

Pedigree of CKCSC/AKC Ch Sheeba's Special Edition

Parents	Grandparents	G-Grandparents	G-G-Grandparents	G-G-G-Grandparents
SIRE: CKCSC, USA/Can Ch Rutherford Elliot of Shagbark	**SIRE:** Can Ch Salador CelticDirk	**SIRE:** Ch Salador Celtic Prince	**SIRE:** Salador Chelsea of Loranka	**SIRE:** Ch Huntsbank Solitaire
				DAM: Salador Crumpet
			DAM: Salador Cherrybird	**SIRE:** Ch Cadeyrn Black Tulip
				DAM: Salador Crumpet
		DAM: Ch Salador Colleen	**SIRE:** Ronnoc True Lock	**SIRE:** Ch Rosemullion of Ottermouth
				DAM: Kerkehove Prolicsome
			DAM: Salador Country Girl	**SIRE:** Salador Clown So Happy
				DAM: Salador Cascade
	DAM: Can Ch Kindrum Alice at Rutherford	**SIRE:** Kindrum Cardinal Red	**SIRE:** Kindrum Danny the Red	**SIRE:** Kindrum Roulette
				DAM: Kindrum Marquisite
			DAM: Kindrum Dixie	**SIRE:** Kindrum Discus
				DAM: Kindrum Marquisite
		DAM: Kindrum Matilda of Biscay	**SIRE:** Ch Salador Crismark	**SIRE:** Salador Clown So Happy
				DAM: Salador Cascade
			DAM: Kindrum Flame Lily	**SIRE:** Kindrum Roulette
				DAM: Kindrum Rose Petal
DAM: Ch Sheeba's Show Special	**SIRE:** Homerbrent Top Copy	**SIRE:** Ch Homeranne Caption	**SIRE:** Homerbrent Henry	**SIRE:** Ch Bredonvale Bernard
				DAM: Homerbrent Dolly Grey
			DAM: Ch Homerbrent Captivation	**SIRE:** Homerbrent Crisdig Reflection
				DAM: Homerbrent Nolana
		DAM: Homerbrent Shirley of Dalvreck	**SIRE:** Silver Shadow of McGoogans	**SIRE:** Ch Rosemullion of Ottermouth
				DAM: McGoogans Polly Pecham
			DAM: Homerbrant Sheba	**SIRE:** Homerbrent Crisdig Reflection
				DAM: Ch Homerbrent Samantha
	DAM: Ch Stonehill's Tanya-Sheeba	**SIRE:** Ch Stonehill's Carl Donavan	**SIRE:** Ch Donavan v/h Lamslag	**SIRE:** Crisdig Carneby
				DAM: Doenja v/h Lamslag
			DAM: Patrice v/h Lamslag	**SIRE:** Ch Samual Pepys of Amantra
				DAM: Bregtje v/h Lamslag
		DAM: Ch Charlotte-Aux-Pommes de la Vigie	**SIRE:** Homerbrent Top Copy	**SIRE:** Ch Homeranne Caption
				DAM: Homerbrent Shirley of Dalvreck
			DAM: Ch Homerbrant Quotation	**SIRE:** Kernewek Trystan of Homerbrent
				DAM: Homerbrent Sophistication

Can Ch Abercorn Admiral, Mrs Reynold's own Can Ch Mostyn Celtic Velvet and later Can/Bda Ch Mostyn Spencer For Hire. In the United States, he sired Can/CKCSC,USA Ch Rutherford Elliot of Shagbark (a tricolour) and CKCSC,USA Ch Ravenrush Tartan (a blenheim). These latter two became top stud dog between them in the States for almost the next 10 years. As a result, many of today's best Cavaliers are descended from one or other (or in some cases both) of these two. On page 156 you will see the pedigree of CKCSC,USA/AKC Ch Pinecrest Kiss Me Kate, top Cavalier for 1996. The pedigree shows Danny's breeding and includes the pedigrees of both Tartan and Elliot. Notice also the strong Kindrum influence, especially among the bitches. Another point of interest is that, if the next generation were to be written in, Ch Rosemullion of Ottermouth would occur at least five times, as he is the sire of Ronnoc True Luck, Kindrum Roulette and Farne Silver Shadow of McGoogans.

Mary Grace and Ted Eubank of the Pinecrest affix are the owners and breeders of CKCSC, USA Ch Pinecrest Kiss Me Kate (see above) and several other very successful Cavaliers. Some of them, including Kate, are pictured on page 155. The Eubanks show great care and skill in picking the puppy with a future and using pedigrees as well as appearance to choose the right stud dog. They have also a shared ownership with Karin Ostman in her outstanding dog Sheeba's Special Edition (pedigree opposite and top

CCKCXC,USA/AKC Ch Sheeba's Special Edition, with judge Joyce Boardman (left) and owners Ted Eubank and Karin Ostman.

Can/CKCSC,USA Ch Laughing Stormin' Norman.
Photo: Vavra's

picture on this page). One of his great-grandsires is the famous Ch Homeranne Caption; his sire is the above-mentioned Elliot, and hence 'Danny' is one of his grandsires.

Can/CKCSC,USA Ch Laughing Charisma. Photo: Vavra's

I also want to mention the Laughing Cavaliers owned by Bob and Barbara Garnett Smith, whom I think I would mention for their wonderful affix alone! They have a number of really nice dogs, many of whom they have bred themselves. They have also chosen to import some dogs from the United Kingdom who have had a very good influence on their stock, the best known of these being English, Canadian and CKCSC,USA Ch Alansmere Rhett Butler of Laughing and English, Canadian and CKCSC,USA Ch Sukev Dolly Daydream of Laughing. Sadly, both these two are now dead, but they have left many notable offspring behind. The photographs show two of Barbara's best known Cavaliers, Can/CKCSC,USA Ch Laughing Stormin' Norman (page 159) and Can/CKCSC,USA Ch Laughing Charisma, both of whom have sired many champions in both Canada and the States.

As I said near the beginning of this chapter, Mrs Joan Twigg has had Cavaliers for many years and her Culloden dogs are well known. She is still breeding and, to quote one of her advertisements, *Our puppies are giving their families tremendous pleasure. And that's what it is really all about.* How true; perhaps sometimes we forget this. The photograph below shows Joan's CKCSC,USA Ch Culloden Unique, or 'Niqui', who was the daughter of Ch McGoogans Tuesdays Child (page 154), her sire being Can Ch Crusader of BJ. She was an American-bred bitch, the only one ever to have been Winners Bitch twice at the CKCSC,USA National Specialty.

CKCSC,USA Ch Culloden Unique.

Tuesdays Child was the top winning bitch of her time and the youngest champion in the States for a few years.

Perhaps one of the most famous Cavaliers of all time was USA/Can/Mexican/American/World Ch Rocky Raccoon of Wyndcrest. He lived from 10 March 1981 until 15 January 1993. He was Canadian bred, sired by Can Champion Amantra Pinball Wizard, and his dam was Can Champion K-Bert Jenny Wren. His breeders were Olive Darbyshire and K Hendrix. He gained his Canadian title at the ripe old age of eight-and-a-half months! Shortly after this, he was acquired by his new owners, Harold and Joan Letterly of San Bernardino, California and his United States career began. To quote from the *CKCSC,USA Bulletin* of May 1993, shortly after his death, *Rocky's appearance defied description. His movement was perfection and as one of his judges commented, 'If you have ever wondered what rear drive looks like, watch this dog. He wrote the book on rear movement!'* He had so many big wins that I cannot list them all. The photograph on the right with all the cups shows him aged about two years winning BIS at the United States of America National Specialty, under judge Susan Burgess.

USA/Can/Mexican/World Ch Rocky Racoon of Wyndcrest at two years old, winning BIS at the USA National Specialty.

Rocky sired 10 CKCSC,USA champions (five winning their own BIS), 15 Canadian champions, four Mexican champions and one International champion. To quote from *CKCSC,USA Bulletin* again, he has left behind him many *pieces of Rock*, offspring who perpetuate his *magnificent qualities: conformation, structure, coat, movement, temperament, melting large eyes, cushioned muzzle, and one-of-a-kind head and face which inspired admirers to coin the often heard phrase, 'That Rocky Look', which is so evident in so many of his offspring*. Rocky has done so much for the Cavalier in America; and, most important of all, was a dog who gave great pleasure to everyone he met.

I cannot end this section without mentioning John Gammon and Robert Scholl, who have bred so many winning Ravenrush Cavaliers. I have already mentioned CKCSC,USA Ch Ravenrush Tartan, and his breeding is clear from the pedigree of Pinecrest Kiss Me Kate (page 156). He has sired a number of champions. Another of their top winners was the ruby dog Am Ch Kindrum

USA Ch Wyndcrest Apollo, at 11 months. Best Puppy in Show at Los Angeles under Dianne Tyssen.

Apollo at 18 months winning RBIS under judge Michael Harvey (left), with owner Harold Letterly on the right.

161

CKCSC/USA/AKC Ch Ravenrush Tailor Made of Pinecrest.

Redcoat of Ravenrush and they also bred Paula Campanozzi's beautiful tricolour dog Am Ch Ravenrush Best Dressed, sire of CKCSC,USA Ch Ravenrush Tailor Made of Pinecrest (pedigree page 157).

There is so much more I could say about the Cavaliers and their owners in North America, but I fear I will have to end by just saying that the Cavalier in America is indeed in good hands. So many truly dedicated owners; and, most important of all, so many beautiful dogs... beautiful in every sense.

The American Breed Standard (Cavalier King Charles Spaniel Club, USA, Inc)

General Appearance An active, graceful, well balanced dog, very gay and free in action; fearless and sporting in character, yet at the same time gentle and affectionate.

Head The skull is slightly rounded but without dome or peak; it should appear flat because of the high placement of the ears.

Eyes Large, round and set well apart; colour a warm, very dark brown giving a lustrous, limpid look. There should be slight cushioning under the eyes, which contributes much to the sweet gentle expression characteristic of the breed. Faults: Small, almond-shaped, prominent or light eyes; white surrounding ring.

Nose There should be a shallow stop and the length from the base of the stop to the tip of nose should be at least one and a half inches. Nostrils should be well developed and the pigment uniformly black. Putty or 'Dudley' noses and white patches on the nose are serious faults, as are small, pinched nostrils.

Muzzle Well tapered; mouth level; lips well covering. Faults: sharp, pointed or snipey muzzle. Full or pendulous lips. Flesh marks ie patches of pink pigment showing through hair on muzzle.

Teeth Strong and even, preferably meeting in a scissors bite, although a level bite is permitted. Undershot mouths are greatly to be discouraged; it should be emphasised however that a slightly undershot bite in an otherwise well-balanced head with the correct, sweet expression should not be penalised in favour of a level mouth with a plain or hard expression. Faults: Weak or crooked teeth, crooked jaws.

Ears Set high, but not close, on top of the head. Leather long with plenty of feathering and wide enough so that when the dog is alert, the ears fan slightly forward to frame the face.

Neck Fairly long without throatiness, well enough muscled to form a slight arch at the crest. Set smoothly into nicely sloping shoulders.

Shoulders Sloping back gently with moderate angulation to give the characteristic look of top class and elegance.

Body Short coupled with the ribs well sprung but not barrelled. Chest moderately deep, leaving ample heart room. Back level leading into strong, muscular hindquarters. Slightly less body at the flank than at the rib, but with no tucked-up appearance.

Legs Forelegs straight and well under the dog, bone moderate, elbows close to the sides. Hindlegs moderately muscled; stifles well turned; hocks well let down. The hindlegs, viewed from the rear, should parallel each other from hock to heel. Pasterns strong and feet compact with well-cushioned pads. The dog stands level on all four feet. Faults: loose elbows; crooked legs; stifles turned in or out; cow hocks; stilted action; weak pasterns; open feet.

Tail Set so as to be carried level with the back. Tail should be in constant characteristic motion when the dog is in action.

Docking Docking is optional, but whether or not the tail is docked, it must balance the body. If docked, tail must not be cut too short; two thirds is the absolute minimum to be left on the body, and the tails of broken colored dogs should always be docked to leave a white tip.

Coat Long and silky and very soft to the touch; free from curl though a slight wave is permissible. Feathering on ears, legs and tail should be long, and the feathering on the feet is a feature of the breed.

Trimming No trimming of the dog is permitted. However it is permissible and often desirable to remove the hair growing between the pads on the underside of the foot.

Size Height twelve to thirteen inches at the withers; weight proportionate to height, between thirteen and eighteen pounds. These are ideal heights and weights; slight variations are permissible, and a dog should be penalized only in comparison with one of equal appearance, type and quality. The weedy specimen is as much to be penalized as the oversized one.

163

Colors The following colors are the only colors acceptable:

1 *Blenheim* – Rich chestnut markings well broken up on a pearly white ground. The ears must be red and the color evenly spaced on the head, with a wide white blaze between the ears, in the centre of which is the much-valued lozenge (diamond) or 'Blenheim Spot'. The lozenge is a unique and highly desirable, though not essential, characteristic of the Blenheim.

2 *Tricolor* – Jet black markings well broken up on a pearly white ground, with rich tan markings over the eyes, on cheeks, inside ears and on underside of tail.

3 *Ruby* – Whole colored, rich red.

4 *Black and Tan* – Jet black with rich tan markings over eyes, on cheeks, inside ears, on chest, legs and underside of tail.

Faults: White marks on whole-colored specimens, heavy ticking on Blenheims or Tricolors.

It is important to remember that a dog can have one or more of the faults listed in the standard, in moderation, and still be an overall typical, gay, elegant Cavalier. On the other hand, bad temper or meanness are not to be tolerated and shall be considered to be disqualifying faults. It is the typical gay temperament, combined with true elegance and 'royal' appearance which are of paramount importance in the breed.

The AKC Breed Standard for the Cavalier King Charles Spaniel

I General Appearance – The Cavalier King Charles Spaniel is an active, graceful, well-balanced toy spaniel, very gay and free in action; fearless and sporting in character, yet at the same time gentle and affectionate. It is this typical gay temperament, combined with true elegance and royal appearance which are of paramount importance in the breed. Natural appearance with no trimming, sculpting or artificial alteration is essential to breed type.

II Size, Proportion, Substance – *Size* – Height twelve to thirteen inches at the withers; weight proportionate to height, between thirteen and eighteen pounds. A small well-balanced dog within these weights is desirable, but these are ideal heights and weights and slight variations are permissible. *Proportion* – The body approaches squareness, yet if measured from point of shoulder to point of buttock, is slightly longer than the height at the withers. The height from the withers to the elbow is approximately equal to the height from the elbow to the ground. Weedy and coarse specimens are to be equally penalized.

III Head – Proportionate to size of dog, appearing neither too large nor too small for the body. *Expression* – The sweet, gentle, melting expression is an important breed characteristic. *Eyes* – Large, round, but not prominent and set well apart; color a warm, very dark brown, giving a lustrous limpid look. Rims dark. There should be a cushioning under the eyes which contributes to the soft expression. *Faults* – small, almond-shaped, prominent or light eyes; white surrounding ring. *Ears* – Set high but not close on top of the head. Leather long with plenty of feathering and wide enough so that when the dog is alert, the ears fan slightly forward to frame the face. *Skull* – Slightly rounded but without dome or peak; it should appear flat because of the high placement of the ears. Stop is moderate, neither filled nor deep. *Muzzle* – Full muzzle, slightly tapered. Length from base of stop to tip of nose is about one and a half inches. Face well filled below the eyes. Any tendency towards snipeyness undesirable. Nose pigment uniformly black without flesh marks and nostrils well developed. Lips well developed but not pendulous giving a clean finish. *Faults* – Sharp or pointed muzzles. *Bite* – A perfect, regular, and complete scissors bite is preferred, ie the upper teeth closely overlapping the lower teeth and set square to the jaws. *Faults* – Undershot bite, weak or crooked teeth, crooked jaws.

IV Neck, Topline, and Body – *Neck* – Fairly long, without throatiness, well enough muscled to form a slight arch at the crest. Set smoothly into nicely sloping shoulders to give an elegant look. *Topline* – Level both when moving and standing. *Body* – Short-coupled with ribs well sprung but not barrelled. Chest moderately deep, extending to elbows allowing ample heart room. Slightly less body at the flank than at the last rib, but with no tucked-up appearance. *Tail* – Well set on, carried happily but never much above the level of the back, and in constant characteristic motion when the dog is in action. Docking is optional. If docked, no more than one third is to be removed.

V Forequarters – Shoulders well laid back. Forelegs straight and well under the dog with elbows close to the sides. Pasterns strong and feet compact with well-cushioned pads. Dewclaws may be removed.

VI Hindquarters – The hindquarters construction should come down from a good broad pelvis, moderately muscled; stifles well turned and hocks well let down. The hind legs when viewed from the rear should parallel each other from hock to heel. *Faults* – cow or sickle hocks.

VII Coat – Of moderate length, silky, free from curl. Slight wave permissible. Feathering on ears, chest, legs and tail should be long, and the feathering on the feet is a feature of the breed. No trimming of the dog is permitted. Specimens where the coat has been altered by trimming, clipping, or by artificial means shall be so severely penalized as to be effectively eliminated from competition. Hair growing between the pads on the underside of the feet may be trimmed.

VIII Color

1 Blenheim – Rich chestnut markings well broken up on a clear, pearly white ground. The ears must be chestnut, and the color evenly spaced on the head and surrounding both eyes, with a white blaze between the eyes and ears, in the centre of which may be the lozenge or *Blenheim Spot*. The lozenge is a unique and desirable, though not essential, characteristic of the Blenheim.

2 Tricolor – Jet black markings well broken up on a clear, pearly white ground. The ears must be black and the color evenly spaced on the head and surrounding both eyes, with a white blaze between the eyes. Rich tan markings over the eyes, on cheeks, inside ears, and on underside of tail.

3 Ruby – Whole colored rich red.

4 Black and Tan – Jet black with rich tan markings over the eyes, on cheeks, inside ears, on chest, legs, and underside of tail.

IX Gait – Free moving and elegant in action, with good reach in front and sound, driving rear action. When viewed from the side, the movement exhibits a good length of stride, and viewed from front and rear it is straight and true, resulting from straight-boned fronts and properly made and muscled hindquarters.

X Temperament – Gay, friendly, non-aggressive with no tendency towards nervousness or shyness. Bad temper, shyness and meanness are not to be tolerated and are to be so severely penalized as to effectively remove the specimen from competition.

The Cavalier in Australasia

Australia

This article was kindly contributed by Jeanie Montford of New South Wales, Australia. Jeanie is one of Australia's most successful breeders. She also judges Cavaliers, both in Australia and New Zealand and in the United Kingdom and North America.

Australia's vast size and its relatively small population of about 17 million people who are mainly concentrated in large cities scattered around the coastline has dictated the pattern of dog breeding and showing. Because of the expense of travelling to shows and sending dogs around the country, many people confine their showing to their own state or major city. This was especially true of the early years but, with the advent of more speciality clubs and more affordable air fares, enthusiasts are making a great effort to support the breed clubs.

Clubs There was sufficient interest in the breed for a club to be formed in New South Wales in 1968, with the Victorian Club in Melbourne following in 1972, the Canberra Cavalier Club in the national capital being formed in 1991 and the South Australian Club in Adelaide in 1993. These Clubs are very active, holding several championship and open shows each year. They publish regular informative newsletters, help to educate new judges, run rescue services, and have regular social days with activities for pet owners as well as exhibitors, and are conscious of the need to educate the general public in the care and welfare of our breed.

Aust Ch Chamanic Centaurus,
a son of Salador Charlock (see page 145).

To become a champion in Australia a dog must win Challenge Certificates, each being worth a number of points depending on the Cavaliers of the same sex exhibited on the day, up to a maximum of 25 at one show. These points may also be gained if the Best of Breed winner takes Best in Group. A total of 100 points is necessary to become a champion. Classification of classes is the same at every show and the breed and groups are organised similarly to those in the United Kingdom.

History The Cavalier presence in Australia began in 1960 with the arrival from New Zealand of a bitch, Soyland Begonia, who was in whelp to Angelo of Crustadele (British import). She went to Mrs Esler (Oakland) in Melbourne. Begonia became Australia's first champion Cavalier and her beautiful eyes and profuse coat are still hallmarks of her descendants. She was closely followed by a bitch, Scarlett (British import), brought out by Mr and Mrs Phillpott (Lancresse). When Mrs Esler's dog Lovage of Ttiweh arrived from England, puppies from Begonia, her daughters and Scarlett provided foundation stock for a number of people.

In Sydney, Mr and Mrs Dixon (Daijon) had brought in Justice of Eyeworth and a ruby bitch Suntop Ida, both from the United Kingdom. Their daughter Aust Ch Daijon Dinky Di Lady was

Blenheims owned by Prue Raffan enjoying the Australian sun: (left to right) Toraylac Elizabeth (lying down), Ch Naffar Uniquely Rosie Too, Fleur de Soleil and Naffar Magenta (behind, standing).

owned by Shirlee Leach (Garaig), who is the longest continuously active Cavalier fancier still breeding and exhibiting today. One of her most notable winners is Aust Ch Garaig Henrietta, who won the Bitch CC under Lady Forwood at the New South Wales Club's 10th Anniversary Show in 1978.

Lovage and Begonia later found their way to Western Australia to join the Pellemelle Cavaliers of Betty Reading and Betty Patterson. These breeders had imported several dogs from New Zealand and, in the mid-1960s, imported Australia's first British champion: Ch Pargeter Trillium of Ttiweh. Many Pellemelle Cavaliers made the journey east to provide stock for several kennels that went on to great success.

In recent years numbers have grown enormously and Cavaliers are among the most popular of Toy breeds. Club shows attract entries of 200–280 dogs, mostly judged by British, New Zealand and Australian breed specialists, and Cavaliers are more than able to hold their own in competition with the other breeds, regularly winning Best in Group and Best in Show at All-breed shows.

Successful kennels and notable dogs abound, too numerous for me to be able to do more than mention a very few of the kennels that have had an influence on the breed.

In tropical Queensland, Eunice Edwards (Grosvenor) has had a succession of imports who have made a sizeable contribution. Ivan and Lyn Domjahn (Ridgeview) and more recently Phil Martin (Sunchant) have also had success.

In New South Wales, early kennels of Shirlee Leach (Garaig), Myra Leach (Leagay) and Helena Hendry (Gaysprite) had enormous influence during the 1960s–1970s, Ch Gaysprite the Regent being the first Cavalier to go BIS at an All-breed Championship show. Gloria Dollin

Aust/NZ Ch Elvenhome Buckthorn. Photo: Cabal

(Gaycrest) has bred numerous champions. Denis Montford's Braganzar wholecolours had a formative and widespread influence on wholecolours, especially in New Zealand. Aust Ch Braganzar Scarteen, a black-and-tan, was the only Cavalier to win Best in Group at Sydney Royal. The Elvenhome Cavaliers of Jeanie Montford have won numerous point scores of the Sydney Club and have produced the top winning Australian-bred Cavalier, Aust/NZ Ch Elevenhome Buckthorn, (eight Speciality BISs, seven all-breed BISs). Also featuring on the list of trophy winners are the Janice Pazikov's Elfkings, Marilyn Madigan's Merseyports, and Brian Mitchell's Zapangus.

In Victoria, Merv Burgamn (Inverglen) is the longest active fancier and has been a consistent breeder of quality dogs since the mid-1970s. The Qualybeaus of Betty and Barry Henry have numerous point scores and BISs to their credit, and in later years David and Raewyn McCulloughs' Caribelle dogs have had outstanding success, notably the much-admired Aust Ch Caribelle Hell's Flame and more recently Aust Ch Caribelle Sweet Charity, three times speciality BIS.

In Tasmania, John Connell (Portcon) has been a long time stalwart of the breed with a particular interest in wholecolours, and more recently the Enrights have had great success with Aust Ch Melloway Main Event, one of the top dogs all breeds in the state.

In South Australia, Helen Porter (Barodaley) and Sally Elliot (Cabrook) have been consistent winners, while Jenny and Bill Egan (Melloway) have imported several dogs, being extremely successful with Aust Ch Homerbrent Catoon (British import), the top-winning all-breed BIS winning Cavalier.

In Canberra, for many years Lyn Costello was a

Aust/NZ Ch Prestonville Giv'm Beans.
Photo: Trafford

regular exhibitor with her Winaways and most notably showed the much-admired and widely-liked Aust Ch Est Royal Windsor, a multiple Speciality winner who had a wide influence at stud. The Le Chevalier dogs of Ralph and Margaret Franze are well known, Ch/Aust Ch Amantra Bohemian Rhapsody winning the first Royal BIS for Cavaliers at Canberra Royal 1979. He was one of a number of British champions imported by the kennel, whose greatest success in recent years has been with the home-bred bitch Aust Ch Le Chevalier Veronique (two speciality BISs, three all-breed BISs). They recently imported Ch Loranka's Dream Lover at Le Chevalier, Best of Breed at Crufts in 1996, who has already become an Australian champion.

New Zealand

This article was kindly contributed by Mrs Dianne Tyssen of Invercargill, New Zealand. Dianne has been breeding Cavaliers since 1973 with great success and she also judges, both in Australia and New Zealand, and overseas.

Cavaliers first arrived in New Zealand in August 1951, which means in effect we are now coming up to our 46th year of the breed. From small beginnings, Cavaliers were in 1997 seventh in popularity of breeds registered with the New Zealand Kennel Club, with 85 litters and 257 puppies registered that year.

Clubs The first Cavalier Club was the Tiki Cavalier King Charles Spaniel Club, formed in 1966 by Mrs Mollie Grocott (Moerangi) and it drew in Cavalier owners throughout New Zealand. In April 1972 a group in Dunedin formed the Otago/Southland Cavalier King Charles Spaniel Club. February 1973 saw Mrs Barbara McDougall (Clanoban) and committee form a branch of the Tiki Club. Another branch became established in Christchurch in the same year, which led to the formation of the Canterbury Cavalier King Charles Spaniel Club in 1975. Reorganisation of the Tiki Club's area of influence to the upper North Island saw the formation of two more North Island Clubs, namely Central Cavalier and King Charles Spaniel Club (encompassing our short-nosed relatives) in Wellington, and the lower North Island and East Coast Cavalier King Charles Spaniel Club in Napier, the middle of the North Island. The Clubs hold two Championship and Open shows to cater for their Cavalier members and to keep their members informed, they all publish regular newsletters. All New Zealand clubs have one championship show per year, with a second championship show granted if there is a sufficient number of Cavaliers shown at previous shows. Cost sharing efforts by New Zealand clubs and our Australian neighbours have, for a number of years, enabled Cavalier Clubs in Australasia to bring out breed specialist judges from the United Kingdom and mainland Europe.

To become a champion in New Zealand a dog must win eight CCs under at least five different judges. Breed and Group classes at all-breeds shows are in age groups similar to the United Kingdom all-breeds scene.

In New Zealand dogs can also gain

NZ Gr Ch Homerbrent Cardinham (Ch Homeranne Carson ex Homerbrent Demelza).

the title of *Grand Champion*. To qualify they must have gained three All-breed Championship show BIS awards and 50 CCs. Four Cavaliers have this title: NZ Gr Ch Homerbrent Cardinham (see previous page), NZ Gr Ch Glengariff Carnaby, NZ Gr Ch Krista Vahl Just Trouble and NZ Gr Ch Old Rowley Topgun.

The Beginning The first two Cavaliers were brought to New Zealand by an Englishman, Tony St John, and were quarantined by Mollie Grocott of Moerangi fame. The rest, as they say, is history. Mollie ended up with the dog Ch Antony of Avoncliffe and the bitch Mingshang Sarah, whose progeny Moerangi Merry Monarch and Mistress became the breed's first New Zealand-bred champions in the early 1950s. Mollie's

Ch/NZ Ch Pageant of Homerbrent.

pioneering efforts and determination to establish Cavaliers in New Zealand led her to import Ch Pargeter Pennypost, Ch Angelo of Crustadele, and the dog who, in Mollie's own words, *has had the greatest influence on the breed*, Ch Eyeworth Professor Higgins, followed by the first British champion to reach our shores, Ch Sugar Crisp of Ttiweh, who incidentally also became the first Cavalier in the world to win BIS at an All-breed Championship show. Later imports were Ch Pargeter Lovebird, Don Camillo of Alumina, Pantisa Guilini and Amanda of Moerangi, Ch Welmor Aegisthus, Ch Alansmere Moonraker, Ch Ronnoc Blake of Moerangi and the wholecolours Ch Pantisa Du Barry of Furbari, Ch McGoogans

Diarmid of Moerangi and Aust/NZ Ch Veresta Ffloyd of McGoogans. These imports and their progeny provided foundation stock for the majority of kennels in New Zealand established from the 1950s to the 1970s. The Moerangi record of 35 home-bred champions has only been eclipsed in the 1990s by the Prestonville kennel's 46 home-bred champions.

Through Mollie's efforts Jean Brodie (Dreva) became interested in Cavaliers and imported Pargeter Elegance (the breed's first New Zealand ruby champion) in the early 1950s, followed by the first tricolour champion, Deanhill Jolly Roger of Ttiweh.

Several other imports came from the United Kingdom in the late 1960s, including Mrs Parker's tricolours Beck Belle and Ch Beau Geste, who both produced well, Dr and Mrs MacLaurin's Ruby Renate of Kormar and Mrs Lucas' Ch Barings Malcoma.

A ruby brought out from the United Kingdom as a pet by Mrs Bloomfield was Merry Musketeer of Eyeworth, sire of the first New Zealand-bred ruby, Ch Moerangi Blunderbus, whose sister Buttercup was dam of the first New Zealand-bred black-and-tan, Ch Moerangi Golliwog, in the mid-1960s.

In the South Island from the late 1960s to the early 1980s Ian Pollock's Somerville kennels produced many champions. The ruby NZ Ch Sir Dougall of Somerville was a BIS winner all-breeds, a first for Cavaliers in the South Island, in the early 1980s. Ian's Australian imports in the late 1960s, the well-broken tricolour NZ Ch Gaysprite Royal Cupid and the heavier marked blenheim NZ Ch Pellemelle Conamara, have had a lasting influence and provided foundation stock for many South Island kennels, including the still-active kennels of Heather Dyet (Bellecourt) and Dianne and Hans Tyssen (Prestonville).

The 1970s to the present The 1970s saw the establishment of many of today's successful kennels, a rise in entries at All-breed and Speciality shows and an increase in imports from Great Britain. Breeders also made use of cheap air travel and no quarantine to send Cavaliers between Australia and New Zealand to be shown and bred from.

More recent wholecolour imports from the United Kingdom were in 1973 Alex Gilchrist and Murray Hutchison's black-and-tan Ch Chandlers Pharamond (winner of BIS at Otago/Southland CKCSC open show under judge Mollie Grocott) and the ruby Merne of Kormar. Through Merne's son NZ Ch Prestonville S'Dubious the successful Prestonville wholecolours were founded. They were followed by Virginia Blakely's Chacombe Croesus, litter brother to Ch Chacombe Camilla, in 1974.

The Wilsons of Bryrose kennel brought their Cavaliers with them from Great Britain but only stayed in New Zealand briefly; however their dogs, Bonnyglen Court Jester of Bryrose and Mandrake of Bembridge and Bryrose, were used, forming the start of David Balfour's successful Bayadere kennel and providing foundation stock for Rae Archibald (Archway), now in Australia, and Bill and Bronwyn Murdoch (Old Rowley).

Jean Fyfe (Mutiara) imported Aust/NZ Ch Matsy Peter Pan, Aust/NZ Ch Leynsord Hatter and Wishwin Rosalind from Great Britain in the mid-1970s. All these left successful progeny in New Zealand, who later found their way to the Elvenhome and Elfking kennels in Australia and contributed to the breed there.

The mid-1970s saw an influx of British imports into the North Island including Barbara Archibald's (Ballinluig) Ch Buckney Firefly, Ch Homerbrent Newsboy and Aust/NZ Ch Salador Country Squire JW, plus an Australian import, the ruby NZ Ch Braganzar Hyperion (a BIS all-breeds winner). Paul Bowden (de Beauvoir) brought back from the United Kingdom the blenheims Ch Amantra Kings Rhapsody (who went on to Glengariff), Ch Kindrum Dodo, and the wholecolours Ch Wertune Red Robin (who went on to Prestonville) and Ch Sorata Lady Jodie. Paul bred from both bitches, who produced champions.

The Glengariff kennel of Ann and Ian Dobie has produced many champions and Speciality BIS winners since the 1970s, including NZ Gr Ch Glengariff Carnaby (a multiple BIS winner all-breeds) and NZ Ch Glengariff Caroline, both progeny of their import NZ Gr Ch Homerbrent Cardinham who has had a widespread influence on the breed, siring many Australian and New Zealand champions. It is interesting to note that Cardinham's grandsires were Ch Homeranne Caption and Ch Crisdig Leading Seaman, and one of his granddams was Ch Homerbrent Samantha. Also imported were Ch Craigowl Rumour and Ch Persephone of Homerbrent (initially by Mary Honey) and Homerbrent Junesta, all of whom have champion progeny.

Bill and Bronwyn Murdoch's Old Rowley kennel was established with Bayadere foundation stock in the 1970s and their lovely Aust/NZ Ch Bayadere Halohoise was a Speciality winner in New Zealand and Australia. Due to many overseas moves, not much breeding was undertaken until they settled back in New Zealand in the early 1990s. Over the years they have imported several dogs, including Aust/NZ Ch Homerbrent Cartoon.

Jenny and the late Jock Graham (Montrose) were very successful with progeny from their 1980s imports NZ Ch Sundance of Homerbrent, NZ Ch Hector of Homerbrent and NZ Ch Homerbrent Polwin (who went on to Glengariff), winning speciality BISs and providing foundation stock for Debbie and Judy Tonkin's successful Krista Vahl kennel with their NZ Gr Ch Krista Vahl Just Trouble winning speciality and all-breeds BISs.

Kaye and Lionel Manners (Monte Carlo) combined their kennels to produce Homerbrent

171

Cardinham's first litter, which produced four champions. Since then they have successfully bred and exhibited several champions and currently are enjoying great success with NZ Gr Ch Old Rowley Top Gun, a multiple BIS winner all-breeds.

The Prestonville kennel of Dianne and Hans Tyssen, established in 1973, has produced many champions in all four colours in New Zealand, Australia and other parts of the world. Their first speciality BIS winner was the lovely tricolour NZ Ch Prestonville L' Janella (BIS at Canterbury Cavalier King Charles Spaniel Club Show 1978 under judge Lady Forwood) followed by the first New Zealand-bred ruby, Speciality BIS winner NZ Ch Prestonville S'Dubois. Their Aust/NZ Ch Prestonville Giv'm Beans (see page 168) was the first New Zealand-bred Cavalier to win Speciality and All-breed BISs in both Australia and New Zealand.

Megan and Keith Wells established their Bosworth kennel in the early 1980s with foundation stock from Prestonville and latterly Glengariff. Their home-bred speciality BIS winner Aust Ch Bosworth High Society was the first of a successful bitch line of Speciality winners, complemented by the importation of Ch Homerbrent Masquerade and Ch/NZ Ch Pageant of Homerbrent (see page 170). Breeding mainly blenheims, they also have an interest in wholecolours, and have campaigned three to their titles.

Shelley and Gary Walker (Redcrest) have since the late 1980s bred a number of champions, including the lovely NZ Ch Redcrest Zara, a well known Speciality BIS winner.

Anja Calder (Drakkar) established her kennels in the 1990s with foundation stock from Prestonville and is enjoying success at present with her home-bred champions and All-breed BIS winner NZ Ch Bellcourt Master Vinn.

Dk/Fin Ch Moorfields Bonheur.

172

The Cavalier in Europe

Finland

This article was kindly contributed by Dr Annukka Paloheimo, a leading breeder in Finland, who has now moved to the United Kingdom where she still shows and wins with her Anncourt dogs. She has been licensed by the Finnish Kennel Club to award CACs and CACIBs to Cavaliers since 1986 and has judged them in many European countries. Dr Paloheimo has also judged in Australia, New Zealand and the United Kingdom.

The very first Cavaliers came to Finland as early as 1952: Quilters Amanda and Pargeter Fanfare, both from Great Britain. They were also the first Finnish champions to be made up in the breed. It was 10 years or more before the breeding of Cavaliers started in Finland. Ms Eeva Kurejoki imported two blenheims, Pargeter Uppish (by Bob Up) and Pargeter Jessica (by Cerdric of Ttiweh). They had five litters, and puppies from these litters were the foundation for the breed in Finland. One of them was Fin Ch Evehill Lovely Lucy, owned by Leila and Annukka Kankaanpaa (Paloheimo).

In the early 1970s came more dogs from Great Britain: Nord Ch Mungo of Ttiweh, Int Ch Highstone Quality Fair (by Rosemullion), Int Ch Tom Brown of Homerbrent and Fin Ch Crustadele Gecko, who established the Anncourt kennel (Annukka Paloheimo), which has bred over 20 champions over the years. Mrs Orvokki Moilanen imported several Alansmere dogs (Fin Ch Alansmere Made to Measure, Fin Ch Alansmere Moonstart, Alansmere Sweet Candy) to establish the Starlet kennel. Fin Ch Charlottetown Imperial Red, Fin Ch Charlottetown Nicholas and Fin Ch Cadeyrn Alexander were some of the many dogs who came to live in Lagoon kennel with Mrs Hilkka Laitamo, who was the biggest

Int/Fin/Dk Ch Anncourt Parasol (bitch).

A 1971 photograph showing Kaironan van Markley, owned and bred by M H Iwes.

breeder for over a decade, and this was where many of the 1980s breeders acquired their foundation stock. In the north of Finland Mrs Marja Hoffren (Mein Heim) and Ms Auli Vesanen (Harrow's) bred many good Cavaliers, using also imports from Holland, perhaps the most influential being Int Ch Fanfare for Cyrus.

Mrs Heli-Anneli Vare (Harmonic) imported Fin Ch Amantra Harbour Grace and Nord Ch Kindrum Calypso, and three dogs from Salador, all of whom both became and produced champions. Mrs Marja Kurittu (Marjaniemen) imported Int Ch Chandlers Lavender Lou, a black-and-tan, who was foundation bitch to a very successul line of wholecolours, one of them Int Ch Marjaniemen Auringonsade, by Fin Ch Fontelania Burnt Almond. In 1990 over 900 Cavaliers were registered. One of the most successful kennels, Crawford (Mrs Irja Poikolainen and Mrs Teija Poikolainen-Dauber), started with a Lagoon bitch, but soon added several Homerbrent imports, most notably Int Ch Homerbrent Limelight, Int Ch Homerbrent Romeo and Int Ch Homaranne Polperro – all influential stud dogs. Mrs Kirsti Maattanen (Panda's) imported Fin Ch Tonnew Tuscany, Fin Ch Deranmar Delusion and Fin Ch Deranmar Raoul and in the 1990s more dogs from Chantiz, the most influential of them being Fin Ch Space Mission via Chantiz, sire of several champions. Another Cocker Spaniel breeder, Mrs Pirjo Lehtonen, established her Breeze-line with imports from Hilarny and Chantiz kennels and is the biggest breeder today. Mrs Anne Lindstrom (Cavannes) imported Fin Ch Hilarny Wurd Perfec, one of the most used sires at the moment.

About 200 Cavaliers were born yearly until in the early 1980s more new breeders started, many of them coming from a Cocker Spaniel background, and the boom began. The registration numbers jumped to over 1100 in 1991, but a decline started in 1994. In 1995 only 790 were registered.

The Cavalier Club of Finland was founded in 1973. Today there are over 1500 members. The Club has established a compulsory heart check programme with the Finnish Kennel Club, starting 1 January 1997, which means that parents must carry heart certificates for their puppies to be registered. The programme runs for five years and should give data for research on heart issues in the breed. The Club holds two championship shows a year, with British judges and entries of around 150. For many years, the BIS award has gone to Finnish-bred dogs, which indicates successful breeding.

The Netherlands

This article was kindly contributed by Mrs Wendy Hilberts-Goodman, who is a top breeder in the Netherlands. She judges in many European countries, including the United Kingdom.

Cavaliers are becoming very popular in the Netherlands and unfortunately are already in the Top 10 of the country's most popular breeds. Often at the championship shows they draw the largest entry in the *Companion Group*, which is similar to the British *Toy Group*. They often gain high placements in the group judging and have frequently won the group.

Mrs C van den Boom, the Countess van Rechteren-Limpurg, was the first person to import Cavaliers into Holland in 1954. She travelled all over Europe showing her dogs and was almost certainly the first serious breeder/exhibitor to own them on the continent. Her affix was *Fanfare*. The first dogs she brought over were from the United Kingdom: the then three-year-old Ch Harmony of Ttiweh (blenheim) and a blenheim bitch named Ttiweh Sorrel of Dendy, who was in whelp to Ch Harmony of Ttiweh. Most of the dogs she continued to import came from Mrs Pitt.

Since 1954, 106 Dutch champions have been made up. To become a Dutch champion the dog has to win a least four CACs under three different judges and the last CAC must be gained after the dog has reached 27 months of age. There are between 13 and 16 shows per year where CACs can be won.

In the early years the Fanfare Cavaliers gained the most titles, later followed by the very successful van Markley kennel owned by Miss R Iwes. She bred on the Fanfare lines and successfully combined them with Crisdig. Around 1972, Hans Boelaars of the Lamslag Cavaliers entered the show ring and certainly made his presence felt with his numerous champions. His first dogs were from Mrs van den Boom, but the imports which had the most effect on his kennel were from Chacombe, Sorata, Crisdig and Amantra. Obviously these were not all

Royal Companion Tri Sensation. Bred and owned by Wendy Hilberts-Goodman. German Bundessiger 1996. Photo: Roberts

Chewing is fun, as demonstrated by Dutch-bred HK Chs Ttitian Tulle and Ttitian Tango. Bred and owned by Barbara Martin.

175

imported by him; several were imported by other breeders on the continent but could be used at stud.

I entered the show scene in 1978 and have built up a very successful Royal Companion kennel entirely based on newly-imported dogs. My success can be mostly attributed to imports from the following lines: Leynsord, Alansmere, Cinola, Kindrum and more recently Loranka. On the wholecolour side, Leelyn has been more dominant.

There are many more breeders in the Netherlands, but the ones I have mentioned are the ones responsible for setting the course here.

Sweden

This article was kindly contributed by Erna-Britt Nordin and her daughter Sara Nordin. They founded the Cavamirs kennel in Sweden and have bred a number of top winning dogs. Erna-Britt has judged extensively all over Europe, including the United Kingdom.

Three generations: (left to right) Su Ch Cavamirs Modesty Blaise, Linvid Black Orchid and Graydyke Graffiti at Linvid, all judged CC quality at the same show by D Fry (Amantra).

The pioneers The first Cavalier registered by the Swedish Kennel Club was imported from Great Britain in 1961. Mrs Kerstin Petersen (Lansmansgardens) bought a ruby dog, Don Diego of Kormar, and a black-and-tan bitch, Sylvana of Restoria. Both became Swedish champions. Mrs Birgitta Ostergren (Stormkappans) bought Kingmaker of Ttiweh, the father of Ch Edward of Knightlow, a blenheim dog that already had two CCs in Britain. He became a Nordic and International champion. Kingmaker was the foundation of many Swedish Cavalier kennels and, as I am writing these lines, we have a litter – the eighth generation after Kingmaker.

But the Cavaliers registered in the 1960s were not the first in the country! There is a picture of King Oscar II of Sweden (1829–1907) and his family, and on the picture is a little blenheim Toy-spaniel of true Cavalier type, with a flat skull, high set ears and a longer muzzle.

Growth in popularity The breed soon became popular in Sweden, and in 1974 for the first time more than a thousand puppies were registered. For many years now, the number of registered Cavaliers has been 1200–1300, which makes them the largest of the toy breeds.

(Left) Modesty Blaise winning BOB with (right) Su Ch Kindrum Gillespie winning Best Other Sex, under judge Shealagh Waters (UK).

In 1984 the Cavalier once again became a royal breed in Sweden, when the Crown Princess Victoria got a Cavalier puppy for a birthday present.

At shows, there are often quite a large number of Cavaliers entered, both at the Swedish Kennel Club shows and at the Cavalier Club shows. The blenheims have been dominant for years, but lately people have discovered the other colours as well.

Cavaliers in the show ring It is impossible to mention all the breeders who have been successful in the rings, but I shall mention a few of the top-winners through the years.

The top winning Cavalier in Sweden has to be Su Ch Sperringgardens Cylvester, a blenheim dog bred by Lolan Nyby-Dahlin and Elin Nyby. Not only did he have numerous victories in the breed ring; he was also very competitive in the group finals, winning several Toy groups and BISs at Swedish Kennel Club shows. In 1985, he was top winning dog all-breeds in Sweden. That same year, the Sperringgardens kennel won the Swedish Kennel Club's Breeder of the Year award. Cylvester then took a

Su Ch Cavamirs Modesty Blaise.

break from the ring for a couple of years, returning as a veteran. And what a come-back that was! That year he won almost everything and became top-winning Cavalier of the year.

Cylvester and Su Ch Sperringgardens Cegovia, also a BIS winner, were both sired by Ch Apricot Fortune, a dog owned by Sperringgardens but bred by Anja Szyszkiewicz, owner of the Apricot kennel, who has had considerable success with dogs from her own, rather small, breeding establishment.

Influential imports The Sperringgardens kennel has imported some dogs from Great Britain over the years. Among the more successful was Su Ch Pennygown Soft Centre, who won numerous BOBs and group placings, even BIS. He was also a very good stud dog, with a lot of top-winning offspring. His grandchild, Su Ch Sperringgardens Coriander, was top-winning Cavalier for two years.

Another group-winning dog who also was a good stud dog was Su Ch Kindrum Gillespie. He was imported by Laila Lansberg Larsson (Rodero's), who also bred his most successful son, Su Ch Rodero's Hackensack, and a daughter who had several placings in the toy-group, Su Ch Rodero's Abigail.

Tricolours All the dogs mentioned above are blenheims, but we really have had some winning dogs in other colours! To start with the tricolours, I must mention Su Ch Bonnyville Trico Tricia, who did a lot of winning during a number of years. Even as a veteran she was often highly placed among the bitches. By Su Ch Kindrum Gillespie, she had a litter of three bitches, all tricoloured, and all of them became champions.

A half-brother of Trico Tricia (same father, Rytonion Oliver Twist), Su Ch Apricot Pacific, was top winning tricolour in 1993. His mother, Su Ch Apricot Marmelad (blenheim) has been among the top-winning bitches for several years, and his litter sister, Su Ch Apricot Penny Lane, also did a lot of winning.

Another top-winning dog is Su Ch Millhill Le Man, imported by the Hackensack kennel. He has been very successful in the ring, also in the Toy group. Now some of his offspring are coming out in the rings, winning classes.

The wholecolours For years, it was rather hard to succeed with the wholecolours in the ring. In the 1970s, we had some very successful dogs, among them Int Ch Tobinne's Lucifer, our own Int Ch Pantisa Willy Wagtail (half-brother to Ch Stellers Eider of Pantisa) and his son Int Ch Dalbovikens Aramis, but then there were some tough years.

Not many of us were trying to breed and show wholecolours, but some of us were struggling on. At the end of the 1980s, we bought the black-and-tan dog Graydyke Graffiti at Linvid, Oivind Jensen in Norway bought the ruby dog Sorata Frank, later to become a Swedish and Norwegian champion, Campanards kennel bought a ruby bitch, Jasenil Erythea, and we also bought the black-and-tan bitch Linvid Black Orchid. Both these bitches went back to the Sorata lines, Erythea through her father Sorata Llewellyn and Black Orchid through her father Graydykes Graffiti at Linvid, a son of Ch Sorata Fissical. They were mated to Frank, and then came the change of the scene! Campanards Twice as Nice, Campanards Teeny Bopper, both rubies, and Cavamirs Modesty Blaise and Cavamirs Willie Garven, both black-and-tans, came out in the show rings and quite quickly became champions. They also won a number of BOBs.

Jasenil Erythea also produced champion offspring in two other litters, with two different dogs, and became a champion herself at nine years of age!

Another memorable event was when Su Ch Corbona's Alexander became the first wholecoloured Cavalier ever to win Toy Group and BIS at the Swedish Kennel Club Show.

Breeders' groups At Swedish shows, we have a class called *Breeder's Group*. Here, a breeder competes with four dogs of their own breeding. They should match each other as much as possible. The best group from each breed competes in the finals in the afternoon. Several Cavalier breeders have been very successful in these classes during the years: Sperringgardens, Rodero's and Gnistans have been in the top five on the year list, and Apricot, Campanards, Bonnyville, Lyalands and some more have had high placings.

France

There are a number of Cavaliers in France, and the French breeders also have their own club, called Club des Epagneuls Nains Anglais (King Charles and Cavalier King Charles). The President is M Jean-Claude Métans, and his address can be found in **Useful Addresses**.

One of the most successful breeders in France is François Huet (pictured on page 113), who owns the only French Cavalier kennel (Arnuettes) to have made up champions in all four colours. I have included a photograph of some of these (opposite page).

Champions in all four colours: (left to right) Fr Ch Hannibal des Arnuettes, Multi Ch Hadèle des Arnuettes, Fr Ch Pamedna Pedro Rosso and Morrocan Ch Indochine des Arnuettes.

Ireland

This section written by the author with some information from Geoffrey Porter, Sean Martin and others.

Brief history The first person to bring a Cavalier to Ireland and show it as a Cavalier, not as a King Charles, was Mrs Bartels who, in due course, had the famous affix Lochfee. Mrs Bartels saw her first Cavaliers at an English show as long ago as August 1952 and, to quote her own words, was 'enchanted' by them. Shortly after this, she bought her first Cavalier, a ruby bitch called Anna, sired by Alexis of Sunninghill, a blenheim; Anna's dam was Kentwater Poppy, a black-and-tan with a lovely head. A year later, Mrs Bartels returned to Dublin and, on St Patrick's Day 1953, showed Anna as a separate breed from the King Charles Spaniel, the first time this had been possible. There were only four Cavalier exhibitors at this show: Mrs Bartels with Anna, Mrs Pitt and Mrs Keswick with Ch Jupiter of Ttiweh, Ch Pargeter Patron, and a younger bitch, Ttiweh Loulu of Sunninghill. The fourth exhibitor was an Irish lady from Wexford called Miss Gardner. Anna was still a puppy. At that show, Mrs Bartels arranged with Mrs Pitt to get a second puppy, and he arrived early in 1954. He was a tricolour named Bluebottle of Ttiweh, and a grandson of Ch Daywell Roger; Mrs Nugent described him as *a great character and solidly built with superb ears.* On Easter Monday 1954, he became the first Irish champion in the breed. Today he has many descendants in the show ring, both in the United Kingdom and in Ireland; his first litter was to Anna.

In 1956, Mrs Bartels took out her Lochfee affix, and a year later Pearl Blaze of Lochfee, followed soon after by Perle of Lenharra, were sent over to England. Perle of Lenharra was sent

Int Ch Sunninghill Perseus of Lochfee as a very young dog. Photo: F W Simms

on breeding terms, so three dogs from Perle's first litter were returned to Mrs Bartels, who registered them with the Irish Kennel Club. Two went to loving homes in Ireland and the third stayed with Mrs Bartels. He became the famous Int Ch Sunninghill Perseus of Lochfee, his father being Ch Aloysius of Sunninghill. Mrs Bartels and Miss Turle went into partnership together, and Miss Turle took Perseus over to England, where he had a very successful show career, going BOB at Crufts when only 18 months old. In 1960, he returned to Dublin for two years. During this time, he mated Clohamon Brownie, the daughter of his

Int Ch Sunninghill Perseus of Lochfee as an adult.
Photo: F W Simms

half-brother Ben Gorm of Lochfee, and this mating produced three champions: Ir Ch Clohamon Patsy of Lochfee, Ir Ch Clohamon Perle of Lochfee and Int Ch Clohamon Heatherbell of Lochfee. They were bred by Lady Levinge (whose affix was Clohamon) and all three produced champion offspring. Heatherbell belonged to Mrs Amy Nugent and, when mated to Mrs Keswick's Pargeter Fling, her daughter Florabell produced many champions, in most cases with different sires. Clohamon Heatherbell and Tnegun Florabel are both in the pedigree of my foundation bitch, Tara. So we are creeping up to the present day…

The Cavalier King Charles Spaniel Club of Ireland was founded in 1959 to *promote, foster and encourage the breed.* The first meeting was held on 6 November 1959 at the home of Mrs Bartels. The constitution was drawn up and an annual subscription of ten shillings (50p) was decided upon. Affiliation to the Irish Kennel Club was applied for. There was great enthusiasm among the members and a determination to see the new club succeed and grow. Judge's lists were obtained from the Cavalier Clubs of England and Scotland and also from The Kennel Club, as the need for specialist judges was realised right from the start. Bulletins and pamphlets from clubs in England and Scotland were passed on to interested members. Mrs Keswick supported the new club by presenting the Pargeter Trophy, still awarded today. In 1965, the club held its first show at the home of the then Chairman, Mrs Gaisford St Lawrence, at Howth Castle, a wonderful venue, and in subsequent years several more shows were held there.

Int Ch Tnegun Flavia. Photo: C M Cooke

Ir Ch Glencross Trojan Boy.

By 1967 there were 22 Irish champions, including six UK and Irish Champions (called International Champions in other parts of this chapter). Three were the Clohamon bitches mentioned above, and ten of the champions were owned by Mrs Nugent, five of them out of Tnegun Florabel. Another champion was the famous Int Ch Sunninghill Perseus of Lochfee. The breed continued to grow in size and popularity and, by about 1975, had become the largest Toy breed in Ireland. A new Club badge was produced and a Club magazine was started.

In 1977, at the Annual Gemeral Meeting of the Club, a Northern member said that she was planning to form a Northern Club, so that it would be possible to have a championship show in Ireland where CCs could be awarded. This new club, called the Northern Ireland Cavalier King Charles Spaniel Club, was formed in 1979 and held its first Championship show in 1984; since then it has held this show in April every year.

How to make up an Irish Champion To make up an Irish Champion, you must have 40 Green Star points. Included in these 40 points you must have four majors of 5 points or more.

The number of points awarded on the day is determined by the number of dogs and bitches shown in your breed. If the dog, for example, wins BOB and the bitch's points on the day were worth more, the dog is awarded the equivalent, and vice versa. If that dog goes on to win the group and an exhibit in that group has more points than he was awarded, his points are made up to equal the one with most points in the group.

Each breed has an index which determines the number of points on offer. This can change from year to year, as the Irish Kennel Club takes into account the number of dogs and bitches shown in that breed in the previous year. Hence, gaining 40 points in some breeds can be very difficult.

Cavalier breeders in Ireland today Mrs Bartels was mentioned first in this section because it was she who effectively brought the breed to Ireland. She is still around today, taking a great interest in all that is happening in the breed; I spoke to her on the telephone while I was preparing this section about her dogs and this book.

Mrs Amy Nugent is also mentioned in the history section as she became a member of the Irish Cavalier King Charles Spaniel Club as early as 1960. She has bred many lovely dogs, including more than 20 Irish champions and five International (English and Irish) champions. Among them is Int Ch Tnegun Charivari, who won his title in Great Britain in 1972. His mother was Tnegun Florabell, mentioned above, and his father Mrs Susan Burgess' famous Ch Crisdig Celebration. Charivari was *a great character and very sweet natured*, to quote his owner. Another is Int Ch Tnegun Flavia (see page 181) who was made up in the United Kingdom in 1968; her sire was Minstrel of Sunninghill, her dam Florabell again, in her first litter. Mrs Nugent describes Flavia as *one of the prettiest Cavaliers I ever bred*. Yet another is Ir Ch Tnegun Marieanne who had the distinction of winning a Challenge Certificate from Amice Pitt. Her owner described her as a *very loving girl*.

Green Stars in all four colours, 1996: (left to right) Moorfields Marron (ruby), Moorfields Mercides (tri), Kragfergus Royal Memento at Moorfields (blen) and Moorfields Merite (b/t).

Paddy Connor took up Cavaliers in 1970 having previously bred Cockers. His three foundation bitches were Tneguns: Febricia, Francette and Dreamsong. Despite an unfortunate start (he lost all the pups from his first two litters) he persevered and was soon successful with Meenan's Inishowen Serenade who became a champion in 1972. He was by Tnegun Dreamsong and Mrs Nugent's Int Ch Charivari. The affix Inishowen was the one Paddy Connor used for his Cocker Spaniels. At about this time, he bought a dog puppy by the famous Ch Rosemullion of Ottermouth (dam: CC-winning Kerkhove Frolicsome) and registered the affix Ronnoc; the puppy was called Ronnoc True Luck, Lucky for short – a very suitable name as it turned out. When he was just a young dog, 'knowledgeable' friends told Paddy to get rid of Lucky as he had too much red on his face and was not a show prospect. In fact, the Connors were not interested in showing, and could see that he was a beautifully coated, medium-sized dog with a most gentle expression and lustrous dark eyes. He turned out to be a prepotent stud dog, siring eight Irish champions including Int Ch Ronnoc Rhum of Sancem. The others were Ir Ch Ronnoc Scarlet Ribbons (one CC), Ir Ch Ronnoc Anne, Ir Ch Ronnoc Brandy, Ir Ch Vandyke True Blue Man, Ir Ch Ronnoc Honoraria (CC winner, Belfast 1979), Ir Ch Tnegun Demoiselle and Ir Ch Ronnoc Rilao.

Int Ch Kindrum Rose Red.

Int Ch Ronnoc Rumba (see page 186), born in 1989, was his grandson. Sheila Smith saw him as an old dog and was so impressed by him that she sent Salador Country Girl to be mated to him. In this litter were Ch Salador Corrigan, Ch Salador Connors and Ch Salador Colleen, which means that his name is found in the pedigrees of a number of the top winning United Kingdom dogs. His name is found also in the pedigrees of many of the top dogs in Ireland today. Paddy Connor only kept a few of these successful dogs, nearly all of them being sold to other breeders in Ireland or overseas.

Kenneth Stevenson, who lives in Northern Ireland, now owns Int Ch Ronnoc Rumba, a lovely dog. His sire was Homerbrent Waltzer, his dam Ronnoc Looby Loo, a daughter of Ronnoc True Luck. In Ireland, he was twice Toy Dog of the Year, also Show Dog of the Year, as well as winning numerous Toy Groups and BISs. He won seven CCs and two RCCs in the United Kingdom and in 1993 was BOB at Crufts. Indeed, a glorious career. Kenneth Stevenson also successfully breeds his own Bacchante Cavaliers, Ir Ch Bacchante Bananarama being perhaps the best known of his dogs.

Sean Meenan and his wife Ethna live in Dublin. Their first champion was Inishowen Serenade, mentioned above as being the first champion to be bred by Paddy Connor. Sean Meenan has bred a number of very successful Cavaliers since. Int Ch Ronnoc Rhum of Sancem, already mentioned, belonged to him, though he was bred by Paddy Connor. Later he was taken over by Molly Coaker, who made him up in the United Kingdom. He also bred Ir Ch Sancem Cirrus and Ir Ch Sancem Emerald Lady, both by Chantiz Half Coin. Ir Ch Sancem Miss Marple was also one of his, a half-sister of Emerald Lady on her mother's side, Ir Ch Ronnoc Tapples; so we see Connor's breeding coming in again. He had his first champion as long ago as 1972, so he has been a long time in Cavaliers and has done a great deal for the Cavalier in Ireland.

Sean Martin first had Cavaliers in the mid-1970s and his Glencross dogs are well known in Ireland. He has made up several champions both in the Irish Republic and the United Kingdom. Perhaps his best-known dog is Int Ch Glencross Kerrywood, a blenheim bitch, who won at all four Club shows in England, Ireland, Scotland and Wales, the only Irish dog ever to do so. Made up in 1985, she

Ir Ch Sancem Miss Marple.

was by Alansmere Country Boy and Sean Martin's own bitch, Glencross Delta Girl, a Ronnoc True Luck granddaughter. Incidentally, Country Boy was a grandson of Ch Crisdig Leading Seaman. Kerrywood's son, Ir Ch Glencross Trojan Boy, won BIS at the Irish Club Show and also won two CCs, one at the West of England Club Championship Show where he was made Reserve BIS. His son, Ir Ch Ronnoc Mr Feathers AN '96, was Top Puppy and Top Cavalier in 1996. He also won several groups in Ireland. (*AN '96* means that he won the most points during 1996.)

Robert and Heather Lamont began breeding and showing Cavaliers more than 10 years ago and have produced several very successful and attractive dogs during this period. During 1996, they won Green Stars with all four colours. The dogs who did this were Moorfields Marron (ruby), Moorfields Mercides (tricolour), Kragfergus Royal Memento at Moorfields (blen), and Moorfields Merite (black-and-tan). They certainly make a lovely picture (see page 183). One of the most recent pups, Moorfields Magny Cours (pictured on page 63), won Best Puppy at the Cavalier Club Show in 1997; to do this he had to beat 153 other puppies. His sire was Moorfield Mercides, his dam Moorfields Charite. Robert and Heather also bred a lovely Irish champion, Moorfields Merci, a tricolour, who won two CCs in the United Kingdom but sadly was unable to continue in the show ring because of an injury.

Geoffrey Porter acquired his first Cavalier in 1973. As a schoolboy, he decided he wanted to buy one as a pet, and saved up his pocket money until he had the £25 needed. He bought a black-and-tan called Feybel Forge Away, sired by Pantisa Rambler, whom he enjoyed as a much-loved pet. When Feybel Forge Away was nearly four, Mrs Nugent saw him and suggested that Geoffrey took him to a dog show. He did so, and from then on he was, to quote his own words, 'hooked'. In 1978 he bought two puppies, Kindrum Rose Red (ruby) from Mrs Thornhill and Ronnoc Scarlet Ribbons (blenheim) from Paddy Connor. Both became Irish champions, and Kindrum Rose Red became a champion in Great Britain as well. Rose Red was the first ruby to become a champion under Irish Kennel Club rules. From these two, Geoffrey bred a number of real quality Cavaliers, both wholecolours and particolours. In July 1989, Ringcreevy Ringlets was born; her sire was Ch Rheinveld Ringold von Salador, her dam one of his own bitches, Ringcreevy Kirby. Ringlets, a black-and-tan, became an Irish champion and won a CC and three Reserve CCs in Great Britain. She has had a number of pups, many of whom are already doing well in the show ring and, do not let us forget, making their owners very happy. Geoffrey is now Secretary of the Northern Ireland Cavalier Club and is doing a great deal for the Cavalier in Ireland.

Hillyacres Clover of Ringcreevy, BIS Parent Club Show 1989. Photo: F Bunce

As everyone knows, politically Northern and Southern Ireland are completely separate countries. However, as far as Cavaliers are concerned, they are shown in both; the average Northern Irish owner goes to as many shows in Eire as in the North. The Southern Irish system is different, as I explained above, and it is only possible for the Irish exhibitor to get a CC at the Belfast All Breeds Championship Show or the Northern Ireland Club Championship Show; otherwise they have to cross to a show on the United Kingdom mainland, as many of them do.

A number always come over to the Scottish Club Championship Show, on the ferry. As the reader will have already noticed, the Irish champions made up in Eire include those living in Northern Ireland. They have to win their 40 Green Star points as explained.

There are many lovely dogs in Ireland and it is a pity we do not see more of them. The breed over there is certainly in good hands and the future looks bright for them.

Ch Ronnoc Rumba. Photo: David Dalton

186

Chapter Thirteen
The last chapter

Rufus, pictured here with new owner Alex Dynnock, had to be rehomed at twelve because his original owner was too old and ill to keep him. He had nearly three happy years with the Dynnock family.

Cavalier rescue

As I said at the beginning of this book, Cavaliers make loving pets and soon become family members. Unfortunately, situations do arise in which it is impossible for even the most loving of owners to keep their Cavaliers. This can happen through illness, death in the family, marriage break-up, a move to an environment unsuitable for keeping a dog, and similar problems. If owners who find themselves in this position do not know anyone who will take their dogs and keep them in the style to which they are accustomed, there is a network of rescue organisations that can take over an unwanted dog and find him or her a really good home. The people who help with this work keep in touch with the dogs in their new surrounding and make sure that all goes well.

In the United Kingdom, the regional clubs run their own Rescue and Welfare services (see **Useful Addresses**). There are also rescue organisations in America and Australia. In the United Kingdom the Cavalier Benevolent Fund, run by the Cavalier Club, helps Cavalier owners with serious problems, usually financial, to do what is best for their dogs.

Rescue relies entirely on donations and money raised by raffles, sales from a special Rescue stall or similar fund-raising events. At most Club shows, somebody goes round with a collecting

187

can for *Rescue*. All the groups have annual parties, where Cavaliers and their owners all have fun together. This helps to raise money, but the main purpose is to get people together in a non-competitive situation. There is always a parade of rescue dogs whose stories are told.

In Scotland, Lettie was in a rabbit hutch when some SSPCA inspectors were closing down a puppy farm. Naturally, they thought she was a rabbit, and only when they took her out of the hutch did they realise they had freed a little dog. She had been in there for about two years, so could not walk or move properly. However, she was soon placed in a truly caring home with Mr and Mrs Vine of Melrose. You can see her in the picture with her friend, Pip.

Pip, a tricolour, was found unconscious, knocked down by a car, very thin and alive with fleas. The local rescue organiser, Liz Smith, took him in. No-one claimed him so, when he had recovered, he too was rehomed with Mr and Mrs Vine, who gave both dogs a loving home. Despite their experiences, both dogs have lovely temperaments.

Letty and Pip taking it (very) easy at home.

There are stories like these all around the country. This vital work is done entirely by volunteers, who devote their energy to helping Cavaliers who have fallen on bad times. Some work involves rehoming when dogs can no longer be kept, but this also means checking out the suitability of the new home and other administrative matters. The rescue teams certainly do a great job, but they could do almost nothing without the big-hearted individuals who give these dogs homes.

The ageing Cavalier

As our Cavaliers get older, we all see certain changes. They may slow up slightly, they may get a little curlier, the hair around the face may go greyish, they often become rather deaf and may not see so well. On the whole, though, Cavaliers keep their enthusiasm for life almost to the very end. They usually want to keep going for their regular walks, and this is good for them even if they are supposed to be taking things easy, though perhaps they should not go so far. They seem to keep their appetites too, though they might be better on a special diet designed for the older dog. Many Cavaliers have lived to 14, 15 or even more, although they are not a particularly long-lived breed. It is said that for a Cavalier to live to 12 or over is a bonus, but many do live longer.

Finally, though, your much-loved friend and companion will be seen to be reaching the end. I feel that as long as Cavaliers have some enjoyment out of life, even if most of the time is spent asleep, and they are enjoying their food, then their life is worth living. Once all interest in food has gone – once there is no interest in anything at all – this is the time to give your dear dog a peaceful end. The best way to do this is to ask your vet to call at the house and give a terminal injection with you there holding your friend to reassure him. If you prefer it, this can be done at the surgery. A caring owner should stay with his or her dog at this time and not just hand the dog over to the vet and go away. We all owe it to our dogs to be there with them at the end, after all the love and devotion they have given us over the years.

Ch McGoogans Tuesdays Child of Culloden, aged fourteen-and-a-half. This picture was taken just a few months before her death. Owner: Joan Twigg.

Tribute to a dog

The one absolutely unselfish friend that man can have in this selfish world, the one that never deserts him, the one that never proves ungrateful or treacherous, is his dog. A man's dog stands by him in prosperity and in poverty, in health and in sickness. He will sleep on the cold ground, where the wintry winds blow and the snow drives fiercely, if only he may be near his master's side. He will kiss the hand that has no food to offer; he will lick the wounds and sores that come in encounter with the roughness of the world. He guards the sleep of his pauper master as if he were a prince. When all other friends desert, he remains. When riches take wings and reputation falls to pieces, he is as constant in his love as the sun in its journey thru the heavens.

Senator George Vest
1870

Appendix A
Top twenty breeds 1997

Order	Breed	Number of registrations
1	Labrador Retriever	34788
2	German Shepherd (Alsatian)	24508
3	West Highland White Terrier	16148
4	Golden Retriever	15214
5	Cocker Spaniel	14541
6	English Springer Spaniel	13869
7	Cavalier King Charles Spaniel	13022
8	Boxer	10993
9	Yorkshire Terrier	9700
10	Staffordshire Bull Terrier	8699
11	Rottweiler	4561
12	Shih Tzu	4207
13	Dalmatian	3786
14	Lhasa Apso	3340
15	Border Terrier	3338
16	Dobermann	2921
17	Shetland Sheepdog	2662
18	Bichon Frisé	2612
19	Bull Terrier	2609
20	Miniature Schnauzer	2504

Appendix B
Definitions of classes
that may be held at a show

Puppies under six months are not eligible for exhibition.

Minor Puppy For dogs of six and not exceeding nine calendar months of age on the first day of the show.

Puppy For dogs of six and not exceeding twelve calendar months of age on the first day of the show.

Junior For dogs of six and not exceeding eighteen calendar months of age on the first day of the show.

Maiden For dogs that have not won a Challenge Certificate (CC) or a first prize at an Open or Championship show (Minor Puppy, Special Minor Puppy, Puppy and Special Puppy classes excepted, whether restricted or not).

Novice For dogs that have not won a CC or three or more first prizes at Open and Championship shows (Minor Puppy, Special Minor Puppy, Puppy and Special Puppy classes excepted, whether restricted or not).

Debutant For dogs that have not won a CC or a first prize at a Championship show (Minor Puppy, Special Minor Puppy, Puppy and Special Puppy classes excepted, whether restricted or not).

Undergraduate For dogs that have not won a CC or three or more first prizes at Championship shows (Minor Puppy, Special Minor Puppy, Puppy and Special Puppy classes excepted, whether restricted or not).

Graduate For dogs that have not won a CC or four or more first prizes at Championship shows in Graduate, Post Graduate, Minor Limit, Mid Limit, Limit and Open classes, whether restricted or not.

Post Graduate For dogs that have not won a CC or five or more first prizes at Championship shows in Post Graduate, Minor Limit, Mid Limit, Limit and Open classes, whether restricted or not.

Mid Limit For dogs that have not won three CCs or five or more first prizes in all at Championship shows in Mid Limit, Limit and Open classes, confined to the breed, whether restricted or not, at shows where CCs were offered for the breed.

Limit For dogs that have not won three CCs under three different judges, or seven or more first prizes in all at Championship shows, in Limit and Open classes confined to the breed, whether restricted or not, at shows where CCs were offered for the breed.

Open For all dogs of the breeds for which the class is provided and eligible entry at the show.

Veteran For dogs of not less than seven years of age on the first day of the show.

Rare Breeds Confined to those breeds not granted CCs in the current year, with the exception of those breeds whose registration is confined to the Imported Register.

Brace For two exhibits (either sex or mixed) of one breed belonging to the same exhibitor, each exhibit having been entered in some class other than Brace or Team.

Imported Register For breeds whose registration is confined to the Imported Register, and which consequently may only be entered in this class.

Any Variety Not Separately Classified For breeds of dog for which no separate breed classes are scheduled.

KCJO Stakes For any variety of dog or bitch exhibited and handled by a member of The Kennel Club Junior Organisation registered, either solely or jointly, in the member's name or in the name of a member of the family, resident at the member's address.

Not For Competition Societies may at their discretion accept *Not For Competition* entries. Societies may accept such entries from breeds of dog not included within the title of the society and at shows held over more than one day. Such entries may be accepted on any day from any breed.

CKCSC,USA/AKC Ch Grantilley English Rose at Laughing.

Appendix C
Colour breeding charts

In these tables, the sire is always the first of the pair and his contribution is always at the top of the box and the dam's at the side. However, the result would be the same either way round.

1 Blenheim x blenheim

Always $a^ta^tees^ps^p$ x $a^ta^tees^ps^p$, so results in **blenheims only**.

2 Blenheim x tricolour

a $a^ta^tees^ps^p$ x $a^ta^tEEs^ps^p$
   can only result in $a^ta^tEes^ps^p$, which means **tricolours only**.

b $a^ta^tees^ps^p$ x $a^ta^tEes^ps^p$ gives

	a^tes^p	a^tes^p
a^tEs^p	$a^ta^tEes^ps^p$ (tri)	$a^ta^tEes^ps^p$ (tri)
a^tes^p	$a^ta^tees^ps^p$ (blen)	$a^ta^tees^ps^p$ (blen)

which gives **tricolours and blenheims in the ratio 1:1**.

3 Blenheim x ruby

a $a^ta^tees^ps^p$ x a^ta^teeSS
   can only result in $a^ta^teeSs^p$, which means **rubies only**.

b $a^ta^tees^ps^p$ x $a^ta^teeSs^p$ gives

	a^tes^p	a^tes^p
a^teS	$a^ta^teeSs^p$ (ruby)	$a^ta^teeSs^p$ (ruby)
a^tes^p	$a^ta^tees^ps^p$ (blen)	$a^ta^tees^ps^p$ (blen)

which gives **blenheims and rubies in the ratio 1:1**.

4 Blenheim x black-and-tan

a $a^ta^tees^ps^p$ x a^ta^tEESS
   can only result in $a^ta^tEeSs^p$, which means **black-and-tans only**.

b $a^ta^tees^ps^p$ x a^ta^tEeSS gives

	a^tes^p	a^tes^p
a^tES	$a^ta^tEeSs^p$ (b/t)	$a^ta^tEeSs^p$ (b/t)
a^teS	$a^ta^teeSs^p$ (ruby)	$a^ta^teeSs^p$ (ruby)

which gives **rubies and black-and-tans in the ratio 1:1**.

4 Blenheim x black-and-tan (cont'd)

c $a^t a^t e e s^p s^p$ x $a^t a^t EE S s^p$ gives

	$a^t e s^p$	$a^t e s^p$
$a^t ES$	$a^t a^t Ee S s^p$ (b/t)	$a^t a^t Ee S s^p$ (b/t)
$a^t E s^p$	$a^t a^t Ee s^p s^p$ (tri)	$a^t a^t Ee s^p s^p$ (tri)

which gives **black-and-tans and tricolours in the ratio 1:1**.

d $a^t a^t e e s^p s^p$ x $a^t a^t Ee S s^p$ gives

	$a^t e s^p$	$a^t e s^p$
$a^t ES$	$a^t a^t Ee S s^p$ (b/t)	$a^t a^t Ee S s^p$ (b/t)
$a^t E s^p$	$a^t a^t Ee s^p s^p$ (tri)	$a^t a^t Ee s^p s^p$ (tri)
$a^t e S$	$a^t a^t ee S s^p$ (ruby)	$a^t a^t ee S s^p$ (ruby)
$a^t e s^p$	$a^t a^t ee s^p s^p$ (blen)	$a^t a^t ee s^p s^p$ (blen)

which can give **blenheims, black-and-tans, tricolours and rubies in the ratio 1:1:1:1**.

5 Tricolour x ruby

a $a^t a^t EE s^p s^p$ x $a^t a^t ee SS$
   can only give $a^t a^t Ee S s^p$, which means **black-and-tans only**.

b $a^t a^t Ee s^p s^p$ x $a^t a^t ee SS$ gives

	$a^t E s^p$	$a^t e s^p$
$a^t e S$	$a^t a^t Ee S s^p$ (b/t)	$a^t a^t ee S s^p$ (ruby)
$a^t e S$	$a^t a^t Ee S s^p$ (b/t)	$a^t a^t ee S s^p$ (ruby)

which gives **rubies and black-and-tans in the ratio 1:1**.

c $a^t a^t EE s^p s^p$ x $a^t a^t ee S s^p$ gives

	$a^t E s^p$	$a^t E s^p$
$a^t e S$	$a^t a^t Ee S s^p$ (b/t)	$a^t a^t Ee S s^p$ (b/t)
$a^t e s^p$	$a^t a^t Ee s^p s^p$ (tri)	$a^t a^t Ee s^p s^p$ (tri)

which gives **black-and-tans and tricolours in the ratio 1:1**.

d $a^t a^t Ee s^p s^p$ x $a^t a^t ee S s^p$ gives

	$a^t E s^p$	$a^t e s^p$
$a^t e S$	$a^t a^t Ee S s^p$ (b/t)	$a^t a^t ee S s^p$ (ruby)
$a^t e s^p$	$a^t a^t Ee s^p s^p$ (tri)	$a^t a^t ee s^p s^p$ (blen)

which gives **tricolours, rubies, black-and-tans and blenheims in the ratio 1:1:1:1**.

6 Tricolour x tricolour

a $a^t a^t EE s^p s^p$ x $a^t a^t EE s^p s^p$
   can only give $a^t a^t EE s^p s^p$, which means **tricolours only**.

b $a^t a^t EE s^p s^p$ x $a^t a^t Ee s^p s^p$
   can only give $a^t a^t EE s^p s^p$ or $a^t a^t Ee s^p s^p$, which means **tricolours only**.

6 Tricolour x tricolour (cont'd)

c $a^ta^tEes^ps^p$ x $a^ta^tEes^ps^p$ gives

	a^tEs^p	a^tes^p
a^tEs^p	$a^ta^tEEs^ps^p$ (tri)	$a^ta^tEes^ps^p$ (tri)
a^tes^p	$a^ta^tEes^ps^p$ (tri)	$a^ta^tees^ps^p$ (blen)

which gives **tricolours and blenheims in the ratio 3:1**.

7 Tricolour x black-and-tan

a $a^ta^tEEs^ps^p$ x a^ta^tEESS

can only give $a^ta^tEESs^p$, which means **black-and-tans only**.

b $a^ta^tEEs^ps^p$ x a^ta^tEeSS gives

	a^tEs^p	a^tEs^p
a^tES	$a^ta^tEESs^p$ (b/t)	$a^ta^tEESs^p$ (b/t)
a^teS	$a^ta^tEeSs^p$ (b/t)	$a^ta^tEeSs^p$ (b/t)

which means **black-and-tan only**.

c $a^ta^tEEs^ps^p$ x $a^ta^tEESs^p$ gives

	a^tEs^p	a^tEs^p
a^tES	$a^ta^tEESs^p$ (b/t)	$a^ta^tEESs^p$ (b/t)
a^tEs^p	$a^ta^tEEs^ps^p$ (tri)	$a^ta^tEEs^ps^p$ (tri)

which gives **tricolours and black-and-tans in the ratio 1:1**.

d $a^ta^tEEs^ps^p$ x $a^ta^tEeSs^p$ gives

	a^tEs^p	a^tEs^p
a^tES	$a^ta^tEESs^p$ (b/t)	$a^ta^tEESs^p$ (b/t)
a^teS	$a^ta^tEeSs^p$ (b/t)	$a^ta^tEeSs^p$ (b/t)
a^tEs^p	$a^ta^tEEs^ps^p$ (tri)	$a^ta^tEEs^ps^p$ (tri)
a^tes^p	$a^ta^tEes^ps^p$ (tri)	$a^ta^tEes^ps^p$ (tri)

which gives **black-and-tans and tricolours in the ratio 1:1**.

e $a^ta^tEes^ps^p$ x a^ta^tEESS

will all contain the genes S and E, giving **black-and-tans only**.

f $a^ta^tEes^ps^p$ x a^ta^tEeSS gives

	a^tEs^p	a^tes^p
a^tES	$a^ta^tEESs^p$ (b/t)	$a^ta^tEeSs^p$ (b/t)
a^teS	$a^ta^tEeSs^p$ (b/t)	$a^ta^teeSs^p$ (ruby)

which gives **black-and-tans and rubies in the ratio 3:1**.

7 Tricolour x black-and-tan (cont'd)

g $a^t a^t E e^{sp} s^p$ x $a^t a^t E E S s^p$ gives

	$a^t E s^p$	$a^t e s^p$
$a^t E S$	$a^t a^t E E S s^p$ (b/t)	$a^t a^t E e S s^p$ (b/t)
$a^t E s^p$	$a^t a^t E E s^p s^p$ (tri)	$a^t a^t E e s^p s^p$ (tri)

which gives **black-and-tans and tricolours in the ratio 1:1**.

h $a^t a^t E e s^p s^p$ x $a^t a^t E e S s^p$ gives

	$a^t E s^p$	$a^t e s^p$
$a^t E S$	$a^t a^t E E S s^p$ (b/t)	$a^t a^t E e S s^p$ (b/t)
$a^t E s^p$	$a^t a^t E E s^p s^p$ (tri)	$a^t a^t E e s^p s^p$ (tri)
$a^t e S$	$a^t a^t E e S s^p$ (b/t)	$a^t a^t e e S s^p$ (ruby)
$a^t e s^p$	$a^t a^t E e s^p s^p$ (tri)	$a^t a^t e e s^p s^p$ (blen)

which gives **blenheims, tricolours, rubies and black-and-tans in the ratio 1:3:1:3**.

8 Ruby x black-and-tan

a $a^t a^t e e S S$ x $a^t a^t E E S S$

will all carry the genes E and S, giving **black-and-tans only**.

b $a^t a^t e e S S$ x $a^t a^t E e S S$ gives

	$a^t e S$	$a^t e S$
$a^t E S$	$a^t a^t E e S S$ (b/t)	$a^t a^t E e S S$ (b/t)
$a^t e S$	$a^t a^t e e S S$ (ruby)	$a^t a^t e e S S$ (ruby)

which means **rubies and black-and-tans in the ratio 1:1**.

c $a^t a^t e e S S$ x $a^t a^t E E S s^p$

will all carry the genes E and S, giving **black-and-tans only**.

d $a^t a^t e e S S$ x $a^t a^t E e S s^p$ gives

	$a^t e S$	$a^t e S$
$a^t E S$	$a^t a^t E e S S$ (b/t)	$a^t a^t E e S S$ (b/t)
$a^t E s^p$	$a^t a^t E e S s^p$ (b/t)	$a^t a^t E e S s^p$ (b/t)
$a^t e S$	$a^t a^t e e S S$ (ruby)	$a^t a^t e e S S$ (ruby)
$a^t e s^p$	$a^t a^t e e S s^p$ (ruby)	$a^t a^t e e S s^p$ (ruby)

which gives **black-and-tans and rubies in the ratio 1:1**.

e $a^t a^t e e S s^p$ x $a^t a^t E E S S$

will all carry the genes E and S, giving **black-and-tans only**.

f $a^t a^t e e S s^p$ x $a^t a^t E e S S$ gives

	$a^t e S$	$a^t e s^p$
$a^t E S$	$a^t a^t E e S S$ (b/t)	$a^t a^t E e S s^p$ (b/t)
$a^t e S$	$a^t a^t e e S S$ (ruby)	$a^t a^t e e S s^p$ (ruby)

which gives **rubies and black-and-tans in the ratio 1:1**.

8 Ruby x black-and-tan (cont'd)

g $a^ta^teeSs^p$ x $a^ta^tEESs^p$ gives

	a^teS	a^tes^p
a^tES	a^ta^tEeSS (b/t)	$a^ta^tEeSs^p$ (b/t)
$atEs^p$	$a^ta^tEeSs^p$ (b/t)	$a^ta^tEes^ps^p$ (tri)

which gives **tricolours and black-and-tans in the ratio 1:3**.

h $a^ta^teeSs^p$ x $a^ta^tEeSs^p$ gives

	a^teS	a^tes^p
a^tES	a^ta^tEeSS (b/t)	$a^ta^tEeSs^p$ (b/t)
a^tEs^p	$a^ta^tEeSs^p$ (b/t	$a^ta^tEes^ps^p$ (tri)
a^teS	a^ta^teeSS (ruby)	$a^ta^teeSs^p$ (ruby)
a^tes^p	$a^ta^teeSs^p$ (ruby)	$a^ta^tees^ps^p$ (blen)

which gives **blenheims, tricolours, rubies and black-and-tans in the ratio 1:1:3:3**.

9 Ruby x ruby

a a^ta^teeSS x a^ta^teeSS
can only give a^ta^teeSS, which means **rubies only**.

b $a^ta^teeSs^p$ x a^ta^teeSS
will all have the genes ee and S, which means **rubies only**.

c $a^ta^teeSs^p$ x $a^ta^teeSs^p$ gives

	a^teS	a^tes^p
a^teS	a^ta^teeSS (ruby)	$a^ta^teeSs^p$ (ruby)
a^tes^p	$a^ta^teeSs^p$ (ruby)	$a^ta^tees^ps^p$ (blen)

which gives **rubies and blenheims in the ratio 3:1**.

10 Black-and-tan x black-and-tan

a a^ta^tEESS x a^ta^tEESS
can only give a^ta^tEESS, giving **black-and-tans only**.

b a^ta^tEESS x a^ta^tEeSS
will all have E and S, giving **black-and-tans only**.

c a^ta^tEESS x $a^ta^tEESs^p$
will all have E and S, giving **black-and-tans only**.

d a^ta^tEESS x $a^ta^tEeSs^p$
will all have E and S, giving **black-and-tans only**.

e a^ta^tEeSS x a^ta^tEeSS gives

	a^tES	a^teS
a^tES	a^ta^tEESS (b/t)	a^ta^tEeSS (b/t)
a^teS	a^ta^tEeSS (b/t)	a^ta^teeSS (ruby)

which gives **black-and-tans and rubies in the ratio 3:1**.

10 Black-and-tan x black-and-tan (cont'd)

f $a^t a^t EeSS$ x $a^t a^t EESs^p$

will all have E and S, giving **black-and-tans only**.

g $a^t a^t EeSS$ x $a^t a^t EeSs^p$ gives

	$a^t ES$	$a^t eS$
$a^t ES$	$a^t a^t EESS$ (b/t)	$a^t a^t EeSS$ (b/t)
$a^t Es^p$	$a^t a^t EESs^p$ (b/t)	$a^t a^t EeSs^p$ (b/t)
$a^t eS$	$a^t a^t EeSS$ (b/t)	$a^t a^t eeSS$ (ruby)
$a^t es^p$	$a^t a^t EeSs^p$ (b/t)	$a^t a^t eeSs^p$ (ruby)

which gives **black-and-tans and rubies in the ratio 3:1**.

h $a^t a^t EESs^p$ x $a^t a^t EESs^p$ gives

	$a^t ES$	$a^t Es^p$
$a^t ES$	$a^t a^t EESS$ (b/t)	$a^t a^t EESs^p$ (b/t)
$a^t Es^p$	$a^t a^t EESs^p$ (b/t)	$a^t a^t EES s^p s^p$ (tri)

which gives **black-and-tans and tricolours in the ration 3:1**.

i $a^t a^t EESs^p$ x $a^t a^t EeSs^p$ gives

	$a^t ES$	$a^t Es^p$
$a^t ES$	$a^t a^t EESS$ (b/t)	$a^t a^t EESs^p$ (b/t)
$a^t Es^p$	$a^t a^t EESs^p$ (b/t)	$a^t a^t EES s^p s^p$ (tri)
$a^t eS$	$a^t a^t EeSS$ (b/t)	$a^t a^t EeSs^p$ (b/t)
$a^t es^p$	$a^t a^t EeSs^p$ (b/t)	$a^t a^t Ees^p s^p$ (tri)

which gives **black-and-tans and tricolours in the ratio 3:1**.

j $a^t a^t EeSs^p$ x $a^t a^t EeSs^p$ gives

	$a^t ES$	$a^t Es^p$	$a^t eS$	$a^t es^p$
$a^t ES$	$a^t a^t EESS$ (b/t)	$a^t a^t EESs^p$ (b/t)	$a^t a^t EeSS$ (b/t)	$a^t a^t EeSs^p$ (b/t)
$a^t Es^p$	$a^t a^t EESs^p$ (b/t)	$a^t a^t EES s^p s^p$ (tri)	$a^t a^t EeSs^p$ (b/t)	$a^t a^t Ees^p s^p$ (tri)
$a^t eS$	$a^t a^t EeSS$ (b/t)	$a^t a^t EeSs^p$ (b/t)	$a^t a^t eeSS$ (ruby)	$a^t a^t eeSs^p$ (ruby)
$a^t es^p$	$a^t a^t EeSs^p$ (b/t)	$a^t a^t Ees^p s^p$ (tri)	$a^t a^t eeSs^p$ (ruby)	$a^t a^t ees^p s^p$ (blen)

which gives **blenheims, tricolours, rubies and black-and-tans in the ratio 1:3:3:9**.

Appendix D
Abbreviations

AKC	American Kennel Club.
AKC Ch	Championship awarded by the above authority.
Aust Ch	Australian Champion.
CAC	Certificates awarded in countries operating under FCI rules that count towards the title *Champion* in these countries.
CACIB	Certificates awarded in countries operating under FCI rules that count towards the title *International Champion.*
CC	Challenge Certificates awarded in Great Britain by The Kennel Club. A dog who has been awarded three of these under three different judges gains the title *Champion*.
Ch	Championship awarded by The Kennel Club (British champion).
CKCSC,USA	American King Charles Spaniel Club, United States of America.
CKCSC,USA Ch	Championship awarded by the above authority.
FCI	Fédération Cynologique Internationale. This organisation is the regulating authority for dog shows in many countries on the European mainland.
Fin Ch	Finnish Champion.
Fr Ch	French Champion.
HK Ch	Hong Kong Champion.
Int Ch	International Champion.
Ir Ch	Irish Champion.
KC	The Kennel Club. This is the overall authority in Great Britain for the breeding and showing of pedigree dogs. Because it was the first such national authority to be formed, it is simply called *The* Kennel Club, with no country.
Nl Ch	Dutch Champion.
Nord Ch	Nordic Champion – a title awarded to dogs that have won CACs in Norway, Sweden and/or Finland.
NZ Ch	New Zealand Champion.
NZ Gr Ch	New Zealand Grand Champion.
Su Ch	Swedish Champion.

Book list

Breed books

Cavalier King Charles Spaniel Club *Interpretation of the Breed Standard* Available from Tom Boardman, *Pelham*, Priory Road, Sunningdale, Berks, SL5 9RE
Cavalier King Charles Spaniel Book of Champions Available from Tom Boardman, address as above.

    Vol 1:   1928–1988
    Vol 2   1989–1994

Evans, John *Cavalier King Charles Spaniels* Crowood Press
Field, Bruce. *The Cavalier King Charles Spaniel* Robert Hale.
Smith, Sheila *Cavalier King Charles Spaniels Today* Ringpress
Town, Ken *Cavalier King Charles Spaniels* Ringpress

Some good older books

Booth, E M *All About the Cavalier King Charles Spaniel* Pelham books.
Burgess, Susan *The Cavalier King Charles Spaniel* KR Books, 1975
Forwood, Mary *The Cavalier King Charles Spaniel* Popular Dogs, 1974
Lytton, *The Hon Mrs* Neville *Toydogs* Duckworth, 1911
Stenning, E M *The Cavalier King Charles Spaniel* W & G Foyle

General

Evans, J M, *MRCVS, and* **White**, Kay *Doglopaedia* Henston
Little, Clarence C *Inheritance of Coat Colour in Dogs* Howell
Page Elliot, Rachel *Dogsteps* Howell
Robinson, Roy *Genetics for Dog Breeders* Pergamon
Turner, Trevor *Veterinary Notes for Dog Owners* Popular Dogs

Useful Addresses

The Kennel Club

The Kennel Club
1–5 Clarges Street, Piccadilly, London, W1Y 8AB. Tel: 0171–493 6651

Breed clubs in Great Britain and Ireland

The Cavalier King Charles Spaniel Club
Secretary: Mrs Ros Loades, Shakespeare Cottage, 111 Kenilworth Road, Balsall Common, Near Coventry, CV7 7EU. Tel: 01676 535545

The Cavalier King Charles Spaniel Club of Ireland
Secretary: Mrs Evelyn Hurley, 14 Grange Park View, Raheny, Dublin 5, Eire. Tel: Dublin 8481621

Eastern Counties Cavalier King Charles Spaniel Society
Secretary: Ms Maryanne Hogan, 1 Foster Close, Old Stevenage, Herts, SG1 4SA. Tel: 01438 317071

Humberside Cavalier King Charles Spaniel Club
Secretary: Mrs R Mochrie, Hillcrest, Hopton, Stafford ST18 0AH. Tel: 01785 253717

Midland Cavalier King Charles Spaniel Club
Secretary: Mrs Mary Rees, Little Oaks, 114 Hawkes Mill Lane, Coventry, CV5 9FN. Tel: 01203 403583

Northern Cavalier King Charles Spaniel Club
Secretary: Mr Ian Sidgwick, Little Bracken, Corby Hill, Carlisle, Cumbria, CA4 8QA. Tel: 01228 561209

The Northern Ireland Cavalier King Charlaes Spaniel Club
Secretary: Mr Geoffrey Porter, Windy Ridge, Ringcreevy Road, Comber, Do Down, NI BT23 5JP. Tel: 01247 872222

Scottish Cavlier King Charles Spaniel Club
Secretary: Mrs Lindsay Gow, 32 Cammo Gardens, Barnton, Edinburgh, EH4 8EQ. Tel: 0131 339 2503

The South and West Wales Cavalier King Charles Spaniel Club
Secretary: Mr A Close, Lamont, Claude Road West, Barry, S Glamorgan, CF62 8JG. Tel: 01446 737733

Southern Cavalier King Charles Spaniel Club
Secretary: Mrs E C Tappenden, *The Firs*, Partridge Hill, Landford, Wilts, SIP5 2BR. Tel: 01794 322507

Three Counties Peke and Cavalier Society
Secretary: Mrs S Jones, 7 Wellesbourne Road, Coventry, CV5 7HG. Tel: 01203 462816

West of England Cavalier King Charles Club
Secretary: Mr J Evans, The Sheiling, Gloucester Road, Standish, Gloucester, GL10 3DN.
Tel: 01453 822599

Cavalier Resue and Welfare Service

Each regional club runs its own Rescue and Welfare Service, and these are the contacts in the various areas:

Co-ordinator	Mrs J Pagan	01245 320488
Midlands	Mrs Mary Rees	01203 403583
Midlands	Mrs E Howard	01905 429457
Midlands	D W Williams	01926 842527
West	Miss C G Greenall	01548 580369
Eastern	Mrs M Jones	01763 853873
North West	Mr Heal	01254 398880
North East	Mr M Spark	01748 834194
Humberside	Mrs J Crossley	01723 864285
Scotland	Mr D Smith	01324 553331
Wales	Mr and Mrs S Harris	01633 680315
Southern	Mrs M Butler	01844 274285
South and West Wales	Mr J Ace	01792 773612

Breed clubs in Australia

Cavalier King Charles Spaniel Club of New South Wales
Secretary: Mr Brian Mitchell, 172 Guntawong Road, Rouse Hill, NSW 2155. Tel: 02 9627 4217

Cavalier King Charles Spaniel Club of Victoria
Secretary: Mrs Helen Murphy, 12 Halley Street, Blackburn 3130 VIC. Tel: 03 98771921

Cavalier King Charles Spaniel Club of South Australia
Secretary: Mrs D Morgan, 44 Germanton Road, Redbanks 5502 SA

Cavalier King Charles Spaniel Club of A.C.T.
Secretary: Mrs Rhonda Lane, 35 MacNaughton Street, Holt 26/5 A.C.T.

Breed clubs in Canada

Cavalier King Charles Spaniel Club of Canada
Secretary: Ms Charlene Kratz, 4910 Maple Street, Niagara Falls, Ontario L2E 2M5.

Breed clubs in Finland

The Finnish Cavalier King Charles Spaniel Club
Secretary: Mrs Paivi Itkonen, Kapytie 1, 12540 Launonen.

Breed clubs in France

Club des Epagneuls Nains Anglais (King Charles & Cavalier King Charles)
Secretary: M J C Métans, Villa Bel Air, Rue P, Curie, 83660 Carnoules

Breed clubs in the Netherlands

Cavalier Club Nederland
Secretary: Mrs O C Zwaartman-Pinster, Doornweg 3, 3235 NJ Rockanje, Westvoorne.

Breed clubs in New Zealand

Tiki Cavalier King Charles Spaniel Club
Secretary: Mr G Duncan, PO Box 5619, Hamilton.

East Coast CKCS Club
Secretary: Mrs J Tonkin, PO Box 3090, Mahora, Hastings.

Central Cavalier and King Charles Spaniel Club
Secretary: Mrs Bronwyn Murdoch, 41 Nicholson Road, Khandallah, Wellington.

Canterbury CKCS Club
Secretary: Mrs J Higgins, 260 Marchland Road, Christchurch 6.

Otago-Southland CKCS Club
Secretary: Mrs V Foley, 11 Darymple Street, Pine Heights, Dunedin.

Breed clubs in Sweden

The Swedish Cavalier King Charles Spaniel Club
Christina Wendel, Drssbodavagen 84, S–906 29 Umea.

Breed clubs in the United States of America

Cavalier King Charles Spaniel Club USA
Secretary: Chris Hansen, S37 W26941 Genesee Road, Waukesha, Winconsin 53188

The America Cavalier King Charles Spaniel Club Inc
Secretary: Martha Guimond, 1905 Upper Ridge Road, Green Lane, PA 18054.

Cavaliers of the North East
Secretary: Charles H Minter, 7 Fairfield Road, Somerset, New Jersey 08873.

Cavaliers of the South
Secretary: Miriam Lovettr, 1943 Robin Hood Road, Winston-Salem, NC 27104.

Cavaliers of the Midwest
Patricia Hutchins, 1258 W Borton Road, Esexville, MI 48732

Cavaliers of the West
Secretary: Harold Letterly, 661 Woodlawn, Devore Heights, San Bernadino, CA 92407

Index

a

Abrasions 132
Abscess 117
Ackroyd, Caroline 147
Alansmere 133–135, 144, 173, 176
Albrecht, Gertrude Polk Brown 151–152
Allergies 117–118
Amantra 135, 171, 175
Anal glands 118
Anderson, *Mrs* J W 153–154
Anncourt 173
Ann's son 32, 34, 36–37, 47
Apricot 177–178
Archibald, Barbara 171
Archibald, Rae 171
Archway 171
Arnuettes 178–179
Arthritis 118
Astraddle 147

b

Baccchante 184
Back 52–54, 60, 93
Bad breath 118–119
Balance 47, 49, 60, 93
Balfour, David 171
Barsac 135
Bartels, *Mrs* 45, 179, 181–182
Barwell, *Mrs* Virginia 147
Bayadene 171
Beauvoir, de 171
Bed 16–17
   Vet-bed 17, 71, 77
Bellecourt 170
Benching 99
Berry, Kevan 144
Birth *see* Whelping
Blakely, Virginia 171
Blaze 21
Bleaney, Ev 154
Bloomfield, *Mrs* 170
Boardman, Tom & Joyce 146–147
Body 48, 54–55, 163, 165
Bonnyville 178
Boelaars, Hans 175
Boom, *Mrs* C *van den* 174–175
Bosworth 172
Bowden, Paul 171
Bowdler, *Mrs* Jane 152
Braganzar 168, 171
Breathlessness 115
Breed clubs 12, 32, 201–203
Breed registrations 190
Breed standards
   AKC 164–165
   CKCSC/USA 162–164
   TKC 47–60

c

Breeding 62–79, 103–113, 193–198
Brierly, *Lt Col & Mrs* 37
Brodie, Jean 170
Brown, Mr & Mrs George 150
Brown, Rainey 152
Brown, Sally 150–151
Bryrose 171
Bunthorne 30–31
Burgann, Merv 168
Burgess, *Brig* Jack 138, 152
Burgess, *Mrs* Susan 138, 152

c

Cages 77, 94–95, 97
Caesarean section 62, 81–83
Calcium 20, 69, 82, 85
Calder, Anja 172
Calladine, Roger 153
Campanards 178
Campanozzi, Paula 162
Canker 123
Car sickness 27
Caribelle 168
Cataract 117
Cavalier Benevolent Fund 187
Cavamirs 176, 178
Chacombe 136–137, 175
Challenge Certificates (CCs) 95–96
Chamanic 137, 166
Chantiz 137, 166, 174
Characteristics 47, 49
Charles I, *King of England* 29–30
Charles II, *King of England* 28
Charlottetown 147–148
Children 8, 61
Cheyletiella 126
Choosing 9–15
Classes 95–97, 191–192
Clohamon 181
Coat 48, 95, 163, 165
Collar 21, 101
Colour 48, 58–60, 91–92, 164–165
   Black-and-tan 48, 60, 91–92, 164–165
   Blenheim 48, 59–60, 91, 164–165
   Particolour 59, 91
   Ruby 48, 60, 91, 164–165
   Tricolour 48, 60, 91, 164–165
   Wholecolour 59, 91–92
Colour breeding 110–113, 193–198
Conformation 60
Connell, John 168
Connor, Paddy 183–184
Constipation 120–121
Convulsions, *see* Fits
Costello, Lyn 168–169
Costs 15, 62
Coughing 119

Coupling 54
Cow hocked 55
Craigowl 137
Crisdig 137, 175
Crustadele 166, 173
Cryptorchid 66
Culloden 61, 81, 150–151, 160
Cushioning 49–50, 60
Cuts 132

d

Daywell 34, 37–39, 42–43
Daywell Roger, *Ch* 37–39, 42–43
Deafness 121
Deanhill 153
Deranmars 147, 174
Diarrhoea 120
Diet, *see* Food
    Diet sheet 19
Distemper 20, 119–120
Diuretic 115, 123
Dixon, *Mr & Mrs* 166
Dobie, Anne & Ivan .171
Docking 48, 56, 163, 165
Dog World 12, 99
Dollin, Gloria .167–168
Donaldson, George .152
Domjahn, Ivan & Lyn 167
Dyet, Heather 170

e

Ears
    Breed standards 47, 49–51, 163–164
    Care 122–123
Ear mites 123
Eclampsia 62, 85
Eczma 189
Edwards, Eunice 167
Egan, Jenny & Bill 168
Eldred, *Mrs* K .37, 42
Eldridge, Roswell 31–32
Elfking 168–171
Elliot, Sally 168
Elsasser, Sandy 154
Elvenholme 26, 168
Endocardiosis 114
Enright, *Mr & Mrs* .168
Epilepsy *see* Fits
Esler, *Mrs* 166
Eubank, Mary Grace & Ted 159
Evans, John 39, 134–135
Exercise 21
Eyes
    Breed standards 47, 49–51, 162, 164
    Care 123
    Staining 23

f

Fading puppies 88
False pregnancy 123–124
Fanfare 174–175
Faults 49, 107

Feather(ing) 22–23, 47–48, 56, 59–60, 92
Feet 48, 52, 56
Fits 126–127
Fleas 124–126
Flesh marks 47, 50–51
Fontenay 37–38, 40
Food
    Adult Cavaliers 20
    Complete 20
    Dried 20
    Nursing bitch .74–75
    Pregnant bitch 69
    Puppies 19–20, 76–79
    Tinned 20
Fontelania 139–140, 174
Forequarters .48, 52–54
Forwood, *Lady* Mary 39, 45–46, 152, 167
Foster mother 88
Fox, Pam & Maxine .149
Fractures 127
Franze, Margaret 169
Freckles 93
Frew, C S 153
Fry, Diane 135
Fyfe, Jean 171

g

Gaisford St Lawrence, *Mrs* 181
Gait *see* Movement
Gammon, John 161
Gardner, *Miss* 179
Garnett Smith, Barbara & Bob 160
Gastroenteritis 130
Gaycrest 168
Gaysprite 170
General appearance 47, 49, 162, 164
Genetics 103–113, 193–198
Gilchrist, Alex 170
Gillies Compston, Caroline 46, 134, 144
Gingell, *Mr* 154
Glencross 185
Glengariff 171
Gnistans 178
Graham, Jenny & Jack 171
Grass seeds 123, 128
Grocott, Mollie 169–171
Grooming 22–25, 98, 102
    Grooming equipment 22–23
Groups 5, 7, 100

h

Hackensack 178
Hall, Alan 39, 134–135
Harper Trois-Fontaines, *Mme* J 37, 41
Head 31, 34, 47, 49–50, 92–93,
                                                162, 164–165
Heart problems 114–116, 119
    Murmur 62, 114–116
Heartworms 132
Heat, On 9–10, 64–65
Heat stroke 127
Heatherside 153

Hendrix, K 160
Hendry, Helena 160
Henry, Betty & Barry 168
Hepatitis 20
Hernia
  Inguinal 127
  Umbilical 127
Hewitt Pitt, *Mrs* A *see* Pitt, *Mrs* A
Hilarny 174
Hilberts Goodman, Wendy 174, 176
Hindquarters 48, 55–56
Hoffren, Marja 174
Homeranne 138, 140–141, 169, 174
Homerbrent 140–142, 147, 169, 171,
                          173–174, 184
House training 18–19
Huet, François 113, 178
Hughes, Loraine 149
Hutchison, Murray 171
Hypothermia 70, 88
Hysterectomy 129

i

Inbreeding 103
Infertility 65–66
Inglis, Norma & Gordon 138
Injury 130
Inman, Hugh & Jocelyn 137
Inoculation 20
Interdigital cysts 128
Inverglen 168
Iwes, *Miss* R 173, 175

j

Jackson, Tracy 135
Jennings, *Mrs* 37, 41–42
Jensen, Oivind 178
Junior Warrant (JW) 100

k

Kendrick, *Mr* 154
Kennel Club, *The* 12, 32, 47, 67–79
Kennel cough 119
Kennel Gazette, *The* 12
Keswick, *Mrs* Barbara . . .39, 43–45, 150, 152, 179, 181
Kidney disease 131
Kindrum 142–143, 155, 161, 171, 174
               176, 178–179, 184–185
King Charles Spaniel (Charlie) . .7, 28, 30–32, 49, 52, 92
Koster, *Mrs* Diana 140
Koster, *Miss* Lucy 140
Kurittu, *Mrs* Marja 174

l

Lactol 19, 72, 74, 77–78, 89
Lagoon 173–174
Laitanio, *Mrs* Hilkka .173
Lamont, Robert & Heather 185
Lamslag 175
Lansberg Larsson, Leila 177
Lansmansgardens 176
Laryngitis 119

Laughing 159–160
Le Chevalier 169
Leach, Myra 167
Leach, Shirley 167
Lead
  Lead training 21
  Show lead 21, 101
Leagay 167
Leelyn 149, 176
Lehtonen, *Mrs* Pirjo .174
Leptospirosis 20
Letterly, Harold & Joan 161
Levinge, *Lady* 181
Lice 126
Lindstrom, *Mrs* Anne 174
Line breeding 103, 106
Linvid 178
Lochfee 179–182
Lozenge 29, 48, 59, 91
Lyalands 178
Lymer, *Mrs* Sylvia 144
Lymrey 143–144
Lyons Brown, *Mrs* W H 151
Lytton, *Mrs* 30–31

m

Maattanen, *Mrs* Kirsti 174
McCullough, David & Raewyn 168
McDougall, *Mrs* Barbara 169
McGoogans 46, 144, 154–155, 189
MacLaurin, *Dr & Mrs* 170
McQuaid, Hilary 149
Madigan, Marilyn 108–109, 168
Maibee 92, 100–101, 143
Maltese (Melitaeus) 28
Mammary congestion 84, 128
Mange 129
Manners, Kay & Lionel 171–172
Marjaniemen 174
Markley, *van* 173, 175
Marlborough, *Duke of* 29
Martin, Phil 167
Martin, Sean 185
Mary, *Queen of Scots* .28
Mastitis 85, 128
Mating 64–65, 67–68
Maxholt 148–149
Meenan, Shaun & Ethna 184
Melloway 168
Merseyport 168
Milk (*see also* Lactol)
  Bitch's 73–74, 76
  Cow's 69, 72, 74
  Goat's milk 74–75
Millhill 147
Milton, Maurene & Jim 139–140
Minerals 69, 73, 80
Miniature Toy Trawler .31
Mismarks 107, 113
Mitchell, Brian 168
Mitral Valve Disease (MVD) 114–116
Moerangi 169–170

Moïlanen, *Mrs* Orvokki 173
Monorchid 66
Montford, Denis 168
Montford, Jeanie 166, 168
Montrose 171
Moorfields 172, 183, 185–186
Mordecai, Ellie 147
Mostyn Walker, *Miss* K 32, 34
Mouth 47, 51–52
Movement 48, 57, 93, 165
Murdoch, Bill & Bronwyn 171
Murray, *Mrs* Daphne 38–39, 41, 46, 152
Muzzle 47, 49, 92, 163–164

n
Nails 24
Neck 48, 52–53, 93, 163, 165
Nits 126
Nordin, Erna Britt 176
Nordin, Sara 176
Nose 47, 49–50, 92–93, 163–164
Nose pigment 50, 93
Nugent, *Mrs* Amy 152, 181, 183
Nyby, Elin 177
Nyby-Dahlin, Lolan 177

o
Oestrus 65
Old Rowley 171
Orange, *House of* 29
Orphan puppies 88–89
Oscar II, *King of Sweden* 176
Ostergren, *Mrs* Birgitta .176
Otitis externa 123
Our Dogs 12, 99
Outcrossing 106

p
Pagan, *Mrs* Joan .145–146
Palfree, Barbara 152
Paloheimo, Annukka 173
Pamedna 149
Papillon 29, 34, 36
Para-influenza 20
Pargeter 39, 43–45, 142, 144, 150,
153–154, 167, 173, 181
Parker, *Mrs* 170
Parvovirus 20
Patterson, Betty 167
Pedigree 14, 64, 103–104
Pellemelle 167, 170
Penney, *Mr* 154
Petersen, *Mrs* Kerstin .176
Phantom pregnancy *see* False pregnancy
Pharyngitis 119
Phillpott, *Mr & Mrs* 166
Pinecrest 155–159
Pitt, *Mrs* A 34–38, 40–46, 141, 144, 152, 179
Pitt, *Miss* Jane .38, 37–38
Pixyline 154
Plantation 37–38, 40–41
Poikolainen, *Mrs* Irja 174

Poikolainen-Dauber, *Mrs* Teija 174
Poisons 128–129
Pollock, Ian 170
Portcon 168
Porter, Geoffrey 185
Porter, Helen 168
Pregnancy 68–69
Prestonville .168, 170–172
Prince Charles (tricolour) 29, 35
Puppy farms 11–12
Purser, Chuck 154
Pyometra 129
Pyramé 30–31

q
Qualybeau 168
Quirk, *Col* Joseph C 150

r
Ravenrush 157, 161–162
Reabsorption 62
Reading, Betty 167
Reagan, Ronald, *President of the USA* 153
Redcrest 172
Registrations, Annual 133
Reid, *Mrs* Joan 137
Rennard, *Mrs* Anne 147
Rennie, *Mrs* Vera .38, 43
Rescue 187–188
Respiratory disease 119
Retinal dysplasia 116
Reynolds, *Mrs* Brigida 154–155, 159
Rheumatism 118
Ricksbury 144
Ringcraft 94
Ringcreevy 185–186
Ringworm 189
Rix, Brian 144
Rodero 177
Ronnoc 183–185
Rooney, *Mrs* Pam 152
Rosemullion of Ottermouth, *Ch* 46, 135, 138–139,
141–144, 148, 159, 173, 183
Roundworms 15, 131
Royal Companion .175–176

s
Salador 144–145, 155, 171, 174, 184
Sancem 184–185
Schilizzi, *Mrs* Diana 136–137, 152
Scholl, Robert 161
Season, In *see* Heat, On
Shinnick, Mick 149
Shoulders 48, 52–54, 93, 163, 165
Showing, shows 90–102
All-breed 95
Championship 95–96
Exemption 96–97
Open 96
Limit 96
Size 48, 60, 163–164
Skin problems 129

Smith, Sheila 144–145
Snorting 119
Somerville 170
Sorata 145–146, 175, 178
Spalding, Elizabeth 151, 153–154
Spencer Churchill, *Lady* 153
Sperringgardens 177–178
Sprains 130
St John, Tony 170
Stanley, *Mrs* Barbara 147
Steel, Poppy 184
Stevenson, Kenneth 184
Stibbard, *Mrs* 153
Stings 129
Stormkappens 176
Stoves, *Mrs* . . . .
Strains 130
Stud dog 64–67
  Stud fee 67
Sunninghill 179–181
Supplements .20, 69, 80, 85
Sutherland 150
Swellings 130

t

Tail 48, 56–57, 93, 163, 165
  Gay tail 56, 93
Talbot, *Mrs* Peggy 148–149
Tapeworms 131
Teeth 24, 47, 51–52, 93, 163, 165
  Tooth abcess 117
Temperament 47, 49, 164–165
Temperature
  Ambient (for puppies) 71, 74, 76
  Body 72
Thomas, Angela 154
Thornhill, *Mrs* Pam 142–143, 152, 185
Ticks 126
Tie 67
Titbits 20–21, 101–102
Tnegun 181–184
Tonkin, Debby & Judy .171
Tonsillitis 119
Toraylac 14, 68
Town, Ken 135, 152
Toxocara canis 131
Toy Spaniel 28–32
Travelling 27, 94–95
  Travelling box 94

Truffle dog 29
Ttiweh 37–45, 134, 141–142,
                              144, 167, 170, 173–174
Turle, Pamela 39, 45, 152, 181
Twigg, Joan & Oliver 150–151, 155, 160
Type 60
Tyssen, Dianne & Hans 169–170, 172

u

Uterine inertia 81
Uterine infection 84

v

Vairire .134–135, 138, 144
Vare, Miss Heli Annali .174
Vesanen, *Miss* Auli 174
Vitamins 20, 69, 80, 85
Volney 146–147
Vomiting 130–131

w

Walker, Sheila & Gary .172
Wall, Barbara 39
Warts 131
Waters, Mrs Shealagh 143, 176
Watkins, Gloria 154
Weaning 76–79
Weight 48, 60, 62, 115, 127, 163–164
  Weighing puppies 72, 74–75, 89
Wells, Megan & Keith .172
Whelping 71–89
  Equipment 71–72
  Problems 81–89
  Whelping quarters 70–71
Whitehead, *Miss* Carolyn 153
Whitman, *Mrs* Harold .150
Whyteplace 90, 147
Wiggins, Marion 90. 121
Wilson, Nancy 154
Winaway 169
Worming 15
Wounds 132
Wyndcrest 160–161

z

Zapangu 168